D1203299

THE TRIUMPH OF TCHAIKOVSKY

THE TRIUMPH OF TCHAIKOVSKY

A Biography by

JOHN GEE

AND

ELLIOTT SELBY

ILLUSTRATED

London

Robert Hale Limited

63 Old Brompton Road, S.W.7

First published in Great Britain, 1959

Printed in Great Britain by Richard Clay and Company, Ltd.,
Bungay, Suffolk

CONTENTS

LIST OF ILLUSTRATIONS

'An artist should not be troubled by the indifference of his contemporaries. He should go on working and say all that he is predestined to say. He should know that posterity alone can deliver a true and just verdict.'

TCHAIKOVSKY.

FOREWORD

READERS of biography have a right to know whether they are being given a reliable account of a life as it was lived, or whether they are being beguiled by fact adulterated with fiction. There is little dispute about the character of Tchaikovsky, and the course of his life is richly documented. Moreover, it has enough natural drama, pathos, and humanity to require no artifice. All that has been necessary has been to extract the tale from the mass of correspondence, diaries and reminiscences in which it is embodied.

No invented speeches are put into the mouths of the people who jostle through this narrative. Where their thoughts or actual words are given, there is always written evidence, a diary note or a witness's recollection, in the background. The same applies to descriptions of places and people. Where we have speculated on Tchaikovsky's or some other person's motives, we have sought to make it perfectly clear that we are doing so.

On Tchaikovsky's sexual deviation, an unembarrassed frankness has seemed to us the only fitting attitude, along with a due sense of proportion. This is the story of a composer of music and of a suffering human being. It is under both aspects that we have to consider him.

The dates given in these pages are those of the modern calendar, not the Julian calendar which prevailed in Russia until the Revolution.

J. G.
E. S.

CHAPTER I

A QUESTION OF SUCCESS

TCHAIKOVSKY drank a glass of water and died of cholera, at the height of his enormous creative powers. His career was a long ladder of disappointments to a heady, exhausting success. His personal life was a progress of calamities, among them a ruinous marriage, three mental breakdowns, and an attempt at suicide. He was seldom free from fear and excessive anxiety, always in shaky health. Yet it is proper to speak of the triumph and not the tragedy of this great and large-hearted man.

In the first place, the major events of such a life as his are musical events. By that measure, his is one of the greatest 'success stories' in the history of the art; and it was his own standard, as well as ours. He had a cloudlessly simple creed as an artist, and lived faithful to it. Although his half-century was all too short, he lived to see himself internationally renowned, and fairly on the way to the position he has ever since held: that of probably the most popular composer of serious music in the world. This he became without compromise, without loss of integrity, without any tainting of his natural simplicity.

Discovering slowly the gift hidden within him, he brought it to light, patiently learning his trade in order to be worthy of it. In spite of laziness, he became an unremitting worker; in spite of unthriftiness, he mastered the business of 'business'; in spite of shyness, he faced the clamour and sometimes the hisses of the crowd. He could not grow a shell, or learn to laugh at the stings.

He went on flinching, never hardened or embittered, to the end.

'The gentlest and kindest of men,' Saint-Saëns called him. His musical rivals were apt to become his staunch defenders.

In an epoch of grandeur, Tchaikovsky was grand; a giant among giants, with touches of absurdity that do not diminish him. Focus the beam of attention on some point in his life and he will very likely be seen as a man suffering some crushing injustice or disappointment, or struggling with an impossible burden, not necessarily his own. Sometimes he is fighting phantoms, psychological ills.

If, for example, we were to look in at a charity concert for famine victims in Moscow, one snowy day in February 1868, we should find a restive audience watching a strange scene. It was Tchaikovsky's debut as conductor, the work being a set of character-dances for his opera *The Voyevoda.* The young musician made a good impression when he entered and bowed. He was tall, upright, with sleek hair already receding above a high forehead: his nose was straight and fine, his mouth rather wide but shapely, his blue eyes of striking, exceptional intensity.

But the stance he took was grotesque. With one hand he was grasping his scraggy beard. With the other he held the baton, but the gestures he was making with it were wild and uncontrolled: he did not appear to be looking at the score at all. The audience began to realise that there was no relation between his antics and what the orchestra was playing.

The players were well rehearsed. Receiving nonsensical indications from the conductor, they took over the responsibility themselves, leaving Tchaikovsky to devote himself to his own task, which was nothing less than preventing his head from falling off.

He confessed this illusion afterwards to his friend and colleague, Nikolai Dmitrievich Kashkin, who was in the audience suffering for and with him. Yet Tchaikovsky was neither mad nor markedly eccentric, as men of genius go.

Kashkin saw him in the artists' room just before the performance and found him unnaturally calm and self-confident. But from his seat he detected in the conductor at the very beginning a scarcely controlled anguish. Tchaikovsky wanted to flee, and the terror he felt passed from one phase to another until it reached a point of absurdity and found him vainly attempting to conduct without letting go of his beard.

Concert-goers were less meek and more demonstrative than those of today; but if the audience were able to see, as Kashkin did, that Tchaikovsky was 'beside himself', they must have felt pity and an embarrassed sympathy alongside the desire to laugh.

He knew how completely he had failed, and it was many years before he attempted to conduct again. He believed for a long time that it was something he could never do. For that reason, in the end, he forced himself to do it, and in the last years of his life conducted great orchestras with notable success in Moscow, Paris, Berlin, New York, London.

At the time of this first attempt, Tchaikovsky was little known. He was just one of many buds in the wonderful springtime of Russian music which had lately begun.

He was then twenty-eight. He came to music comparatively late, and died at the age of fifty-three. His output embraced seven symphonies, eleven operas, various symphonic poems, ballets, concertos, overtures, orchestral suites, string quartets, marches, cantatas, liturgies, songs, and many miniature compositions for the piano: little of it unchallengeably supreme in its kind, except his ballet music, but including work that enlarged the boundaries of music.

Our more meagre age can only listen and wonder. This was not ephemeral creation, and there can be no composer whose work is more often performed, or in more lands, today.

Tchaikovsky's private life was always difficult, and he committed some great follies. He was homosexual, but like so many homosexuals, he was conventional and conformist in his general outlook and had no wish either to defy or deceive society. He fought a painful battle against the trend of his nature, but found it was something he could neither quell nor transform. His attempt to appease society by getting married almost cost his sanity and his life. In a career subjected to ever-increasing publicity, he was always in danger of disgrace. It appalled him. This was not something he could take lightly. He wept—and recorded some new temptation and fall.

It was part of Tchaikovsky's temperament to accuse himself of many faults, from hypochrondia to cowardice. Everyone who knew him testifies to his transparent goodness, his charm and innate dignity. His weaknesses were never mean ones. He was always giving, outpouring.

His publisher tried to extract a promise that he would stop giving away his manuscripts right and left. But, said Tchaikovsky, of course he must have the right to give them away, to friends, to the directors of the opera-house! But, on the other hand, if he were convinced that the publisher's interests really suffered—well, in that case he would not do it again.

He let money slip through his fingers, he poured out his emotions in diaries and letters, he spent himself unsparingly in friendships, and in his teaching, an activity which he did not like, but which apparently he did uncommonly well. Above all, he gave himself to, and in, his music. Nothing short of total collapse could dam up the music that welled and flowed. No sooner had he decided, as he repeatedly did, that it was all over, that the well was empty, than a freshet broke and he was down to work again, giving it form, and feeling a new pride in himself. For of course he was not ignorant of the stature of his gift. When in his early twenties he gave up his job at the Ministry of Justice to give his life to music, his eldest brother Nikolai reproved his recklessness, but he answered: 'The day will come when you'll be proud of me.'

He was modest in manner and no one could have been more ready to submit to criticism, or striven harder to be objective about his own works. This was not easy and there was usually a swing from extreme partiality to distaste for his latest composition, and balanced judgment came only when the pendulum had stopped. Such is the way with most artists, no doubt. Sometimes Tchaikovsky made astonishing generalisations, as for instance that he had never been able to master form; or such candid admissions as when he told the Grand Duke Constantine: 'There is a lot of padding in my works: an experienced eye can see the stitches of my seams, but I cannot help it.'

In the early stages of his development he carried humility to excess, and was far too willing to accept the harsh judgments of others; to alter or even destroy his compositions at the word of someone who may not have understood his work, or who may have had a jealous motive which Tchaikovsky in his innocence was incapable of suspecting.

The failure of his debut as conductor, the shame of which stayed with him so long, was only one and by no means the first of his disappointments. Some he brought upon himself, some were due to the malice of others; some were simply the consequence of a new talent making its appearance and encountering the conservatism of public taste; some must be put down to sheer bad luck, which pursued him so unremittingly that he might well have asked, with Gerard Manley Hopkins: 'Why must disappointment all I endeavour end?'

We may here glance at some examples of his woes.

A certain number of them came from two dictatorial geniuses, the brothers Rubinstein: Anton, his teacher, and Nikolai, his employer. Thus, Tchaikovsky hoped to burst upon the world at a concert of the Russian Musical Society; Nikolai Rubinstein, who was the Moscow founder and subsequently head of the Conservatory into which it grew, had given this young member of his staff an opportunity to have one of his works played, and Tchaikovsky had written a *Concert Overture in C minor*. He was distressed to find that Rubinstein had discarded it and substituted an earlier piece which Tchaikovsky felt he had already left behind in his development.

This was a mild shock compared with what happened to his *First Symphony*, which he called 'Winter Day Dreams'. The symphony was no product of calm reverie, in spite of its title, but was born in anguish, when the composer was prostrate with nerves and insomnia. When it was still unfinished, he was rash enough to submit it to the two leaders of the St. Petersburg Musical Society, Anton Rubinstein and Nikolai Zaremba. They savaged it with what seemed to the composer to be absolute brutality. The features he liked best, they hated most. His creative judgment struggled with their opinions and he would have liked to refuse the formidable revisions they commanded. But they had been his masters in his student days: they were used to obedience from him, and he was accustomed to submitting. Reluctantly, he set about the task.

But even when he had made the desired alterations, Anton Rubinstein rejected the symphony. Eventually it was his brother who gave it a hearing, but conducted the middle two movements only, and it was not a success. The music was too novel, in form and matter, for the audience of the day, as it had been for the St. Petersburg musicians. It is difficult for us to put ourselves in the place of an audience unfamiliar with Tchaikovsky's music and that of the individuals and schools which have succeeded him.

Later on, Tchaikovsky determined to restore the symphony to the form in which he had originally composed it. He deleted most of the changes he had made. But—a sad footnote to the story—when he wanted to reinstate the second theme, to which Zaremba in particular had objected, it refused to be recalled. He was obliged to publish the work with a substitute theme, which, rightly or wrongly, he felt to be inferior.

This incident had considerable importance in his life. It cut the apron-strings of St. Petersburg, the city of his upbringing and the musical centre of Russia. Henceforward Tchaikovsky began to look towards Moscow, not at first without misgivings, as a place where the winds might blow less harshly about his head.

When the symphony was played in Moscow, two years after these troubles in the northern capital, it had a welcome that confirmed him in this.

Distresses, sudden reversals of fortune, inexplicable failures and equally improbable successes—these are to be found in the careers of most artists, but Tchaikovsky had surely more than his share: so much so, that one wonders whether he did not rather 'ask for' cruelties; as there is always one child at school who is bullied far more than the rest. To energetic, masterful men like the Rubinsteins, fighting their way in the world, determined to create a proper standing for Russian music and musicians, he may have seemed maddeningly gentle and easy to wound. There were occasions, though, when they made amends and had second thoughts about his work. Tchaikovsky never experienced a more bitter castigation in his life than Nikolai Rubinstein dealt out to the *B flat minor Concerto*; one consequence being that it was played in public for the first time in Boston, Massachusetts, instead of in Russia. Yet two years later Nikolai Rubinstein introduced it to an appreciative audience at a concert in St. Petersburg—in spite of the composer's refusal to rewrite it as he had demanded.

Sometimes it was the caprice of the public that made Tchaikovsky suffer. The treatment accorded to his first opera, to take one more instance from his early days, was harder to bear than any outright refusal. *The Voyevoda* went up like a rocket and came down like the stick.

It was produced in Moscow, a year after the fiasco of the dances from it which Tchaikovsky had tried to conduct. The first-night audience received the opera with enthusiasm. The composer had to go on the stage to receive a bouquet, and was given fifteen curtain-calls. His head must have been in the stars.

The opera ran for just five performances. According to some accounts it was poorly sung. Tchaikovsky's boyhood friend, the critic Herman Laroche, wrote a hostile critique, although not long before he had declared, 'I consider yours the greatest musical talent of Russia's future.'

Tchaikovsky tore up Laroche's notice. Not long afterwards he tore up the score of his opera too. This act might be thought to vindicate the critic! But the composer refused to speak to him again for two years.

His behaviour in this case, and in that of the *Concerto* and *First Symphony* was not that of a coward or a man without pride in his work, easily mortified though he was. Innovators learn that they have to create their public, since there is none ready-made for them, by conflicts and conquests, making enemies and influencing people, at peril of getting tough or cynical.

Tchaikovsky, though, was extremely resilient, his downcast spirits could always rise again, he was incapable of cynicism, and was always capable of starting a new and trusting friendship.

By the time he had reached what should have been only middle age, Tchaikovsky was recognised as one of the glories of his native land, despite all that rivalry and calumny could do against him. In his naïve way he was surprised to find, travelling abroad, that he was known wherever he went.

Out of the blue sky of comparative contentment he had to take a staggering and totally unexpected blow: the defection of his patroness Mme. Nadejda von Meck, who had encouraged and supported him, emotionally and materially, for thirteen years.

This famous friendship, which will have its due place later in this narrative of the composer's life, was one of the strangest ever known. The two parties made a pact never to meet. They never spoke to each other, and when their carriages chanced to pass, they drove on without stopping.

They corresponded voluminously, and in loving terms, though Tchaikovsky refused the intimacy of 'thou' instead of 'you'. They rhapsodised about their emotions, and about music; they continually gave each other advice; and in the end undoubtedly came to rely a great deal on each other.

All the more remarkable was the break, which came from Mme. von Meck's side. The composer died without ever really understanding her motives, and they are still not perfectly clear. But some insight has been gained into the matter, and more evidence is available to us than was known to Tchaikovsky. There has been a good deal of astute psychological speculation, but there can be no certainty.

She had pensioned him, commissioned works from him, striven through various channels to increase his fame, rented an Italian villa for him, entertained him—in her absence—at her splendid home. She had fuelled his genius, given him security, made him declarations of innocent love that involved no responsibility except to pursue his art.

Suddenly this whole golden ambience she had created for him vanished. No more money, no more communications, no decently adequate explanation. Tchaikovsky was left like the Sleeper Awakened in the *Arabian Nights*, when the Caliph's prank is over.

Viewed from outside, theirs was an impossible friendship. There are too many elements of make-believe about it, and the parties seem a little like two surrealists, conspiring to construct a dream. On the other hand, they wrote much sound sense to each other: she, on such matters as Tchaikovsky's marriage, on where it was best for him to live, and whether he should accept this or that commission on certain terms; he, on his music and that of others, and on the character of his associates. They exchanged good, enlightened, nineteenth-century views on religion. Neither of them betrays any sense of the oddity of their bodiless relationship—and yet other people must surely have remarked on it and questioned them about it. But the full extent of their soul-baring and of their financial relations were known only to themselves.

Remarkable as it was, and bitter as was its ending, it is necessary to keep this friendship in perspective. It was by no means the whole of Tchaikovsky's personal life. In spite of the intimate tone of the correspondence with Mme. von Meck, Tchaikovsky never told her anything directly about the homosexual part of his nature, or the territory into which it led him. Nor did she discuss with him her emotional conflicts over her eldest son, which may be the clue to her ultimate change of heart. Tchaikovsky's life was rich and full of people, and he had lived thirty-seven years in this world before he heard of Mme. von Meck. She meant much to him, and he to her; but not everything. Although he had written to her that he did not believe he could produce another line of music without her, yet in point of fact he went on composing after her desertion, without any loss of inspiration.

One element that might have spared him some of his sufferings was certainly lacking from Tchaikovsky's character: a sense of humour. His feelings could have the purgation of anger, sometimes;

of tears, often; but almost never of laughter. He could be exuberant, he could play tenderly with children, he could drink 'like a Russian', he could enjoy card-games and small-talk when he knew the company well enough and was not too shy. His manners, dignified and gentle, were found charming. But he very seldom smiled.

There are many witnesses to his charms, one of whom declares that 'everyone fell in love with him'—men, women, grandmothers and children alike. Neither an aristocrat nor a man of the people, he was without snobbery or condescension, and cared nothing for ancestry. He sometimes had to wear borrowed clothes, but he never knew real poverty or hardship. He was singularly free from greed for money, and from the temptation to be corrupted by it.

In politics Tchaikovsky was mildly conservative, strongly patriotic, and conventionally filial towards the Tsar.

Tchaikovsky wrote quite a quantity of words, apart from letters and journals. He wrote opera libretti, two textbooks of harmony, some youthful poems, a mass of reviews and musical criticism, many translations, and an autobiography—now lost.

He was fond of calling himself lazy, though the remark became an affectation in the end. While young he was sincerely worried about his indolence. He more than anyone else except his master Rubinstein made music a professional matter in Russia; he detested what he considered the dilettantism of the dominant St. Petersburg school of composers. But his own entry into music was amateur and casual.

At the age of twenty-one, he wrote to his sister, Alexandra (Sasha), describing himself as the possessor of 'uncommon talents . . . power and capacity', but said he was 'afraid of want of purpose'. He accused himself of 'idleness, fragmentariness' and said he feared he was 'easily done for'.

But what a student he became! Rubinstein said of him later: 'Once in the composition class I told him to write out contrapuntal variations on a given theme, and mentioned that in this sort of work not only quality but quantity was important. I thought he might write about twelve variations. At the next class he gave me over two hundred.'

Demoniac energy indeed, in the slender, none too robust frame of this nervous, self-critical, self-doubting young man. There are two or three explanations, complementary to one another, for his power, throughout his life, to work in this way. One, which is no explanation at all, is that he was a genius, with the well-known proportions of perspiration and inspiration. Since the term cannot be defined, it had better be taken as one of the axioms of the case. Another explanation is that the artist is a man who harnesses the powers of chaos in the beauty of order, starting with the chaos in himself. Tchaikovsky quickly found his idiom and method, releasing the torrents within him. He knew at once that this was the way for him to keep sane, to hold his personality together, to justify his existence in his own eyes. It was very necessary, for he felt he had many wayward impulses, many reasons for guilt, could easily go to pieces, could surrender to the temptation to escape from life and become a drone. He says he even contemplated the monastic life; and this was certainly no impulse of piety, but simple escapism (he was never near enough the church to think he had any religious vocation).

The other explanation is connected with his love of Russia, his relations with the Rubinsteins, his response to the spirit of his times and the desire of eager men of talent to enhance Russia's glory and compel the world's admiration. Such a crusading programme demanded a great output. Tchaikovsky felt strongly that the men who had the gifts to create their nation's music should throw themselves wholly into the task and not treat their art as merely the hobby or fancy of a gentleman, a landowner, an officer, a courtier, or a bureaucrat. He himself had taken the risk and given up everything for music, determined to be thoroughly professional about it. He thought others should do the same. It meant working hard, and not only writing according to your inclination but fulfilling the tasks that offered, even if they were boring. Hardly ever did he refuse a commission, even when he despised the kind of thing he turned out. (No critic of the hackneyed *1812 Overture* could be more severe than Tchaikovsky himself: he called it 'showy and noisy' with 'no artistic merit, because I wrote it without warmth and without love'.)

Should an artist do hack-work to order, 'without warmth and without love', work that may debase the currency, debauch the taste of inexperienced audiences?—it is a debatable question. But it is clear that Tchaikovsky's own motive was not base; he made it a point of professional honour to meet the demands made upon him, as many painters, composers and sculptors and some writers have done. He had always enough surplus energy to do these commissioned works quickly and effectively so that he could get on with his own proper labours.

Except for church music on the one hand and folk song on the other—in both of which Tchaikovsky showed considerable interest—the native art of music in Russia was young. Italians, Germans, Frenchmen were the country's music-makers until Glinka virtually founded the Russian school not long before Tchaikovsky's birth.

There is a striking story of how Anton Rubinstein found out the insignificance of his art in the eyes of official society. The parallel in England was the old law that classified actors as rogues and vagabonds.

Rubinstein, a Jew whose parents were baptised in the Christian faith, went to the cathedral for confession, which was compulsory every three years, and when asked his rank and vocation replied that he was 'a musician, an artist'.

The deacon asked whether he was employed in the theatre? Did he give lessons in some school? Was he in the government service? He replied no to all these questions. The deacon was in a quandary. No category existed for one of the world's foremost pianists.

'I know not how it would have ended', Rubinstein says, 'had it not occurred to the deacon to say, "May I ask your father's profession?"—"A merchant of the Second Guild."—"No, then, we understand!" exclaimed the deacon, greatly relieved. "You are the son of a merchant of the Second Guild, and as such we shall inscribe your name."'

The questions and the answer left an indelible impression on his mind. The title of musician, universally respected in other lands, had in Russia no definition, no standing.

In such a society, how strongly the young musicians must have felt the need to raise the prestige of their art.

In accordance with this purpose, Tchaikovsky steeled himself as the years advanced to appear before the public, to meet his great contemporaries, to accept the honours done him by foreign lands. He came to be known as 'the hermit of Klin', but that was a phase, an episode only; even in that quiet country place he received friends and lived a tolerably social life; and in truth it was chiefly a base for his constant journeys.

It is sometimes said that Tchaikovsky wore himself out, worked himself to death. It is a matter of opinion whether an artist *can* do such a thing. Tchaikovsky died of a disease which has nothing to do with hard work and everything to do with contaminated water.

The story of Tchaikovsky's life is full of crises, and its dramas were played in a great variety of settings. He swam through an extraordinary tangle of personal relationships. He loved and hated (though he could not hate for long), was incensed, enraptured, moved to tenderness or sorrow from hour to hour, and expressed these feelings with a freedom that the modern person, particularly the Englishman, may find astonishing.

Not everything is known about him, the devotion of scholars notwithstanding; nor ever will be. He himself destroyed some of the evidence, and some of it was suppressed by his brother, the well-named Modest, one of his earliest biographers, who was concerned with the composer's good name. Probably the missing data is of no great importance and would do no more than fill in details of the picture of the man, which is clear and coherent in its outline.

A study of his life confirms what musicians feel about his work: that except for increasing mastery, there is no radical change over the whole creative period. His music records spiritual growth but not transformation. His life shows him always struggling with the explosive forces that were mixed in his make-up, and always much the same simple, mercurial person as in early days. It is worth noting that he idolised Mozart, who—though in a classic instead of a romantic vein—poured out end-in-itself music that registered no great psychological development; and he felt little sympathy with Beethoven or Wagner, in whom such development is of major importance.

These are different *types* of composer, not degrees of greatness, of course. The objection may also be made that Tchaikovsky was as unlike his hero Mozart in other respects as possible. Mme. von Meck made that very point, protesting in her letters that he had nothing in common with 'that epicurean Mozart'—whose music she was not the person to appreciate.

He replied, 'You say that my worship for Mozart is quite contrary to my musical nature. But perhaps it is just because—being a child of my day—I feel broken and spiritually out of joint, that I find consolation and rest in Mozart's music, wherein he gives expression to that joy of life which was part of his sane and wholesome temperament, not yet undermined by reflection.'

That last phrase—'not yet undermined by reflection'—seems the link between the diverse musical temperaments of Mozart and Tchaikovsky. Elsewhere, Tchaikovsky wrote, 'Mozart was an inspired being, childishly innocent, mild as a dove and modest as a maid'. The description would fit Tchaikovsky himself, in spite of the sins for which he blamed himself so harshly. He did feel 'out of joint' and sometimes broken up; but he, too, was an inspired being and knew how to give voice to the joy of life, as well as its pathos.

Sensitive, thoughtful, idealistic: he was all these things; he was also, one can't help seeing, uncommonly unsophisticated. In fact, the one thing he never acquired was sophistication, a quality which many of his associates, like Laroche and the Rubinsteins, seem to have had from their birth The lack of it may show a limitation in him but is inseparable from the pure-hearted quality which, shining through the texture of his music, endears it to millions of ordinary people. In Tchaikovsky's uninhibited flow of melodies and sonorities we feel his goodness. A certain amount of the emotionally lush is not an exorbitant price to pay.

CHAPTER II

THE PLUNGE

THE family into which Piotr Ilyich Tchaikovsky was born was singularly unmusical. Not only was there no encouragement to him to become a musician, but he did not have the immense advantage enjoyed by many composers of hearing music played and talked about with enthusiasm in his childhood, taking in its rudiments with the air he breathed. Modest, his brother, became a successful playwright and librettist, but he, too, found little in the home atmosphere to foster his interests.

But the home was comfortable and hospitable, and possessed the degree of culture appropriate to its time and its class. To say it was unmusical is a comparative term; for in those days when music was made in the home a little executant capacity was a necessary 'accomplishment'—like needlework—for young ladies. Tchaikovsky's mother sometimes played and sang to him. Besides the piano there was a mechanical music-maker, a pioneer invention called an orchestrion—a musical box with stops, which imitated the sounds of several instruments. It played Mozart, Donizetti, Rossini, and Bellini, and thus implanted in the little boy his earliest tastes.

Tchaikovsky was born on May 7, 1840, in the province of Viatka, the son of a mining engineer, and grandson of a physician. 'There are a number of Poles bearing my name,' he wrote. 'I myself am probably of Polish descent, though I don't know positively who my ancestors were.'

His father, he said, lost his capital by putting it into the hands of 'an adventuress, who promised him mountains of gold'. So instead of retiring his father had to go back to work for another fourteen years, finding a job with the St. Petersburg Technological Institute, from which he was finally pensioned off. Tchaikovsky himself was later liable to fits of insecurity and the fear that he would have to begin again as a teacher, even when his affairs were thriving.

His mother, he wrote Mme. von Meck, 'was a fine, clever woman'. After her death, his father remarried and 'my stepmother, a half-educated but very intelligent and extremely kind woman, succeeded in inspiring us all with a sincere respect for her tender, unselfish devotion to her old husband'. (This was his third wife.) 'I have four brothers. The eldest, Nikolai, works on the railway and lives at Kharkov. He is married but childless. After him, I come; after me, my brother Hippolyte, who lives in Odessa, married and also childless. Then come the twins, Anatol and Modest.' The twins, just ten years younger than Piotr, were the objects of his own devotion, whom he sought to guide and help throughout their childhood, and whom he loved all his life. There had been a daughter of his father's first marriage, who was eleven years older than Piotr, and played little part in his life. It was his younger sister, Sasha, two years his junior, who shared his secrets, and to whose home he used to flee in times of trouble. On the whole, they seem to have been an affectionate family.

They were not nobility but they were 'gentlefolk' who could mix unselfconsciously in any society.

What kind of a child was Tchaikovsky? Sweet and lively, dull, untidy, capricious, in phases, like any other. He cried easily, was hysterical sometimes and had mysterious ailments, no doubt nervous in character.

He was not especially good-looking, being one of those people whose looks improve steadily as they mature, as his photographs bear witness. A picture of him at eight conveys a delicate charm, however, and his governess called him 'a porcelain child'.

The governess, Fanny Durbach, a French protestant, was one of the two women whom the child adored. The other was his mother, Alexandra Andreyevna, herself of French ancestry, as her grandfather was a refugee from the Revolution, although she was born in St. Petersburg and educated in an orphanage there.

A fact of significance in her ancestry is that her grandfather was epileptic, and there may have been a tendency to this condition in the composer.

Fanny Durbach was twenty-two when she was engaged to live in the Tchaikovsky household and give lessons to six-year-old Nikolai and his cousin Lydia, who was living under the same roof. Little Piotr begged to join in and was allowed to do so. He learned rapidly, and is credited with being fluent in German and French by the age of six. He was certainly the brightest of the three pupils, and in the sunny affection between him and the governess his mind flourished. Unfortunately, the governess did not encourage him in music, though she tried to teach him to paint, to write French verse, and Russian prose. She thought he had literary talent. But she considered he reacted in an unhealthily emotional way to music, and did her best to damp him down. Once he cut his fingers by drumming rhythms on a window-pane until he broke the glass. Once she found him crying in bed after listening to music at an adult party: he begged her to 'save him from the music', and held his head saying, 'It's in there, it won't let me rest.'

He was happy under her sway, and she saw he had unusual

qualities. He loved her sincerely, despite her tendency to sandbag his strongest emotions with commonsense.

At his first home, at the town of Votkinsk, living was expansive. The composer's cheerful father, a Lieutenant-colonel and chief inspector of mines, was an important person in the neighbourhood and was commander of a hundred Cossacks. Even after the move to St. Petersburg, the home was not poor, but the change in circumstances was great for Piotr, for he was shortly afterwards sent, at the age of eight, to boarding-school.

Failing to recover normally after an attack of measles, he was described by a doctor as suffering from 'spinal brain disease' and was ordered six months' rest. He wrote pathetic little letters to his lost governess, saying 'I can understand nothing'.

He cried and moped, but gradually his health returned.

His father, meanwhile, had taken a job east of the Urals, and removed to Alapayevsk, in the province of Perm. Piotr's education was temporarily in the hands of his half-sister, Zinaida, whom he did not care for. Eventually he was found a new governess, his mental development was again encouraged, and once again he responded eagerly. He was able to resume long-interrupted piano lessons, and we get the first glimpse of his ruling passion. He writes to Fanny that he is hardly ever away from the piano, and that this 'comforts me a great deal', adding that he is sad much of the time.

Aged ten, Piotr was sent to the St. Petersburg School of Jurisprudence. When it came to parting from his mother, who had taken him there and was leaving to return to Alapayevsk, he grew hysterical, wept and kissed and clung to her, and even ran after her carriage and seized the turning wheel. He used to recall that parting as the most terrible moment of his life. It was two years before the family moved to St. Petersburg, and his sense of exile was assuaged.

Men of genius, it has been said, have wonderful mothers and tragic lives. There does not appear to have been anything particularly wonderful, objectively speaking, about Tchaikovsky's mother: but she seemed so to him.

Her contribution to her son's musical education was possibly more important than it looks—just because he loved her so much, and every association with her had a sacred intensity. She took him to the opera: it was Glinka's *A Life for the Tsar*. He spoke of this with enthusiasm in the only two of his thirty-nine letters in his first two school years that made any mention of music. He played Alabyev's arrangement of *The Nightingale* and wrote to his mother that 'immense sadness overwhelmed me. I recalled how I played it at Alapayevsk while you listened . . . how you sang it with me. . . . I remembered that this was always our favourite piece.' And the sole musical composition of his childhood, in which Sasha collaborated, was a song called *Our Mamma in Petersburg.*

Piotr, affectionately known as Petia, was fourteen when his mother died of cholera, the scourge which had already once influenced the family fortunes by making the Tchaikovskys decide to move to St. Petersburg rather than Moscow, where it was raging. From the day her illness began she survived for a month, which is an unusually long time, but the best medical attention of the time could not save her. Towards the end she was given a warm bath, then recognised as the last resort, and which her son in his turn was to receive. In neither case did it make the slightest difference.

It was more than two years before Tchaikovsky could bring himself to speak of his mother's death and the suffering it caused him—even in his letters to Fanny Durbach, his beloved governess. When he came across his school letters to his parents, twenty-five years later, he could not sleep at night for thinking of his mother and the pain of losing her. Later still, he entered in his diary, 'Anniversary of Mother's death, thirty-five years ago'.

'She loved her children passionately,' he said. He certainly loved her with passion. No woman throughout his life ever inspired a comparable feeling in him. This powerful mother–son bond is common with homosexuals; though whether as cause or effect is another question.

Tchaikovsky made good progress at his school, in general subjects as well as in his piano lessons. From singing soprano he ripened into alto, and about this time formed the first of his strong attachments. One of these early friends, Vladimir Stepanovich Adamov, destined to become an official of the Ministry of Justice, shared his musical interest. So, a little later, did Alexander Nikolayevich Apukhtin, who became a lyric poet of distinction. They did much opera-going in their student years, and Apukhtin dedicated a poem to Tchaikovsky, which said:

> 'Music was our worshipped idol then,
> And life a fleeting dream to us.'

Tchaikovsky was thinking more and more about music, and at fourteen composed his first original work—a waltz (now lost) dedicated to his second governess. He also considered writing a comic opera, but dropped the subject for a characteristic reason—because there were too many recitatives and arias and too few concerted numbers in the libretto. He also persuaded his father to engage a private musical tutor for him.

This was Rudolf Kundinger, a teacher of repute, who remarked later on that Tchaikovsky had a good memory but made little progress under him. Asked by Tchaikovsky's father whether he thought the boy would be justified in making a career of music, he said 'No.'

Such a life in Russia was a hard one, he truly said. His pupil did not seem to him to have any of the marks of genius. At this time Tchaikovsky was almost certainly unaware of his great gifts, though he felt stirrings and questionings within him and knew that music had the power to arouse his strongest feelings.

The family went to live with a hermit-like uncle of the composer, who found himself among a new assortment of cousins. He also became friendly with an old Neapolitan singing teacher named Piccioli, who used rouge and dyed his hair, and who taught him to love Italian opera. Under his influence, Tchaikovsky wrote an Italianate song and published it at his own expense. It was undistinguished, according to his brother Modest.

At the age of nineteen, his vague hopes of a musician's career having to be abandoned, he left the School of Jurisprudence and became a clerk in the Ministry of Justice. In private life he differed very little from other young men of fashion. His dress was dandyish and he followed the usual amusements—the plays, operas, ballets, and the evening parties, at which he played and would, perhaps, improvise a polka.

At one such affair occurred a trifling incident which may have been a genuine turning point in his life. A cousin in the Mounted Grenadiers, showing off his own musical talents, demonstrated the ability to modulate from any key into another in three chords.

Tchaikovsky was immensely interested and impressed. This technical skill put him on his mettle. Where did his cousin acquire it? At the classes of the Musical Society. Tchaikovsky decided that he would join those classes.

There, of course, his serious musical education really began, and his capacities engaged with something more than waltzes, ballads, and polkas. He found himself crossing a mountain-pass of the mind, and suddenly a great kingdom lay before him. He trembled, doubtful of his moral stamina, doubtful of his strength to go forward and make it his own. But the power was in him, driving him on, overcoming his fears and hesitations, stripping his life of its frivolities and inessentials, dedicating him.

The tussle was not a slight or simple thing. Modest refers to it as his brother's 'dark hours' and says it went on, hidden from the sight of his acquaintances, for more than two years. In pessimistic moments he thought it was already too late to start a musical career—as he told his father, soon after his twenty-first birthday.

That summer, 1861, a temporary escape from his problems came his way. A friend of his father was going on a business tour of Western European capitals, and knowing that Piotr had some facility in languages offered to take him along as interpreter.

Until the coming of a new and more liberal Tsar, Alexander II, foreign travel had long been difficult for ordinary Russians. The opportunity was therefore a doubly 'alluring dream', as he put it, to the young man, and he went off in high excitement.

They visited Berlin, Brussels, Paris and London among other cities. There were many evenings at the opera, there were plays, cafés, concerts—the travellers heard Patti sing. They spent six weeks in Paris, which Tchaikovsky liked better than any other place he saw. It rained in London, and he did not care for Berlin. He came, though, to dislike the man he was travelling with, and they quarrelled.

Tchaikovsky blamed himself for acting the spendthrift, wasting money on 'vulgar pleasures', and described the whole 'dream' tour as 'a colossal piece of folly'.

He now threw himself strenuously into his duties, both at the Ministry of Justice, where he had already climbed to senior assistant to the chief clerk, and in the music classes, where he studied under Zaremba, learning thoroughbass, counterpoint, and the church modes. Besides the piano, he took organ lessons and he began to appear in public as an accompanist. He had neither time nor money for the pursuits of fashion and pleasure. The Tchaikovskys were having a thinner time than ever before, for his father had at last retired, and the younger children were still at school. An occasional hand of cards with the old man was now the composer's main relaxation.

The pressure on Tchaikovsky to stay in his safe job must have been great. But his conscience had to listen to another appeal besides that of responsibility to the household: that of his responsibility as an artist. The day of decision was near.

'Sooner or later I shall abandon my present job for music,' he wrote to Sasha, and went on: 'Whether I become a famous composer or a struggling teacher does not matter. My conscience will be at peace, and I shall no longer have the unhappy right to grumble.'

In the piano class he made a new friend, Herman Augustovich Laroche, a witty young man of only seventeen—the coming critic, who was to upset Tchaikovsky so painfully by his attack on *The Voyevoda*. He was as precociously in advance of his years as Tchaikovsky was in arrears. Tchaikovsky's modesty and willingness to learn gave Laroche a chance to display his brilliance. They took to each other at once, with the older tending to be the disciple of the younger, rather than the other way round. Laroche was a straggle-bearded, hawk-nosed young man, with a narrow, nervous, intellectual face and high forehead.

He had the perceptiveness to realise early that whereas his own talents were critical, Tchaikovsky's were creative, and on no trivial scale, either. He helped to sustain Tchaikovsky's confidence in himself at this crucial time in his life, and he was the author of a letter which helped to secure for him his first job as teacher.

All Tchaikovsky's friendships tended to take on strong emotional colouring. His attachment to Laroche blotted out all other intimacies, and he made the young man his 'dearest companion and friend,' says Modest.

Laroche knew much more about the literature of music than did Tchaikovsky and was an eloquent talker, his conversation being backed by wide general reading. At this early period Tchaikovsky showed many curious musical antipathies, which he later outgrew. His dislikes were not for particular composers, but for certain qualities of sound. He hated the combination of piano and orchestra, the timbre of string quartets and quintets, and most of all the piano with one or more stringed instruments.

'Not once but hundreds of times he vowed in my presence never to compose a piano concerto, nor a violin and piano sonata, nor any work of this class,' his friend says. Laroche uses the rather suspect word, 'morbid', applied so frequently by other writers to an element in Tchaikovsky's music: a hearty pejorative term which often does duty for a judgment, condemning all introspective and melancholy moods. A strange and revolutionary composer Tchaikovsky might have become, if his early antipathies had developed instead of dying away.

Tchaikovsky was working furiously but erratically at his lessons under Zaremba and Anton Rubinstein, and the latter taught him to think in the language of the orchestra, a habit and attitude which put him profoundly in his teacher's debt. As a mature composer, Tchaikovsky usually conceived both the theme and its instrumentation simultaneously. He did not, of course, set down the orchestration at once, but none the less it arrived as part of the original creative thought; and this he owed to Rubinstein—whose own musicianship was supreme as a pianist.

Kashkin says it was Anton Rubinstein who first became impressed by the exceptional ability that Tchaikovsky showed as a student, but Laroche gives the credit to Zaremba. In view of the story of the two hundred variations it was most probably Rubinstein. He then performed one of those acts of psychological statesmanship which mark a great teacher. He asked the pupil to stay and talk to him when the class was over. He accused him of carelessness, that 'fragmentariness' which Tchaikovsky had recognised as his own weakness. At the same time he told him plainly and emphatically that he had a vocation, a destiny, and a corresponding duty. He should be ashamed to treat his gift in an irresponsible way. He must apply himself to it more completely.

This chimed perfectly with what Tchaikovsky was in the habit of telling himself: delivered by the head of the Conservatory, it was a profound shock, of the most bracing kind. He went away and took it to heart.

Whatever wounds these men, Zaremba and Rubinstein, inflicted on him in later years, out of narrowness, envy, or lack of imagination, Tchaikovsky never forgot what wonderful teachers they had been, in their severity and complete seriousness, or denied how much he owed to them.

A small factor helped to settle his future: he failed to get a hoped-for promotion in the government service. So, at twenty-three, with Laroche giving him encouragement, he resigned from the Ministry of Justice. He never again worked at anything unconnected with music.

Anton Rubinstein found him some private pupils to eke out his livelihood, for his father, now living on a small pension, could do nothing more than provide his son's meals. Tchaikovsky lived and worked in one small room containing only a bed and a writing-table, where he sat up late, night after night, at his studies, straining to live up to Rubinstein's expectations. Materially, it was the poorest time of his life. It was also the happiest.

Anton Rubinstein piled ever harder and heavier tasks upon him. The more he did so, the more Tchaikovsky expended himself in labour, even sitting up all night on some piece which he wanted to hand in the next day. His friends and the idler, less dedicated students looked on in astonishment. They said among themselves that Rubinstein had cast some magic spell over the pale, red-eyed young man, who was slaving so madly and looking so pleased to do it.

The students, Tchaikovsky included, were, naturally, irreverent towards the master, and made fun of his various foibles. These included his ungrammatical way of speaking, his total inability to expound a problem logically, the 'fascinating disorder' of his lectures, and the fact that he appeared not to know even ten minutes beforehand what he intended to talk about or how he would say it. Rubinstein was at ease in several languages, but could not speak a single one of them correctly. But he spoke with verve, on the inspiration of the moment, and carried his hearers with him, in spite of their impulse to mock. It was not mere spellbinding: they were made aware of the knowledge and experience behind his words, and were truly impressed. Tchaikovsky despised the master's numerous and insipid compositions as well as being amused by his peculiarities; but he also had an unshakable regard for him as a teacher and a man.

In giving himself up wholly to music, Tchaikovsky had made the first big break of his life; the second, the transition from St. Petersburg to Moscow and from pupil to teacher, was to follow less than three years later. It involved the greater emotional wrench of leaving home.

During those three years he had one musical encouragement, and one harsh discouragement to balance it. The heartening event was the acceptance of his *Dances of the Serving Maids*—the set of dances later incorporated in *The Voyevoda*—for performance at an open-air concert, when they were conducted by Johann Strauss: decidedly more successfully by the waltz king than when he himself attempted it.

The blow was an attack by Rubinstein on an overture which he composed to Ostrovsky's play, *The Storm.*

His teachers did not like Tchaikovsky to be stormy, free, highly coloured. They were opposed to the big orchestra and to all unconventional combinations of instruments. It is clear to us, looking back, that Tchaikovsky needed the full modern orchestra, the post-Meyerbeer orchestra, to speak with his true voice; but it was not at first obvious, even to himself, let alone his teachers; he early developed a preference for it, but did not easily acquire mastery of it, although in the end his understanding of the capacities of the instruments and the range of their combined powers was incomparable.

Rubinstein had already reprimanded Tchaikovsky severely on one occasion when, having asked him to orchestrate Beethoven's *Sonata in D minor* in four different ways, he was offered an arrangement including English horn and various other novel features.

Now Anton Rubinstein not only understood the resources of the big orchestra perfectly but explained them conscientiously and scientifically to his pupils—not in the hope that they would compose for it, but that they would have nothing further to do with it! He must have been often disappointed; as he certainly was in Tchaikovsky.

The 'heretical' combination for which Tchaikovsky scored *The Storm* Overture included tuba, English horn, harp, tremolo for violins *divisi*, i.e. split into sections instead of playing in unison as was customary. It brought down Jove's thunderbolt—but not on his own head, which was not there to receive it. He sent in the composition by the hand of his friend Laroche, being away, and officially unwell, perhaps really so, after an extraordinary spell of dissipation and glory which came to him that summer.

This adventure seemed to him like a fairy-tale, an unaccountable dream.

One of Russia's aristocrats, Prince Alexis Galitsin, meeting Tchaikovsky, took a sudden affectionate interest in him, and invited him to spend the summer on his Kharkov estate, Trostinetz. There the student, completing his daring composition with which to defy his mentors, found himself honoured as never before, and as he would not be again until years of labour and struggle had passed. It pleased the host to treat the young guest as the great man he actually was—probably a princely whim, rather than a divination of his genius.

July 11 was Tchaikovsky's name-day, and the prince made that the climax of the entertainments. It was splendid weather, and the whole day was given over to homage to the young composer.

First there was an attendance at early service. Then came a breakfast that was a banquet, and further entertainments all the day, till darkness fell.

Then the prince led his guests to the forest. Lights were flickering among the trees: they found the paths illuminated with flaming torches. They trooped down the avenues of light and found that in the middle of the woods the prince's servants had erected a marquee, and in it had served a feast, of royal and Russian magnificence. There was music, folk dancing, choral singing on the green sward surrounding the great tent.

Tchaikovsky, the flushed and nervous youth, still only trying his musical strength, found himself praised and fêted in the torchlit glade like a pagan bard. If he thought about the work he had just completed for Rubinstein, he must have known how soon he would be made to feel rather like a human sacrifice.

Very humanly, if not very heroically, he took to his bed instead of returning to St. Petersburg. He sent the overture by post to Laroche, asking him to take it to Rubinstein.

It was Sunday morning when Laroche complied with this innocent-seeming request. 'Never in the course of my life have I had to listen to such a homily on my own sins as I then endured vicariously,' he said.

Rubinstein burst out in fury, and he was a master of invective.

'How dare you bring me such a specimen of your own composition?' he began, oblivious of the fact that the man before him was nothing more than the bearer of the manuscript. Laroche felt like the bearer of bad tidings to Cleopatra, who got beaten for his services.

A few days later Tchaikovsky appeared in person, having recovering from his illness and come down from fairyland. Hearing from Laroche what Rubinstein thought of his effort, he went with his heart in his mouth to present himself before the master.

But by this time, Rubinstein had forgotten his wrath. Lightning never strikes twice on the same spot. Tchaikovsky was received with mildness.

On second thoughts, discouragement is the wrong word to apply to this experience of Tchaikovsky's: he would know from earlier experience and his understanding of Rubinstein's tastes and standards, that he was inviting anger in submitting such scoring. It was a defiant gesture, the manifestation of youthful genius struggling against irksome bonds and fumbling for its natural freedom of expression.

Anton Rubinstein was himself a young man at this time, no more than thirty. But there was the gulf of a generation in taste between him and Tchaikovsky.

Understanding and musical sympathy, as distinct from admiration and respect, could not cross the gap.

Incidents like the reception of this overture helped to make it clear to Tchaikovsky that however much he admired Rubinstein, to break clear of such teachers at the right time was just as important as it had been to quit the Ministry of Justice.

Meanwhile he went on learning things, with enormous appetite.

In those early days of the Conservatory there were few pupils who could play any instrument well except the piano and the violin. Rubinstein's ambition was to create a Conservatory orchestra, and he set about the task by encouraging some specialisation among the pupils. To achieve this, he put up the substantial sum of 1,500 roubles for free tuition in the instruments required.

Tchaikovsky chose the flute, and after two years became proficient enough for orchestral purposes.

In spite of Tchaikovsky's love of his art and his ever-increasing self-discipline in its service, he wavered sometimes in his resolve to live for music, because of the uncertainty of being able to live by it. One of his friends, aware of his doubts, told him of a post that had fallen vacant, that of a meat inspector. Bizarre as it appears, Tchaikovsky actually gave the proposal his serious consideration. But in the end he stayed his course, though he no longer had a well-to-do family behind him, or any other security, and the future was doubtful. He felt he had committed himself, however, and he did not turn back.

Apart from the brief but wonderful visit to Prince Galitsin's country seat, there were interesting encounters in these years. There was Dostoievsky, for instance, giving his opinions on music, talking 'at length and very foolishly', in the opinion of these students. There were elderly people at Tchaikovsky's sister's country home

Tchaikovsky at the age of twenty-two

Tchaikovsky's parents

who remembered Pushkin and Gogol. There was also a girl, Vera Vasilyevna Davidova, the sister of Sasha's husband, to whom Tchaikovsky dedicated his piano composition *Souvenir of Hapsal* and who was suspected to be in love with him. He told Sasha he would be 'gravely displeased' it it were true.

He composed a string quartet and an overture and then, as a graduation offering, a cantata on Schiller's *Ode to Joy*. It nearly remained unperformed, as the composer was too scared to attend the *viva voce* public examination as required, and Anton Rubinstein threatened to withhold his diploma. But in the end the cantata was performed, and awarded a silver medal, and Tchaikovsky got his diploma in his absence. The composition, needless to say, was heartily loathed and abused by the St. Petersburg musicians, including Rimsky-Korsakov, Balakirev, Serov, Cui—and trounced, to Tchaikovsky in person, by Rubinstein himself.

Tchaikovsky's twenty-fifth year ended, and a new life began.

The *Ode to Joy* was no bad choice of a theme, for it was written in a time of hope: not merely in the composer's personal life, but in that of Russia generally, and the young of Tchaikovsky's generation felt that ideals were not foolish, nor optimism a fallacy. It was 'the thaw'. The serfs had been liberated, censorship had been eased, the rule of the secret police had diminished, the land was full of gifted writers and composers; the arts were even receiving official support.

Old feudal Russia was having its renaissance. The national consciousness was high, the rivalry of artistic centres was great. Battles of the mind raged everywhere and there was much talk of romanticism and realism, Reason and Spirit.

St. Petersburg, as Tchaikovsky came to realise, was not the place for brilliant innovators, but an enclosed city with a rigid pattern of life. Everybody knew everybody else in the upper circle of its society and all were on visiting terms with each other, as Tolstoy observed. There were, however, distinct sets of which the upper circle was composed—the official set of ill-assorted persons curiously bound together by laws of social etiquette; another pretentious level consisted of pious, virtuous, ugly old women and clever, learned ambitious men which called itself the conscience of St. Petersburg. Yet a third level was the smart set, the world of balls, dinners, and brilliant toilets, which revolved about the court.

Paradoxically, it seems that ancient Moscow, less fashionable, was able to be more open-minded to receive new ideas, and hence was a better environment for Tchaikovsky. A parallel can be seen in the way that the composer, coming late to his art and from a family without a musical tradition, possessed none of the dogmatic views of people with those advantages. He did not grow up either musically sophisticated or hidebound and had no qualms about breaking the rules.

The musical life of St. Petersburg had been brought to a focus by the creation of the Russian Musical Society in 1859. It both arranged concerts and launched classes for professional training, quickly becoming known unofficially as the St. Petersburg Conservatory. The inception of this very important institution came from the intimacy between Anton Rubinstein and the Tsar's aunt, the German-born Grand Duchess Yelena Pavlovna, a great patroness of music. He became her music-master, toured Europe in her company, and discussed with her the possibility of elevating the standing of Russian musicians. Through the Grand Duchess, the Tsar gave his patronage to the venture. Tchaikovsky was one of the earliest pupils at its classes; and just as he had completed his student life, this institution, which had 'hived off' in Moscow, opened up the next stage for him, providing the opportunity for the learner to become a teacher.

The Moscow enterprise, though it had not the prestige and scope of its St. Petersburg parent, also enjoyed the imperial blessing, and its principal, Nikolai Rubinstein, was as energetic and as dedicated as his brother. It had been giving concerts for nearly six years when it received the Tsar's sanction to hold classes. The composer Serov was engaged as its harmony teacher, but he failed to take up the appointment. The reason for this has to do with the difference between Moscow and St. Petersburg in musical tastes, a factor of the greatest moment in Tchaikovsky's own career. Moscow audiences were comparatively cool to one of Serov's operas which had been received with terrific enthusiasm in St. Petersburg. Serov thereupon revoked his decision, and left Nikolai Rubinstein with only a matter of weeks in which to find a substitute.

In this quandary, Nikolai wrote to his brother asking him if he could recommend someone and Anton suggested Tchaikovsky. Zaremba, though, dissented and thought Nikolai should engage someone more mature. If Nikolai Rubinstein needed any endorsement of his brother's advice it was provided by Kashkin, who was one of his staff and a friend of Laroche. It so happened that Kashkin had in his possession a letter from that eloquently expressive young critic, which he showed to his principal.

Tchaikovsky, the letter said, was 'the future star of Russian music'. Rubinstein at once wrote and offered Tchaikovsky the vacant post of teacher of harmony, which he promptly accepted, at the small salary of fifty roubles a month.

It meant a great uprooting for him. Apart from leaving the loved landscape, and that bare room where he had worked so happily, the friends with whom he had made music and the teachers who had moulded him, he was leaving his twin brothers, Modest and Anatol, now fifteen years old. When he first saw them, Tchaikovsky wrote to his governess that these babies 'seem to me to be angels come down to earth', and his adoration never diminished. He wrote later to Mme. von Meck, speaking of their mother's death when the twins were only four: 'I was no mother, but from the first moment of their bereavement I wanted to be to them what a mother is, because experience has taught me what an indelible imprint a mother's tenderness and caresses can leave on the soul of a child. And from that time, between them and me such a bond has grown that I love them more than myself, and am ready to make any sacrifice for them. They are boundlessly devoted to me.'

In his first winter away, he wrote to the twins from Moscow saying he had been imagining their miseries on returning to school after their holidays—'Modka's head under the bedclothes to hide his tears—how I longed to comfort him!' He went on with advice to Modest to 'study, study, study,' and to choose reliable friends. He begged them to write, and ended: 'a kiss for you both.'

The letter, with its kisses and diminutives, is in a tone that clearly says the twins are still children in their elder brother's eyes; but the knowledge that they were passing out of childhood and the need for his 'mothering' helped him to decide that he would accept the Moscow opportunity.

It was some years time before Tchaikovsky mentally settled in Moscow: his loyalties lingered in St. Petersburg, and he felt at first that he could not face 'without horror' the idea of staying in Moscow for years, perhaps for life. In the end it was Moscow's warmer enthusiasm for his music that won him over.

He arrived there in January 1866 and he and a violinist named Shradik were lodged in the house of the Principal, Rubinstein.

He was a stranger, socially bashful, unsure whether he could do what was required of him (he always underrated himself as a teacher) and short of money and clothes. The ancient capital, with its glittering onion domes, its bell-tongued towers and mighty walls, seemed as cold and intimidating as the snows that carpeted and surrounded it.

But he had youth and hope and talent: one imagines that the 'horror' of the situation was not unmitigated. Looking at the wonderful old city, did he also see it as the stage where his triumph and tragedies were to be acted out, and where his name would one day be known and honoured by everyone?

Nikolai Rubinstein was not impressed with Tchaikovsky's wardrobe. He appeared in a borrowed and very shabby fur pelisse. Feeling that the school must maintain a certain sartorial standard for its teachers, the Principal presented him with a second-hand frock coat left behind by a visitor. It fitted very badly, but Tchaikovsky was exceedingly proud to wear it as he entered the pillared portico of the handsome Conservatory to face his first class.

Not surprisingly, he had a severe attack of nerves. But he knew his subject surpassingly well; he had good looks and charm, which have their rôle in the art of teaching; he was dignified, and his serious attitude commanded respect. There was never any criticism, except his own, of his work as a teacher.

Laroche wrote to encourage him, in the same strain as the letter to Kashkin which secured him his job.

'I consider yours the greatest musical talent of Russia's future,' he reiterated, 'stronger and more original than Balakirev's, loftier and more creative than Serov's, much more refined than Rimsky-Korsakov's.' He forecast that it would be five years before Tchaikovsky's truly original works began to appear, but when they did they would 'surpass anything we have heard since Glinka'.

In his new environment, Tchaikovsky began to make friends. One of the first and best was Kashkin, who was Moscow's most popular teacher, and who with his wife offered unstinted hospitality. Another was a beautiful girl whom he pretended to be a little in love with—'she is nicknamed Mufka, and I am wondering whether I dare call her that, too.' There was a playful rivalry over Mufka between Tchaikovsky and Rubinstein (who was only five years his senior): 'I am very much taken with her, which causes Rubinstein to be a perfect nuisance. . . . Rubinstein has also been in love with her, but his sentiments have now cooled.'

He made friendships among the young men whom he was teaching. He also became acquainted with the head of the Moscow opera, Vladimir Petrovich Begichev, and his wife, a former singer, who had two sons by a previous marriage. The younger of these, Vladimir Shilovsky, then fourteen, was later to become Tchaikovsky's protégé and favourite.

Soon after settling in Moscow, Tchaikovsky got to know the rugged and virile Ostrovsky, the dramatist for whose play he had written an overture, and whom he greatly admired. They met at the Artists' Club, which Ostrovsky had founded.

It is characteristic of Tchaikovsky that with all the tumultuous impressions of a new city, new job, new friends and colleagues pouring in upon him, he yet began composing during his first week in Moscow.

The work that occupied him was the *Overture in C minor* which, as already mentioned, brought him his first rebuff from Nikolai Rubinstein. Anton Rubinstein, to whom he sent it in the second place rejected it no less decisively. Tchaikovsky apparently came round to their opinion of the piece, later on, for he wrote the words 'terrible rubbish' across the score.

Nikolai Rubinstein showed better perception than his brother where the older *Overture in F minor* was concerned, for he had Tchaikovsky rescore it for larger orchestra than the St. Petersburg teacher would countenance. It was performed with success, and the composer was loudly applauded at the supper party which followed the concert. He was already planning his first symphony, and his prospects seemed set fair. But within his mind, clouds were gathering.

One reason may have been overwork. He was both teaching and studying music, as well as reading in foreign languages, and taking on such extra commissions as the composition of an overture for a Danish royal visit. (The Tsar's son was marrying a Danish princess: the music was written and duly performed, and the Tsarevich presented a set of gold and turquoise studs to the composer, who sold them immediately for ready cash.) But the deeper conflicts of his nature and the problems of his adjustment in his complex new environment are to be seen as the causes of the coming storm. If overwork contributed, it was only in so far as it led to insomnia, which in turn exhausted the nerves.

Far into the quiet night Tchaikovsky was working at his music. In the noisy daytime, he found it difficult, even when his teaching duties were not demanding his time. Other people's violin and piano classes filled the air with their maddeningly repetitious din.

He found a partial solution when he came across a quiet inn, the *Great Britain*, not far away but out of earshot of the music-makers. There every spring morning he would sit and work in peace for a while. But this respite never lasted long. The students knew the inn, too, and as soon as they were liberated from their classrooms they would flock in, bringing youthful pandemonium. Tchaikovsky would put away his music-paper, pay for his drink, and quietly depart.

Summer holidays ought to have brought relief and averted the crack-up. Strangely enough, they had no such result.

Tchaikovsky's symptoms were becoming ominous. Sleeping badly, he now complained of violent headaches, and then of apoplectic strokes, which may have been a hypochondriacal exaggeration.

They may on the other hand have been severe migraine attacks, or mild epileptic disturbances, inherited from his maternal great-grandfather: a recurrence of the undefined nervous affliction of his childhood. He wrote to his brother that he feared he would die with his first symphony unfinished.

July came, and reunion with his family, though not a general reunion at Kamenka as he had hoped. Instead, he went with Modest to visit some of the Davidovs at Peterhof, near St. Petersburg. Vera, the girl who was in love with him, was there. He had the peace of the sunny countryside, his father was near at hand but not on the spot, he was in a pleasant house, there was a piano which he could play all day long if he wished, and there were no noisy students to interrupt his labours. Nobody was demanding hack compositions, there was no timetable, the company was agreeable, doubtless the food was good and the beds were comfortable. All pressures appeared to be lifted from him at exactly the right time. The only one that remained was the inner pressure of his creative impulse, compelling him to go forward with his first symphony.

Instead of improving, his state dramatically worsened. What little sleep he could get was filled with nightmares, from which he awoke in terror. Hallucinations set in.

The composition of his first major work had already ceased to be a joyous creative act and was a nightmare of struggle with intractable material. Soon it became impossible. Staring and feverish, Tchaikovsky suffered his first complete breakdown, and his frightened relations sent for a doctor.

If doctors in that age of purging and bleeding knew little about the causes and right remedies of the body's ills, they knew even less how to 'minister to a mind diseased, pluck from the memory a rooted sorrow'—or to follow the tricky interplay between sicknesses of psyche and soma. Modern psychiatry could probably have helped. The physician of 1866 could only tell Tchaikovsky's relations that he was very near to the madhouse, and that he must have complete rest, with no more piano-playing or composing for the present.

The patient was frightened into obedience. He knew that he was in truth swaying on the brink of insanity, and that he was no longer fit to take his own decisions: he craved the authority of the doctor's orders, and found release in submission. He realised, too, that in his sick, confused state it was impossible to force himself by mere will-power to complete his symphony. More was at stake than this recalcitrant piece of music.

Tchaikovsky gave up what had become a useless struggle, and allowed himself to slide into passivity.

Body and mind relaxed in thankfulness, maybe just in time, and the tide turned. Almost at once, health and courage began to creep slowly back.

CHAPTER III

THE DIVIDED SELF

TCHAIKOVSKY'S homosexuality, whatever pleasures it may have brought him, was a burden and terror to him and he waged a long, vain struggle against it.

When the first memoirs of Tchaikovsky were published, this was an undiscussable subject. It remained so for over thirty years. References were oblique and guarded: as, for instance, in the entry under Tchaikovsky in Grove's. Rosa Newmarch, in a memoir written six years after the composer's death, and therefore in the lifetime of many who knew him, gracefully avoided the subject, contenting herself with such phrases as 'possessed with an almost feminine craving for approval and encouragement', and 'the almost feminine sensibility of his nature'. Gerald Abraham, as late as 1944, is to be found positively declining to believe that Tchaikovsky had a physically as well as emotionally homosexual side to his life. 'Despite the unusual amount of affection he often showed towards males,' he says, 'there is little ground for supposing that he was a practising homosexual'.

If this were the case, and Tchaikovsky had experienced only temptation, not fulfilment of his desires, he would have had no cause for either remorse or dread of discovery.

More recently, English public opinion has undergone one of its periodic rapid changes, and with amendments in the law foreshadowed, newspapers, radio, and television have begun to talk openly and even open-mindedly about homosexuality and no longer feel obliged to treat it as necessarily either a state of moral degeneracy or a disease.

Official views thus appear to be moving towards conformity with private conversation and daily social practice.

There is still much conflict of learned opinion on the origins of homosexuality. It is sometimes regarded as a neurotic state, originating in infancy; recent statistical evidence suggests that it may be innate; some authorities say it is a thing of glands; some point to evolutionary history and the vestiges of the opposite sex in each person's body; some grade the temperaments all the way from extreme to extreme, and find them all 'natural'; some consider homosexuality a fixation in a stage of development that should be left behind at adolescence. It is not limited to a single form and there are probably many causes. Psychiatrists seem to have had little success in attempting to 'cure' it, and prefer nowadays to try to adjust the homosexual to his life and make him accept himself.

Most authorities would agree that conflict with the environment, the dread of public opinion, the constant vigilance imposed on speech and behaviour, the necessity to crush strong feelings or to hide their consequences, put a huge strain on the psyche. The ultimate agony, though, lies in the homosexual's submission to public censure and judgment which may drive him to condemn his own nature, twisting this way and that in a vain effort to escape it.

That was Tchaikovsky's plight. He was irrevocably homosexual, but it was no part of his programme to 'épater le bourgeois': to be an artist was in itself sufficient deviation from the common run for his liking, and moreover he did not want any other sort of clash to upset his relations with the public whom he had to win over to his new kind of music.

Homosexuality was not uncommon in the Russia of his time (if it has ever been uncommon anywhere). But as in Victorian England, it was regarded as shameful, and Tchaikovsky never dared to name it in his correspondence or his diaries: in the latter he denoted it by the letter 'Z'.

His brother Modest was also an invert, unlike the other twin, Anatol. Their sister, Sasha, appears to have known all about Modest and Piotr, but did not receive explicit confidences. Such a safety-valve as Modest provided must have been of the utmost help to Tchaikovsky, especially in his formative years. Throughout his life this was one person to whom he could confide without fear.

There was no psychiatrist to guide his understanding of the problem, or to mediate an acceptance of his nature. 'My predilections are my greatest, my most insurmountable obstacle to happiness,' he wrote. 'I must fight against nature with all my might.'

In his diaries he cries, 'What should I do to be normal?'

He found out by the desperate trial and error of marriage what he must not do.

At the time of that event, ten years after the breakdown described in the previous chapter, he wrote to Modest saying, 'There are people who cannot help despising me for my vice, if only because they learned to love me before they had any suspicion that I was a man with a lost reputation. Sasha is one of them. I know that she guesses and forgives everything. A similar attitude is revealed by many other people, who are either loved or honoured by me.

'Can you possibly think that the consciousness of their pity and forgiveness for actions for which I cannot be held responsible is not a difficult cross to bear? Or that the thought that those who love me may at times be ashamed of me does not torment me? And such occasions have arisen a hundred times and will arise a hundred times more.'

Actions for which I cannot be held responsible. He had been driven to the point of formulating it like that. At the same time he still hoped to achieve a self-conquest that would make him 'normal'. The marriage which brought him to the brink of suicide and madness should have ended all such hopes, though it was an expensive way to learn: but he was still wondering whether it could be done, a decade later.

This may be the occasion to mention that Tchaikovsky was not the effeminate type of homosexual, whose voice and appearance proclaim him for what he is. He had every good reason to believe that his audiences, his pupils and his musical acquaintances would accept him as a normal person, unless some scandal reached their ears.

One may perhaps find a betraying touch of the feminine in small characteristics. 'Burned perfume', says an entry in his diary: he was very fond of scent, and used to experiment with different blends. He readily burst into tears: but we must be careful how we assess that faculty. It was the high romantic period, when a man was considered to lack sensibilities if he did not weep on all suitably affecting occasions. Literature from the late eighteenth century to the late nineteenth is dripping with manly tears. The fashion has changed, in both life and letters, but in spite of hard-boiled realism and the stiff upper lip, tough men do weep, to this day, on more occasions than they will publicly admit; and not from any deficiency of male hormones.

Tchaikovsky was above average height, well proportioned, with a masculine voice, bearded, upright in bearing, quiet, and gracious in manner. A rather surprising fact is that he was able to put away great quantities of alcohol without being any the worse for it. At one time he made himself out to be actually 'taking to drink', but he was exaggerating: it never had a serious hold on him.

He could get very indignant, and could fly into rages sometimes. Habitually, he was gentle, but hysteria was not far below the surface, as he well knew.

No evidence exists to show when Tchaikovsky first discovered he was homosexual, or when he first yielded to his impulses. It has been suggested that this happened when he was in his early twenties. It may have been some years earlier, but according to Modest—a plain young man, not much like his brother in looks, except for a wide skull and disenchanted eyes—soon after Piotr became a government clerk, there was 'some unknown event in his life'. He goes on to explain that at that time Piotr (aged twenty) was feverishly pursuing vicious pleasures that led to agonising despairs. These generalised phrases presumably refer to homosexual passions and disappointments which his brother did not think fit to specify. There is, however, no particular reason to suppose that the unknown event was the first of its kind, if in fact it was a homosexual affair. His friendship with Piccioli in 1855 is a more likely starting-point.

Tchaikovsky's hidden and hopeless struggle with his sexual tendencies had certainly been going on for years by the time of his first breakdown. The situation may have felt more acute to him in Moscow than in St. Petersburg, if only because he had the responsibility of a teacher instead of the irresponsibility of a student, and because he was becoming known also as a young composer. The attraction of the boys studying at the Conservatory may have intensified his sense of peril, and he may conceivably have heard of gossip which was circulating in that quarter. Possibly there was nothing so immediate, only the knowledge of the divided self, the moral tension contributing its share to the forces threatening his reason.

The most astonishing thing about the breakdown is that with no treatment but rest he recovered so quickly and completely. By the time the new term began at the Conservatory, in September, he was back there with his confidence restored. His salary had been raised. The Conservatory had moved into a larger building, and a banquet was held to celebrate the expansion. Tchaikovsky surprised everybody, including himself. He not only proposed a toast to the parent body in St. Petersburg, rhapsodising in praise of his old teacher Anton Rubinstein, but he sat down and played from memory Glinka's Overture to *Ruslan and Ludmilla*, declaring that he must insist that Glinka's should be the first music to be heard in the new building. He was warmly applauded. Somehow or other, he had recovered his balance and mental vigour, and even, for once, overcome his stage-fright.

The breakdown had halted Tchaikovsky's labours on his *Winter Day Dreams* symphony. Anton's harsh rejection of this work alienated Tchaikovsky's sympathies from St. Petersburg, for he perceived that Nikolai, for all his caution, was less obdurate than his brother, and that his talents would have freer play in the newly blossoming Moscow Conservatory.

The symphony was at last performed as a whole under Nikolai's baton almost two years later and this time the audience liked it. But it was not repeated for another sixteen years, and was never to be popular.

Paradoxically, Tchaikovsky's health, mental and physical, which had cracked up in the midst of a calm holiday, now held out splendidly against a run of ill luck. After the rejection of the first symphony came the tribulations of the first opera, which, as already mentioned, ran for only five performances.

Following up the advantage of his acquaintanceship with Ostrovsky, the composer asked him if he would be prepared to write a libretto based on his play *The Voyevoda*, or *A Dream on the Volga*.

He consented, and two or three months later he gave the first act to Tchaikovsky, who began work on it immediately. But he interrupted himself to carry out another task, a piano composition which became his Opus 1—*Scherzo in Russian Style*. Then, in the utmost confusion and dismay, he went to confess to Ostrovsky that the libretto text was lost or accidentally destroyed.

The amiable dramatist agreed to rewrite it. But Tchaikovsky proved so constructive a collaborator, so full of ideas and suggested alterations, that after completing one act, Ostrovsky gave up, and left the composer to do the rest himself.

This Tchaikovsky manfully did, and was orchestrating the last act of the opera by the time his first symphony was played, though travel and other work had intervened. He was never a good librettist but he would always undertake a literary task, like any other, if he felt it was required of him. To be able to write words for music was a part of all-round musicianship, in his view: if your librettist let you down, you did the writing yourself.

He did not find this half as intimidating as being asked to make a speech of homage to the aged Berlioz at a Moscow dinner. But that, too, he accomplished without disgracing himself.

An ordeal of another kind was being stranded, near-penniless and freezing, on the coast of Finland. It happened to him and his brother Anatol when they went on holiday together, taking too little money and spending too quickly. They had to use their last sou for the cheapest boat passage to Hapsal, Estonia, a bitterly cold voyage, to reach their relations the Davidovs, who put them up for the rest of the summer vacation.

The musical fruit of this holiday was the *Souvenir of Hapsal* among which is the *Chant sans Paroles*, the first of Tchaikovsky's compositions to become world-famous.

Vera Davidova was no doubt more than flattered at the dedication of the *Hapsal* music to her. It must have seemed to her a distinct encouragement to hope that the composer returned her affections. The rest of the family looked at it in the same light. But the time had not yet come when Tchaikovsky would consider marriage as a possible solution to his problems.

He wrote to his sister the following spring on the subject of Vera. 'I quite see how all this ought to end,' he said. 'But what can I do if I sense that my feeling for her would turn to hatred if the question of marriage ever became serious?'

He was already becoming very much attached to young Vladimir Shilovsky, the frail, handsome son of the former opera-singer. Vera never had the same kind of hold over his feelings, fond though he was of her. Whether she knew it, how much she suffered, we cannot tell. Her life was of no interest to posterity: there was no one to put her thoughts on record. Her song remains without words.

Tchaikovsky was giving music lessons to Vladimir, now sixteen years old. When the summer came, Begichev, the boy's step-father, decided to take him abroad for a holiday and invited Tchaikovsky along so that the teaching could continue without interruption. They went to Berlin, and then to Paris, where Vladimir was seen by specialists, who found him threatened with consumption.

Parting regretfully from his companions, Tchaikovsky returned to Russia. He visited his twin brothers and the Davidovs before leaving for Moscow, where the autumn classes at the Conservatory, the rehearsals for *The Voyevoda*, and plans for a second opera were waiting to consume his time and energies.

Before the summer tour Tchaikovsky had made his bow as a music critic, in a way which finely exemplifies his fairmindedness and generosity of spirit.

It must be remembered that he was an enemy of dilettantism, the vice of which he accused the nationalist school of composers at St. Petersburg—notably the Five: Balakirev, Cui, Mussorgsky, Borodin, and Rimsky-Korsakov. Moreover, though most patriotically Russian, he was culturally cosmopolitan, where they were self-consciously and narrowly nationalist in their work. (Twenty years later Tchaikovsky said of himself that in Germany 'many people, without any real foundation, regard me as a representative of the ultra-revolutionary party in music, just as in Russia I am often placed, equally without grounds, in the ranks of the retrogrades'.) The Five returned his opposition in good measure. They also attacked the Rubinsteins and denounced their Conservatories as 'music factories'.

Both parties had their critics and supporters, all armed with sharp pens. The controversy may be said to be still in progress, *mutatis mutandis*, at the present day, when all the original protagonists are dead.

The lines were clear-cut until Tchaikovsky did the unheard of thing: came out in defence of one of the enemy. His action was dictated by sincerity, not sensationalism, but it caused a stir in both Moscow and St. Petersburg.

The circumstances were these: at the concert at which he tried to conduct his *Voyevoda* dances, Rimsky-Korsakov's *Serbian Fantasia* was also played. An anonymous critic, partisan of the antinationalist front, wrote a notice of the concert in a magazine called *Entr'acte*, praising Tchaikovsky's dances for lofty aims, orchestration, masterly handling of themes and so forth. He dismissed Rimsky-Korsakov's work as lifeless and colourless.

Having learnt to admire the *Fantasia* at rehearsals, Tchaikovsky wrote a long analytical critique expressing great admiration and sent this to another journal, which published it in full.

Neither faction could quite understand this quixotic act on the part of the man whose work had been praised at Rimsky-Korsakov's expense. The article was much discussed in the rival cities. It won the personal goodwill of the St. Petersburg group, which was clinched by Tchaikovsky's personal charm when they met him. The war of ideas continued, but with respect and mutual friendship, as far as Tchaikovsky and the Five were concerned.

An important consequence was Tchaikovsky's friendship with Balakirev, who suggested to him, during a forest walk one sunny day in May, that he should compose an overture based on *Romeo and Juliet*. Tchaikovsky agreed, and his fantasy overture, ultimately recognised as one of his finest achievements, is dedicated to Balakirev—as also is the posthumously-published symphonic poem *Fate* which Balakirev said bluntly did not please him.

The *Romeo and Juliet* overture, to glance ahead for a couple of years, brought the composer yet more disappointments. Once again it was partly sheer mischance.

Barren of ideas for some months, Tchaikovsky was busy with routine work in 1869 when Balakirev was living for a time in Moscow. The suggestion of an overture to *Romeo and Juliet* reawoke his sleeping muse and the composition developed fast.

Balakirev, who looked the perfect boyar, was another of those monstrous egoists—like the Rubinsteins—with whom Tchaikovsky seemed fated to get involved. They were drawn by his own humility. Balakirev knew talent when he saw it, and he was well-disposed in a personal sense, but it did not occur to him that the malleable Tchaikovsky was a composer of twice his stature. Back in St. Petersburg, he not only sent detailed instructions on how the overture should be written—on the lines of his own *King Lear* overture—but sent him half a dozen bars of an allegro with which to start it.

When the overture was completed, in November, and the parts were being copied, Balakirev insisted that the composer should send him the principal themes.

Admitting that there were 'many beautiful things' in them, Balakirev nevertheless wanted drastic alterations. The introduction should sound less like Haydn, more like Liszt. The love melody was not spiritual enough. And so on.

The following year Tchaikovsky made some of the revisions suggested, and some which he himself thought desirable, before the work went into print. Even then, Balakirev wrote that it was a pity that Rubinstein, who had arranged publication of the work in Germany, had 'rushed' matters as there were other changes he wanted Tchaikovsky to make. He still hoped that an 'improved version' could be published at some future time.

Balakirev, had his attitude been questioned, could have called in evidence the reactions of the Russian public, and those of audiences abroad. It is an amazing fact that the overture was actually hissed when first performed in Germany, France, and Austria, and for almost ten years it was unacceptable to the public in almost every European country, according to Tchaikovsky himself.

But something quite extraneous to questions of public taste marred its first performance in the spring of 1870. Rubinstein conducted, but it so happened that on the previous day he had appeared in court as the defendant in an action brought by a girl student, who claimed that she had been wrongfully dismissed from the Conservatory. Rubinstein was ordered to pay a small sum in damages, and that appeared to his students and admirers to call for a demonstration of their loyalty at the concert. The noise and the incessant cheering destroyed the evening as a musical occasion. It was a public triumph for Rubinstein—and a total eclipse for Tchaikovsky and his new work. The overture was played, of course, but went unnoticed.

Incidentally, the composition was eventually restored to its original form, most of the later revisions being excised.

As for Balakirev's self-importance, it must be borne in mind that the Five were men with a mission, and it was a sacred duty with them to assert their views forcibly. They were radical exponents of a nationalist art, and like many another clique they cheered each other on, clamouring for public recognition and seeking converts. Tchaikovsky was one of the unconverted, but since he showed himself friendly and open-minded, he should be guided to the right road if possible. One thinks of the tactics of religious sects, of political factions, of art groups like the Pre-Raphaelites, or of the Irish Nationalists. Balakirev's attitude must be seen in a similar context. The Five, in case their belief in their loudly proclaimed 'invincibility' should waver, had a powerful theorist for ally, the critic Stassov, to whom Tchaikovsky later dedicated his symphonic fantasia *The Tempest*. Stassov coined the name 'the mighty handful' for the Five, and encouraged them to assert their might.

When the fantasy overture *Romeo and Juliet* was completed, neither Balakirev nor Tchaikovsky's closest friends recognised that he had written a masterpiece. Knowing Tchaikovsky's tendency to cruel self-doubts it is perhaps not incomprehensible that he himself was unaware he had produced a work that pronounced him a genius. He was then twenty-nine and had much to learn—about himself and other people.

His synthesis of the dramatic elements in Shakespeare's play was scored for a modern orchestra, including the harp and *cor anglais* and already suggests the methods Tchaikovsky was to employ in his later orchestral writing, particularly the familiar antiphonal exploitation of related instruments.

The fate of Tchaikovsky's *Fate* is on a different level from the *Romeo and Juliet* affair, as the composition is not of comparable merit. Tchaikovsky did not publish it, and later destroyed the score. The posthumous publication was a reconstruction from the separate orchestral parts. Balakirev's criticism of *Fate* asserted that it had been too hastily written and that the form was 'completely unsuccessful'. He informed Tchaikovsky, 'you know too little of modern music. You will never acquire freedom of form from the classics—nothing new is to be found there.'

When the Grand Duchess Yelena Pavlovna, patroness of the St. Petersburg Conservatory, sought to oust Balakirev from his role of concert director, Tchaikovsky defended his fellow composer and criticised the Grand Duchess for interfering in artistic matters. In writing his most famous song, *None but the Lonely Heart*, to Goethe's lyric (Nur wer die Sehnsucht kennt), Tchaikovsky dedicated it to a singer named Khvostova. Balakirev, however, persuaded her not to sing it at a recital lest it should 'ruin by its presence a programme graced by the names of Mussorgsky and company'.

These two incidents are not exactly parallel; but they very clearly exemplify the narrow zeal of Balakirev and the magnanimity of Tchaikovsky.

It will have become apparent that when Tchaikovsky yielded to the persuasions of others and revised his work, he sometimes had third thoughts later on and took out the 'improvements'. Nevertheless, he sometimes destroyed a score altogether, as ruthlessly as Cézanne ditched his canvases when the composition did not meet his perfectionist standards. He would occasionally abandon a project before its completion on the advice of some experienced musician. Casting about for an operatic subject in 1869, he was offered a libretto called *Mandragora*, a fantasy by Professor Sergei Rachinsky, and began to work on it. Kashkin, having heard his first chorus for this and admired it, warned him that the material would serve for ballet but would never make an opera. Tchaikovsky became angry, but after a heated dispute he accepted Kashkin's judgment and wrote no more of *Mandragora*. The one completed number, the *Insect Chorus*, was successfully performed on various occasions, however, and a doubt remains whether such well-meant and sincere warnings as Kashkin's were true wisdom or merely the voice of orthodoxy raised against novelty and experiment. Tchaikovsky at the time was again suffering from nervous disorders and his self-confidence was easily shaken. If he had received encouragement from the friend and colleague whom he valued so highly, might he not have gone on to create a new kind of fantastic opera, which later generations would have called ahead of its time?

Speculations of this kind are usually reproved as 'idle', but unless one takes the determinist view that what *did* happen is the only thing that *could* have happened, an artist's career is full of tempting ifs and ans. Especially so in the case of a man like Tchaikovsky, versatile and suggestible, living in an age when his country's music was developing in diverse ways, and change was in the air.

Like most great artists, he looked back without regret at the holocausts of his youth, and had none of the small man's sentimental tenderness for his own juvenilia.

Later, when Mme. von Meck inquired whether he had written any early works that were never published, he replied that there were many, 'and how I bless the fates that did not permit me to find an amateur who might have been willing to publish all that infant lisping, which at the time I considered serious composition'.

A few of his early compositions had been preserved, but most of them he had burned, he said. Among these he mentioned *The Voyevoda*, from which the dances were saved, and *Undine*, which was rejected by the directors of the St. Petersburg theatres—'at which I was much offended, but later I was thankful enough that the directors had rendered me this service. It was an atrocious opera, and I threw it in the fire without a regret.'

In another letter to his patroness at the same period he elaborated his views on operatic and symphonic style, and their relation to public taste.

'The composer of an opera', he said, 'must never for a moment forget the stage, he must realise that in the theatre more is required than melody and harmony; action must exist for the satisfaction of an audience which comes not only to listen but to look. Lastly, operatic style must correspond to the style of mural or scene painting: it must be plain, clear and colourful. Put a Meissonier painting on a theatre stage and all the charm of its delicate detail will be lost. And the same with music: small, fragile, intricate harmonies are overlooked in a theatre, where what is needed is brightly-outlined melody and clear harmonic design. Writing *The Voyevoda*, I lost

(*Right*)
Tchaikovsky's birthplace at Votkinsk

(*Below*)
Tchaikovsky's Conservatory diploma, certifying "that he is a member of the professions"

ВЫСОЧАЙШЕ УТВЕРЖДЕННАГО РУССКАГО МУЗЫКАЛЬНАГО ОБЩЕСТВА

С.ПЕТЕРБУРГСКАЯ КОНСЕРВАТОРІЯ

ДИПЛОМЪ.

[illegible]

Президентъ

Директоръ Консерваторіи

Désirée Artot

Nadejda von Meck

sight of the stage and its requirements and busied myself tracing a thematic filigree.

'Naturally, these theatrical requirements paralyse to a great extent the composer's purely musical inspiration, and that is why symphonic or chamber music is far superior to operatic music.

'Writing a symphony or sonata, I am free, I feel no constraint and no false limitation. On the other hand, opera has an advantage in that it speaks to the masses in a language they can understand. Also, the fact that opera may be performed forty times in a season, gives it preference over a symphony which may be heard once in ten years!

'After hearing an opera several times, a hostile listener may become friendly to the work—but what a long time it takes for the masses to appreciate a good symphony! In spite of the temptations of the operatic siren, I take far greater pleasure in composing symphony, sonata or string quartet.

'To return to *The Voyevoda*, the orchestral effect is far too massive, and overrides the voice parts. These defects were all due to inexperience. To reach perfection, a whole series of trial-and-error is necessary, therefore I am not ashamed of my failures. They served their purpose as lessons and signposts to further effort. You may gather from all this, dear friend, how stubbornly I refused to recognise my own faults. . . .'

Which is unlikely to be the conclusion that anyone would draw from this letter, or from the record of his actions; there is characteristic humility in the turn of phrase. Here we have the mature composer reading the morals of his experience, and candidly explaining why the operatic form continued to draw him, in spite of the greater attraction of purely orchestral music. *The Queen of Spades* and *Eugene Onegin* are admirable achievements, but they are neither the greatest of operas nor the best of Tchaikovsky's works. They were the product of his desire to reach a mass public. Incidentally, he held that Wagner was 'a symphonist by nature', a man with a 'glorious talent' who strained himself by pursuing the impossible in the theatre.

As far as his symphonies are concerned, Tchaikovsky was never able to assert himself against structural elements that belonged to the norm of traditional writing. As a romantic, the arch priest, if you like, dedicated to the elevation of the lyrical in music, he could not but apprehend, not necessarily in the beginning, that the classical symphony was alien to his nature and inspiration.

The sonata form and its prime employment in the opening and closing movements was a bridge that echoed to his uncertain footsteps and here was begun the agony of creation he endured in setting down the first of his symphonies. This, and the two which followed, are no more than wan relations of the last three symphonies, which are plainly autobiographical and in which Tchaikovsky becomes truer to himself and his limitations. The dramatist and colourist of his own emotional nature, he found the freedom offered, in both form and content, by the two middle movements much more to his taste. Within their compass can be found in his three symphonies truly glorious examples of Tchaikovsky at his finest—the superb command he exercised over the resources of every instrument and the craftsmanship he employed to achieve the effect he desired.

Since artists grow by a law of uneven development there came between the first and second symphony the *Romeo and Juliet*, which foreshadowed the achievements to come much later.

If Tchaikovsky in his maturity ever recalled 1869 as the year he wrote his now famous fantasy overture, he would almost certainly remember the prima donna Desirée Artôt, whose dazzling personality apparently swept him off his feet, in an episode as brief and sudden as a summer storm. One more disappointment, this: a human instead of a musical one; for this, too, he may have had cause to 'bless the fates'—though he was preserved only for a worse error, later on.

It is a strange story: the behaviour of both parties is curious and their motives are not easy to explain. Superficially, this is the one orthodox romantic passion in Tchaikovsky's life. The reality is not quite so simple.

CHAPTER IV

THE HIGH ROMANCE

ACCORDING to Tchaikovsky himself, he had been introduced to Desirée Artôt in the spring of the previous year and attended a supper given after her benefit performance, but was not sufficiently interested in her to call again.

'When she returned here in the autumn I did not visit her for an entire month. Then we met accidentally at a musical soirée,' he wrote to his father. 'She expressed surprise that I had not called and I promised to do so, a promise I should never have kept (owing to my shyness with new friends) if Anton Rubinstein . . . had not dragged me to see her. After that I constantly received invitations, and fell into the habit of going to her house every day.'

It will be observed that in this account, Tchaikovsky is the one who is being courted, and the beginning of the acquaintanceship is very much a matter of chance.

We know, however, that Tchaikovsky saw her on the stage in September, not long after his return to Moscow to resume his teaching, after his travels with young Vladimir Shilovsky, and his visit to the Davidovs. A fortnight after his visit to the theatre, he was claiming the singer's friendship and praising her 'magnificent personality'.

The performance he attended that autumn evening was a great theatrical occasion. Grand equipages filled the approaches to the Bolshoi Theatre, and a befurred and bediamonded audience flocked into the auditorium. The opera was Rossini's *Otello*, and Morelli's Italian opera company was highly esteemed. Despite the nationalists the musical public of Russia still regarded the Italians far more highly than the native school, not without reason.

A vanished world! that link-lit scene of still feudal splendours; of tinkling harness and cracking whips, of gems and orders and gold-frogged uniforms; and walking among them the sombrely dressed figure of the young composer with his middle-aged gravity and his gentle air, a little known, a little noticed, and yet unsuspected of being the greatest man among them.

His musical friends were there, and his Conservatory colleagues; and the Bolshoi was soon to stage his own first opera: he walked in a glitter of promise.

Desirée Artôt sang Desdemona, and Tchaikovsky was greatly moved by her performance. Whether or not he had to be 'dragged' to see her in person, he was soon spellbound by her witty conversation, her presence, her flattering response to his shy attention.

She was a woman of renown, and daughter and granddaughter of well-known French musicians. At the time Tchaikovsky met her, she was thirty-three, and not at all beautiful, but she turned every young man's head. Her voice was said to be 'more like an oboe than a flute'. She sang all types of soprano role: her range was as great emotionally as vocally.

People began to say that Tchaikovsky was courting her, and for once, the idea did not shock him. For the first time, marriage appeared as a possibility before him.

It was an infatuation, a flutter of tender emotion, a sense of exhilaration in the singer's company, and an equal lack of earthly desire and realistic thinking about the relationship. What he experienced was dreamlike, rainbow-coloured, deliciously exciting, born of the theatre; there is no sign that it touched the deeper springs of his being, or of hers. But like children with a toy, they played with the idea of marriage.

In the letter to his father already quoted, written in January of the next year, he talks in a worldly wise way about it all: 'Naturally, the question of marriage, which both of us desire, arose at once, and if nothing prevents it, our wedding will take place this summer. But the trouble is that there are several obstacles. First, there is her mother, who always stays with her and has much influence over her daughter. She does not favour the marriage, considering me too young and probably fearing that I should expect her daughter to remain in Russia permanently. Secondly my friends—Nikolai Rubinstein in particular—are trying everything to prevent my marriage. They insist that if I marry a famous singer I shall play the pitiful role of "his wife's husband"; that I shall live at her expense and follow her about Europe; and finally that I shall lose all opportunities for work, so that when my first love has cooled I shall have nothing but disillusionment and depression.'

He goes on to say that she refuses to give up her profession, which is very lucrative: and that he is not willing to risk sacrificing his own future.

He is to visit her near Paris in the summer, 'when our fate will be decided'. He adds: 'You see, Papa, my situation is extremely difficult. On the one hand I love her, heart and soul, and feel that I cannot exist without her any longer; on the other hand, cool commonsense tells me to weigh more carefully the misfortunes with which my friends threaten me.'

This letter, which drew excellent paternal advice on thinking out his position and acting wisely, is disingenuous, for Tchaikovsky was unable to tell his father the truth. He lists the 'obstacles', her mother's opinion, their respective careers, but not that aspect of his life which in his diaries he calls 'Z': his emotional attachments to his own sex, the impossibility for him of physically desiring a woman, the factor that made him in the case of the devoted Vera 'sense that my feeling for her would turn to hatred if the question of marriage ever became serious'. In other words he omits the major obstacle, compared with which all the rest are trifles. His father knew nothing of Vladimir Shilovsky.

Why did Tchaikovsky not recognise the same danger that his feelings might turn into hatred if marriage with Desirée Artôt became 'serious'? There are alternative possibilities: one being that he knew in his heart that it would never become serious at all; that the whole thing was wonderful make-believe, to be repeated on another plane in the long paper-rhapsody for Mme. von Meck, later on: and that he was secretly glad of those weighty difficulties created by their rival careers and their different fatherlands.

Another possibility is that he genuinely lost his heart and his head to the singer, and believed that with her, a complete marriage would be possible for him. In that case we must take at fullest value his fear that he would be unable to do his life's work, fulfil his destiny as a composer, if he had to follow her star about the globe. For nothing else in his life except his work could have been important enough to merit consideration, as against the chance of 'normalising' himself. Again and again it is made clear that he was not the kind of homosexual who lightly accepts his condition: he hated and condemned it, he was ashamed of the double life it forced upon him, and he lived in fear of discovery and disgrace. A successful marriage, canalising his sexual impulses into the accepted channel, freeing him forever from the curse laid upon him would be worth almost any price. Any but one; his other fulfilment, his fulfilment as an artist. That was the one price that could not be paid.

But if this was really the situation, if these tremendous issues were in the scales, would not the tone of his letter have been utterly different, if it could have been written at all? It cannot possibly be seen as that of a man wrestling in his soul over its profoundest division. 'First, there is her mother . . . you see, Papa, my situation is extremely difficult. . . .' And a little later to Anatol: 'I am now very doubtful that I shall ever tie the hymeneal knot. Things have begun to go a little wrong. . . .'

Yet another possibility is that Tchaikovsky was already considering marriage as a mask, a pinch of incense on the altar of orthodoxy, a way of stilling the tongues of gossip. Many homosexuals marry for such reasons, sometimes with the knowledge and connivance of their brides, sometimes without. This question will arise again when we come to discuss Tchaikovsky's actual marriage. It is certain that he never considered such a stratagem where Vera Davidova was concerned. Artôt was a celebrity, worldly wise, and older than he; they had common interests, a marriage of true minds might be theirs: from several points of view she was the kind of woman whom a marriage on a very slender sexual basis might be possible, and who might be sufficiently understanding to accept the proposition.

The weight of probability seems to me to rest with the first of these interpretations—namely, that Tchaikovsky and Artôt performed a dance, a skater's waltz, gaily, sentimentally, talked lightly of their love and marriage, kissed (if her mother was ever absent), longed for each other's company when apart, made and abandoned many flimsy plans for the future, spoke of marriage, played up to other people's romantic excitement, fought lively battles with their friends and relations and reported back to each other on what was done and said; shed tears, sometimes; but never in their inmost being really moved towards one another, never imagined themselves one flesh. They were content to let the world talk on. Somewhere inside them, they knew better than to marry.

There remain some puzzles in the behaviour of Mme. Artôt, but there is nothing which conflicts with that view.

Tchaikovsky never went to the château near Paris where his fate was to be decided. His fate reached him on wings of its own, in the middle of a rehearsal.

Mme. Artôt and the company in which she had scored so great a hit with the Muscovites packed up and departed on tour.

She went with the pleasant knowledge of a conquest: a charming man of promise adored her. But desired she was not, in spite of her name. Something very soon occurred to wipe out the memory of those drawing-room dreams and *conversations galantes*. She found a different type of lover—a Spanish baritone in the company, Marian Padilla y Ramos.

Tchaikovsky had meanwhile plunged into work—daily rehearsals for *The Voyevoda*, plans for a second opera, transposition of a set of Russian folk songs for piano duets. His beloved was singing, receiving bouquets and sparkling for the salons of Warsaw, the first capital on the company's itinerary.

Tchaikovsky was not satisfied with the progress of his rehearsals, with a small orchestra, shabby scenery and singers who could not master all his desired effects, but he was hopeful that all would be well by the first night.

As he stood on the Bolshoi stage at rehearsal one day doing his best to coax his music out of the company—only a few days before the opening performance—Nikolai Rubinstein walked up to him, a telegram in his hand. Desirée Artôt had married the baritone.

Tchaikovsky blanched, but seemed surprised rather than hurt. Rubinstein attempted to console him for the blow by assuring him it was for the best, that Russia needed him and could not afford to lose him to a famous foreigner. He did not answer his well-meaning comforter, who undoubtedly knew even stronger reasons why it was better that he should not marry. Without a word, he walked out of the theatre.

The singer returned to Moscow a year later. Tchaikovsky went to the theatre with Kashkin to hear her, and, says his friend, kept his opera-glasses to his eyes till the end of the performance, 'although it is doubtful how much he could see, because the tears ran unheeded down his cheeks'. There is no reason to doubt the sincerity of those tears, even if one questions the depth of the emotion.

Seven or eight years elapsed before chance threw the couple together again, and it was an embarrassing encounter.

Tchaikovsky had gone with Kashkin to call on Nikolai Rubinstein at the Conservatory. They were told, though, that he was engaged with a lady in his private room and they sat down in the anteroom to wait until he was at liberty. Not long afterwards the door opened and Desirée Artôt appeared.

Tchaikovsky saw at once who it was and rose from his seat, agitated and very pale. She gave a little cry of distress and in her confusion began to fumble for the door, but it was not easy to open in that half-lighted room. He did not help her. She got out at last and fled without a word.

But the wounds healed and the story has a gay ending. The composer and the singer met again twenty years later, in Berlin at a banquet.

'Whom should I sit next to but Artôt!' Tchaikovsky wrote to his brother. 'She was in evening dress, and as fat as a bubble. We were friends instantly, as though the past had never been. I was inexpressibly glad to see her, and found her as fascinating as ever.'

Her marriage had been a successful one, and her daughter Lola became a famous singer in her turn. Tchaikovsky could not boast of any such luck. Mme. Artôt gave him a photograph of herself, signing it with her married name and inscribing it: 'à Pierre Tchaikofsky, souvenir de profonde admiration'.

In his second venture into opera Tchaikovsky had no more success than with the first, leaving out of account the discouragement of the unfinished *Mandragora*. The new subject was a poem, *Undine*, of which he was fond, and from which a libretto had been contrived by Count Vladimir Alexandrovich Sollogub. Having rapidly completed this opera, Tchaikovsky sent it to the St. Petersburg theatre directors, where it suffered a truly Russian fate. It was handed over by the directors to an official of the Marinsky

Theatre; next, the composer was told it could not be played that season; then it was rejected outright; finally it was mislaid by someone's carelessness. Not till three years later did it turn up again, only to be sent back to the composer.

By that time, some excerpts having been badly received, it had fallen out of favour with its creator himself, and he burned it. Three numbers survived, and found rebirth in *The Snow Queen*, in *Swan Lake* and in the second movement of the *Second Symphony*.

It was his next opera, *The Oprichnik*, which he began early in 1870, that was to prove to Tchaikovsky and to the public that he could succeed in that medium. It cost him much time and effort, but it represented a break-through of importance to him, even though it was not destined to have any great interest for future generations. Its story, dealing with the dissolute robber-barons who formed Ivan the Terrible's bodyguard, is highly melodramatic, and the music wavers between Italianate and Russian influences. Tchaikovsky embodied in it some material salvaged from his failures.

The writing of it took him longer than he had anticipated and still more time elapsed before it was staged. Meanwhile he hurried on with other work, not only composing and teaching but writing musical criticism and a textbook of harmony. Finally, he became irritated and depressed by all these activities, and, as his nervous tension grew, so did the danger of hysteria. He began to imagine that he was unfitted to be a teacher and that nobody took any interest in his music.

'I am an unbearable hypochondriac,' he confesses, but, nevertheless, in these bouts of utter dejection he was able, quite often, to coin his melancholy into his art, as in *None but the Lonely Heart*, one of his first half-dozen songs.

The tragic frailty of life and love were epitomised for him in the consumptive youth, Vladimir Shilovsky. The drama of the previous summer repeated itself when Tchaikovsky, planning a holiday with his sister and his twin brothers, was suddenly told that Vladimir was once again in the hands of French doctors, gravely ill, and was asking for him.

Dropping everything, he rushed to Paris—an agonising journey, fearing all the time that he might be too late.

But the lad was not dying, and with Tchaikovsky at his bedside he rallied. After a fortnight in France, Tchaikovsky took him to Germany, to Soden, near Frankfurt on Main, a resort for tubercular patients, and there they idled the summer away, in concert-going, sadness, sentiment, heat, and boredom. Once, Tchaikovsky went over to Wiesbaden to see Nikolai Rubinstein, who was gambling and losing but convinced that he would break the bank—like that other inveterate Russian gambler, Dostoievsky, in the same casino, in that same decade.

In the middle of this sultry season, in which Tchaikovsky and his hollow-eyed companion had little to do but take life easy and keep ennui at bay, a war burst upon them: the Franco-Prussian War. Sickness or no sickness, they had to pack in haste and scramble into a refugee train. They had no idea what it was all about.

With hundreds of other foreigners in the same plight as themselves, they arrived in Interlaken. They remained in Switzerland six weeks before returning by way of Vienna to Russia, in time for Tchaikovsky's autumn term. The stay in Switzerland did more for the health and spirits of both than the drowsy summer in Germany—or perhaps the war crisis had shocked them out of themselves, in a salutary way. At any rate it got Tchaikovsky back to work. He revised the score of *Romeo and Juliet*, and returned to the problems of *The Oprichnik.*

The following summer he again went abroad with Vladimir, to France and Germany, and gave out that he was visiting his sister. He warned Anatol that nobody *except Rubinstein* was to be told the truth. This seems confirmatory evidence that the secrets of his temperament were not hidden from his worldly-wise Principal, and that Tchaikovsky was aware of it.

The attachment to Shilovsky did not last. By the time the young man was twenty, Tchaikovsky found his company 'very trying'.

There was no positive break between them, though money matters later gave a sordid tinge to their relationship and there were recriminations.

It was Shilovsky who in 1875 sent the piano score of *Carmen* to Tchaikovsky after attending its performance and communicated to him his own burning enthusiasm for it. Modest speaks of his brother's 'almost unwholesome passion for this opera'. This may be merely an indication of how strongly Tchaikovsky had influenced the taste of his former pupil, attuning it to his own. The rich young man had intelligence and sensibilities, certainly; and the shadow of an early death which seemed to be upon him increased his appeal to Tchaikovsky's melancholy and sympathetic heart. But he did not actually die until a few months before Tchaikovsky himself, in 1893. In the meantime, the deterioration in their friendship is indicated by a letter which Tchaikovsky wrote in 1879, in which he says:

'I have learned from reliable sources that you are complaining to the whole world of my ingratitude, adding that you have given me 28,000 roubles!!! I would be lying were I to say that I am completely indifferent to the *rumours you are spreading*. I find them unpleasant—but accept them as just punishment for my indiscriminate methods of obtaining money and for my genuine interest in you. In rare instances similar money transactions between friends one of whom is rich, the other poor, entail neither punishment for the recipient nor poisonous accusations and misunderstandings from the giver. Ours evidently is not one of those rare instances. I am guilty, therefore, not because I took the money (I see nothing *dishonourable* or *shameful* in that) but because I took that money from *you*; that is, from a man who, I well knew, would sooner or later tell of it *à qui voudra l'entendre.*

'And so the fact that you are now revealing our money relations to all and sundry wounds me to some extent but does not surprise me in the least—I have always expected it. I am, however, greatly astonished by the arbitrary figure with which you so generously endow your gifts to me. . . . I do not consider it superfluous to point out that you have magnified the sum total of your generosity—and proportionately the degree of my black ingratitude—most unsparingly. I have an exceptionally fine memory in such matters, and I shall tell you to a kopeck exactly how much I got from you. . . .'

Before detailing the gifts, he exempts from the reckoning certain items—a piano, a bed, a screen, his salary as teacher, and money spent on trips abroad in 1868 and 1870: he says that in the latter trip he acted 'in the capacity of something between companion, teacher and uncle'. But he includes in the account the cost of the 1871 trip to Nice. He makes it, altogether, 7,550 roubles—'both a great deal and very little. Very little if one takes into consideration the innumerable spiritual tortures this money cost me; very little when one remembers that you are a rich landowner and I a poor artist; very little indeed when one recalls your endless protestations of love, and readiness to make sacrifices for my sake. . . .'

Nevertheless he admits: 'You rescued me from great difficulties and God knows I was grateful to you and still am grateful. At the same time I submit, is it becoming to a gentleman to brag of having been my "benefactor" and, while doing so, to sin so against truth, by magnifying the sum *fourfold*?'

The letter ends with a request, not for himself, but for an old man, 'poor, pitiful and sick', to whom Tchaikovsky had been in the habit of giving regular sums of money, which he could not afford to keep up. He asks Shilovsky to provide the old man with a life pension of twenty-five roubles a month, and promises in exchange not to be offended if he continues to spread his rumours! The letter concludes: 'I hope you have a pleasant summer.'

After this they saw less and less of each other, though Tchaikovsky continued to have professional dealings with Konstantin Shilovsky,

Vladimir's elder brother, who collaborated on the libretto of *Eugene Onegin.*

In his latter days Tchaikovsky heard apparently unmoved of the death of Vladimir Shilovsky.

There remain two piano pieces, the *Humoresque in G major* and the *Nocturne in F major* which are dedicated 'To my friend Vladimir Shilovsky'—an epitaph to a love that did not endure. They were the outcome of one of the trips to Nice, preceding that less pleasing sequel, the reproachful accounting ('to a kopeck!').

Tchaikovsky in his early thirties moved from Nikolai Rubinstein's house into a small apartment, where at last he had quiet in which to write. He lived modestly, with a manservant, a young rustic who could cook only one dish—cabbage soup with groats. The furnishings were a large sofa, some cheap chairs, a picture of Louis XVI and one of Anton Rubinstein. Tchaikovsky improved the décor later, however, although he was never interested in luxury. He cared about cleanliness and was horrified by lice, bugs, and rodents, all of which during his travels he encountered in plenty. But he seldom complained of physical discomforts, unless a concomitant of nerves or emotional upsets of his own.

He dressed neatly and quietly, went about with mild outward dignity, unless something betrayed the excitable nature underneath. He was a considerably admired person. A young person, we should say nowadays; middle-aged, by the standards of his time; even beyond that, in his own eyes.

'I am old and can no longer enjoy anything. I live only on memories and hopes. But what is there to hope for?' he writes self-pityingly at the age of thirty-one. This, with all his major work ahead of him!

But his volatile spirits leap up again, he finds a great deal to hope for, many things to do, and the air full of music. He wakes to the singing of a workman plastering a wall, under his window: an enchanting tune! Tchaikovsky writes it down. Presently he asks the labourer to sing him the words. (Another version of this story makes it a baker, and the place his sister's country home, Kamenka.) As when Queen Victoria sent to inquire the name of a delightful melody, only to be told it was 'Come where the booze is cheaper', so Tchaikovsky may have been a little let down when he found the words of the song to be nothing more inspired than this:

> 'Vanya sat on the divan
> And smoked a pipe of tobacco.'

But from the old folk-melody which bore this splendid statement along, he wrote the Andante Cantabile of his first *String Quartet in D*, and so immortalised it.

The *Quartet* had a very practical *raison d'être.* The composer wanted funds for his holiday abroad, and Nikolai Rubinstein proposed: 'Why not a benefit concert, of your own work, including something new for the occasion?'

This seemed to Tchaikovsky a brilliant notion and he determined to overcome his habitual stage-fright and put himself before the public in this fashion. The hall must be small and cheap, there would not be room for an orchestra; he therefore decided that the new composition must be a string quartet—a form that not very long before he had found intolerable, according to Kashkin. (He said he could scarcely keep awake through Beethoven's *Quartet in A minor.*)

Well-known musicians, including Nikolai Rubinstein and a popular singer, helped to make a success of the concert. The unexpected presence of Turgenev in the audience gave a fillip to Tchaikovsky's prestige.

He filled his pockets sufficiently to be able to make his summer tour, visiting his brothers, Vladimir Shilovsky, and Sasha. His stay at his sister's home at Kamenka bore a wonderful fruit, for there he wrote a little ballet for the children to perform. It was the first brief version of *Swan Lake.*

Half a dozen years later he elaborated the four-act version. But with this once again the farcical tale of Tchaikovsky's misfortunes repeated itself: miserable, second-hand costumes, whole sections cut out because the dancers and musicians could not cope with them, scraps from other ballets spatchcocked in to fill the gaps: a bored, puzzled audience, unused to anything on the scale or of the quality conceived by Tchaikovsky.

Tchaikovsky, self-critical over the whole affair—he said later that he considered *Swan Lake* 'simply trash' in comparison with Delibes' *Sylvia*!—allowed it to be dropped from the repertoire without a protest on his part. The sad truth was that the full-scale work as staged at the Bolshoi had given him far less pleasure than the artless performance of his sister's children at Kamenka. It was only after Tchaikovsky's death that Petipa and Ivanov worked out a new choreography for *Swan Lake* and firmly established it as a classic.

Had Tchaikovsky been a different type of person, with more vanity and with the temperamental capacity to assert himself like the Rubinsteins, many of these disasters of his would have been averted. He would have held others, not himself, responsible for any possible failure, and thereby put them on their mettle. A Rubinstein would have insisted on better materials and workmanship and would certainly not have blamed himself for what could be put down to the inadequacy of the interpreters. There are always lazy, slipshod people to take advantage of such a character as

Tchaikovsky. Ballet too, like opera, had to contend against prejudice towards the home-grown: small orchestras and old costumes were considered good enough for it, while the best of everything was reserved for Italian companies.

Humourless and easily led, Tchaikovsky was a born victim for comic as well as pathetic situations.

During the summer of 1872, he was travelling with Modest by diligence from Kamenka. They stopped at an inn for a change of horses, and had a meal with plenty of wine. When the landlord told them that no fresh horses were available, Tchaikovsky stood on his dignity and asked, 'Are you aware to whom you are speaking?' The landlord was unimpressed, but the wine had stirred Tchaikovsky's blood and his daring. He called for the visitors' book, wrote in it a complaint about the service, and signed it in the style of a courtier—'Prince Volkonsky, Page-in-Waiting'.

'The result was brilliant,' Modest says. Horses were ready within a quarter of an hour and the head ostler sharply reprimanded.

But when the travellers reached the next stage, Vorozhba, where they were to part company, Modest to catch a train and Piotr to go to Shilovsky's home by road, Piotr discovered that he had left his pocket-book behind at the inn. It contained not only his money but also his passport and visiting cards.

The brothers discussed their plight. To face the innkeeper now was more than Piotr could bear. Modest left by train, first giving his loose change to his brother, who stayed the night at the nearest inn, and asked the post driver to bring his wallet back to him the next day. He was unlucky in his night's lodging, with his horror of rats and mice: the place was infested with them. They scampered over his bed, squeaking like so many demons sent to punish him for his small act of deception. Sleep was impossible, and in a tottering state he came out of the room the next morning to meet the coachman.

Alas, the innkeeper had refused to hand over the wallet to anyone but Prince Volkonsky himself!

There was nothing for it: Tchaikovsky had to go back to the post-house. It tortured him to think that his wallet had been opened and his masquerade become known. He faced the innkeeper with none of the imperiousness he had displayed the previous day. But he was treated with deference, and since all seemed well, he thanked the man and asked his name.

'Tchaikovsky!' was the shattering reply.

But the innkeeper was not taking revenge for having been duped. His name *was* Tchaikovsky; he had not opened the wallet; and the avenging furies of conscience had been, after all, only rats and mice. . . .

CHAPTER V

PIANO CONCERTO

PASSING from holiday to professional tours, Tchaikovsky became a much-travelled man in the years of his maturity. But there never was such a homesick voluntary traveller. He had none of the globe-trotter's characteristics. He was not physically tough, or given to the exultant conquest of hardships; he was frightened of strangers, and often wearied by their talk or upset by their opinions; he had not even an exploring mind, and his notes on the places he sees are mostly commonplace and studded with exclamations of dissatisfaction and boredom.

'With the exception of Glinka, who gave but one concert in Paris, and Rubinstein, who, thanks to his gifts as a virtuoso, won laurels on all the platforms of the world, I was the first Russian to introduce my works personally abroad,' Tchaikovsky boasted.

The melancholy fact behind this invaluable pioneering is the restlessness of a man with no home of his own. His marriage failed to provide him with one, and he could be only, at best, a visiting uncle at the homes of others—his sister, in particular, and the Shilovskys for a time. A bachelor apartment with a manservant did not meet his contradictory needs. He loved small children, and longed for the untidy, hospitable, solid homes of his childhood, when his father was a man of substance, with the generations swarming around him. Yet he needed a working solitude, too. Again, he liked the quiet of the country, but was forced to live mostly in the noise of the town, and the stress of opera-house and rehearsal room.

One of his favourite oases of peace was Kamenka. This rustic place on the banks of the Tiasmin river, in Kiev province, was by no means a beauty spot, but it had its quiet charms. The Davidov family, into which Sasha had married, owned the property, and there he was always a welcome visitor, whether as a distraught fugitive from the city and his troubles, needing sisterly comfort and understanding, or as amiable Uncle Petia, with his head full of new music and his pockets full of presents for the children.

His sister's husband was the son of Vassily Davidov, a prominent Decembrist, as those revolutionaries were called who rose against the Tsar in December 1825 in protest against harsh laws and serfdom. When the rebel was exiled to Siberia, he left the estate to his elder son, Nikolai, who in turn left the management of it to the younger son, Leo, Tchaikovsky's brother-in-law.

When the old Decembrist was dead, his widow wore as an iron bracelet a length of her husband's prison chain. Tchaikovsky liked this proud old woman and she had considerable influence over him.

The place itself might have served as setting for *The Seagull*, or *A Month in the Country*, or any other Russian drama of frustration and decay. It had shady lawns, mouldering grottoes, noble memories of long gone by: in its heyday, Pushkin had been a frequent visitor.

Tchaikovsky, who described his sister as 'an irreproachable and wonderful woman, in every sense of the word,' used to find himself longing for her company, and her easy-going household, whenever his tensions mounted.

'I look forward to summer and Kamenka as to the Promised Land,' he would write.

That was what it remained: the Promised Land of rest and calm that could be enjoyed only in holiday times, or emergencies, or in daydreams: Tchaikovsky's conscience did not allow him to do much lotus-eating, and his unsettled spirit often drove him away from the places where he was most at ease.

However, at home or abroad, in season and out, he continued to write music.

In the spring of 1872, he composed a cantata for an exhibition being organised for the two hundredth anniversary of Peter the Great, a commissioned work. Apparently it was performed once only, then it was lost, and Tchaikovsky did nothing to recover it. He had received the fee, he cared little for the composition, and he was soon off and away to Kamenka, there to begin work on his second symphony. He continued this later in the summer at Ussovo, the home of Vladimir Shilovsky.

In the autumn, Tchaikovsky moved into a new apartment, resumed his duties at the Conservatory, negotiated for production of *The Oprichnik*, did a season's solid professional work as music critic, wrote some songs, and completed his *Symphony No. 2 in C minor* (the 'Little Russian').

After this spell of work it is not surprising to find him feeling a little weary and complaining of eye-strain. In December he wrote, characteristically, that he had 'abandoned himself to idleness', lacking inspiration and the creative urge. No less characteristically, his spirits rallied when he heard hopeful news of the prospects for his opera, and on the occasion when he played the last movement of his new symphony to a boisterously enthusiastic Petersburg gathering of musicians at the house of Rimsky-Korsakov. They almost tore him to pieces in their delight, he said. Among them was Stassov, who shortly afterwards suggested the subject of *The Tempest* to Tchaikovsky.

When we learn that Stassov proposed a detailed programme, it begins to look like Balakirev's dictatorial behaviour all over again. But Stassov himself disavows this. The critic says that knowing he had suggested subjects for overtures, operas, and symphonies to various composers, Tchaikovsky begged him for this favour, which he at first refused to grant as 'I did not feel I knew his tastes and disposition well enough'.

After several pressing letters, he gave in, and offered various subjects, beginning with Scott's *Kenilworth*, and ending with *The Tempest*, which Tchaikovsky chose. 'He accepted my programme in all its details, without the least change, and the work, he said, must and should be dedicated to no one but myself.'

But before Tchaikovsky could begin to carry out this task, another one came his way.

The Grand Duchess Yelena Pavlovna died suddenly. Not long before she had commissioned Serov, as her favourite composer, to write an opera based on Gogol's *Christmas Eve Revels* and a libretto, under the title of *Vakoula the Smith*, had been written by Polonsky, the same poet who wrote the *Festival Cantata*. But Serov himself died before he could carry out the project.

The Russian Musical Society then decided that the opera should be written in honour of Serov and the Duchess, and they offered substantial prizes for settings of the Polonsky libretto.

Tchaikovsky decided he would enter only if sure to win. He made inquiries to assure himself that his chief rivals, Rimsky-Korsakov, Anton Rubinstein, and Balakirev, were not intending to compete. He found they were not, and so went to work at top speed.

An unhappy incident over this composition was, perhaps, the first and the last to cast any doubts on Tchaikovsky's personal integrity. He mistakenly believed the closing date of the competition to be August 1874; actually, it was August 1875. He composed the opera in a month, finishing it a whole year earlier than he need have done; then he submitted it in St. Petersburg, and did not find out his error until his return to Moscow. So far, no harm was done. But unfortunately he then tried to induce the directors of the St. Petersburg Opera to have *Vakoula the Smith* produced before the competition was judged. The relevant Grand Duke was incensed at this conduct and Tchaikovsky was upset when he realised the bad impression he had created.

Explaining himself, he wrote: 'In my impatience to have my work performed (which is far more to me than any money) I inquired, in reply to a letter of Kondratiev's, whether it might be possible to get my work brought out independently of the prize contest.' (G. P. Kondratiev was director of the Marinsky Theatre, St. Petersburg.) 'Now I see that I have made a stupid mistake, because I have no rights over the libretto of the opera.' He had previously written to Modest: 'You cannot imagine how much I am counting on this work. I think I might go mad if it failed to bring me good fortune.'

Modest comments that this incident shows 'how imperfectly he realised the importance of silence in such an affair as a competition, in which anonymity is the first condition of impartial judgment'. Tchaikovsky did not even keep to himself the inquiries he had made as to the other competitors. The fact that he committed these follies with no attempt at concealment is what saves him from the suspicion of anything worse than naïveté and egoism.

The panel of judges accepted his explanation, and no more was heard of the matter. Both the first and second prizes were awarded to Tchaikovsky and the opera was successfully produced in November 1876 at the Marinsky. But the success was not a lasting one. Though Tchaikovsky was quite in love with this work when he first wrote it, he was later to recast it and rename it. It has been suggested that one reason why the original production did not establish a firm hold on public favour is that people expected a French puff-pastry comic opera, and found *Vakoula* too nationalist for them.

Before it was staged, Tchaikovsky played the score over to a group of his intimates. They were expectant hearers, predisposed in his favour: but he was so nervous that he gave a lifeless performance, and his friends were disappointed.

Yet when the score appeared in print, and when a competent company performed it on the stage, they reversed their opinions and found it had merits which Tchaikovsky's own poor rendering had hidden from them.

At about this time the composer completed another work to commission, and received a satisfactory fee for it. This was the music to Ostrovsky's *The Snow Queen.* It was not remembered for long, partly because of its poor libretto. The Rimsky-Korsakov opera on the same subject a few years later was destined to supersede Tchaikovsky's entirely, in the theatre.

Tchaikovsky and his colleagues and friends celebrated his *Snow Queen* with a splendid picnic among the spring blossoms, the peasants gathering round to watch 'the quality' eating on the grass. Nikolai Rubinstein gave the peasants sweets and wine, and persuaded them to sing old songs and perform folk dances.

A little later Tchaikovsky left Moscow for the country estate of Shilovsky and it was there he composed *The Tempest* in ten days. His friend was absent and, indeed, not a soul was about, and

Tchaikovsky 'roaming the woods and wandering on the measureless steppe', was able to compose, as he says, 'effortlessly, as though inspired by some superhuman force'.

The Tempest, though inferior to *Romeo and Juliet*, has many felicities and when Nikolai Rubinstein first conducted the work it was, for once, both an immediate success and a lasting one, at any rate throughout the composer's lifetime.

Tchaikovsky was now writing criticism as well as music, and continued to do so over the years. His evaluations are not of much intrinsic interest. He was always conscientious, always thoughtful, and frequently wrongheaded, from the standpoint of today. (The same, it must be admitted, can be said of far greater critics.) His admiration for Mozart has already been mentioned: it was unbounded. He showed a conventional regard for Haydn, did less than justice to Wagner and had a blind spot for Brahms. He was much influenced by Schumann, but showed himself surprisingly perceptive of his limitations—the 'pallor and dryness' of his orchestration, and so on. His opinions of his Russian contemporaries have already been indicated. One may add that he held the same view of Glinka—that he was really a symphonic rather than an operatic genius—as he held about Wagner. Fundamentally, it was his opinion of himself, too. Repeatedly, in his letters, he speaks of the theatre as a siren, a temptress to his talent. 'The stage and all its glitter beckon me irresistibly.'

Two men who were to have great importance in Tchaikovsky's musical career had by this time come into his life. One was Piotr Ivanovich Jurgenson, his publisher. Not much older than Tchaikovsky, he was dark, handsome, and gentle-eyed. He founded his business in Moscow when the composer was twenty-one and very early took an interest in this budding talent. Jurgenson became one of the founders, too, of the Moscow Conservatory, and the principal publisher of the rising school of Russian composers. At his death he had in his store-rooms 70,000 engraving plates of Tchaikovsky's music, covering almost all his works.

The other significant figure in the building of Tchaikovsky's reputation was the great German pianist Hans von Bülow, first husband of Cosima Liszt. He paid a triumphant visit to Russia and was acclaimed by Tchaikovsky and many of his fellow composers. What is of greater moment is that von Bülow realised that Tchaikovsky was the outstanding talent in contemporary Russia. He began to play his works and also to write about him in the German newspapers. This praise made Tchaikovsky happier than any other he had ever received.

It was von Bülow who first performed the *Concerto in B flat minor*, as a result of that astounding piece of Rubinsteinism already mentioned

—a full-scale assault by the 'thunder-hurler' as Tchaikovsky called his chief, on what has become one of the best-loved compositions in the world. Tchaikovsky smarted for years from the attack, as he testified in a letter to Mme. von Meck. It is true, of course, that we have only Tchaikovsky's own version and that Rubinstein's account might have been very different. He was by no means the first and last critic of the work. Yet the time came when he was to play it many times in Europe. And Tchaikovsky, despite his avowal that he would not alter it, did make some revisions.

Here is his famous description of his mortifying experience:

San Remo, January 21, 1878.

. . . In December, 1874, I wrote a piano concerto. As I am not a pianist, I needed a virtuoso's opinion as to what was technically impractical, difficult, unplayable and so on. I needed a serious but friendly critic, but only for the pianistic aspect of my composition. Rubinstein is not only the first pianist of Moscow, but is truly a perfect pianist; knowing that he would be deeply offended if he thought I had ignored him, I asked him to listen to the concerto and give me an opinion on the piano part, although some inner voice protested against my selecting him as judge. It was Christmas Eve of 1874. We were both invited to a Christmas tree that evening at Albrecht's [1] and Nikolai suggested that we go to one of the classrooms at the Conservatory beforehand. And so we did. I arrived with my manuscript, and after me Nikolai and Hubert.[2] Have you any idea, my friend, what the latter is like? He is very kind and clever, completely lacking in independence, very talkative, needing a whole preface to say yes or no, incapable of expressing an opinion in a simple way, always backing the one who at the moment expresses himself bravely and decisively. I hasten to add that it is because of lack of character, not servility. (*A delicious backhanded compliment!*)

I played the first movement. Not a word, not a remark. If you only knew how disappointing, how unbearable it is when a man offers his friend a dish of his work and the other eats and remains silent! Well, say something, scold, in a friendly way, but for God's sake, one sympathetic word, even if uncomplimentary!

While Rubinstein prepared his thunder, Hubert waited for the situation to clarify, so that he would know which way to jump. The point was that I did not want a verdict on artistic merits, but advice as to piano technique. Rubinstein's eloquent silence had great significance. As much as to say, 'My friend, can I speak of details, when the thing as a whole disgusts me?'

[1] Karl Albrecht, a member of the Conservatory staff.

[2] Nikolai Albertovich Hubert, also a Conservatory teacher.

I armed myself with patience, and played it through to the end. Again silence. I stood up and said: 'Well?'

Then from the lips of N.G.R. poured a torrent of words, first quiet, then more and more the tone of Jupiter, lord of the thunderbolts. It appeared that my concerto was worthless, impossible to play, the themes had been used before, and were clumsy and awkward beyond the possibility of correction; as a composition it was poor, I had stolen this from one source and that from another. There were only two or three pages that could be salvaged, and the rest must be thrown away, or completely altered! 'For example, what is *that*?' (And he plays the part indicated, caricaturing it.) 'And that? Is it possible',—and so on. I cannot convey the tone in which it was all spoken. An outsider, dropping into the room, would have thought me a madman, without talent, ignorant, a worthless scribbler who had come to trouble a great man with his rubbish.

Hubert, who noticed that I was silent and amazed, was shocked that a man who has written many works already, should be subjected to such a denunciation, to such a humiliating sentence, without appeal—a condemnation that would not be justified in the case of a mere untalented student unless his work had been very carefully examined. Hubert started to explain N.G.R.'s opinions, not differing, but only softening what His Excellency had put so harshly.

I was not only astonished but embarrassed by the performance. I am no longer a boy, trying his hand at composition. I no longer need lessons, especially lessons delivered in so sharp and hostile a manner. I need and will always need friendly criticism, but this was nothing like friendly criticism. It was a decisive, total condemnation, expressed in such a way as to wound me deeply. Speechless with agitation and fury, I walked out of the room without a word and went upstairs.

Rubinstein appeared soon afterwards and seeing my disturbed state, asked me into another room. There he repeated that my concerto was impossible, and having pointed out many places needing radical changes, he told me that if I would alter it according to his wishes by a certain date, he would do me the honour of performing it at his concert.

'I will not alter a single note!' I replied. 'I will print it exactly as it is!' And so I did.

This incident caused Rubinstein to look upon me as a *frondeur*, a secret enemy. He has grown colder towards me since then, though it has not prevented him from repeating on all occasions that he is terribly fond of me and ready to do anything for me.

After the serious alienation of feeling caused by the clash described in Tchaikovsky's letter, he cancelled the intended dedication of the concerto to Rubinstein and substituted von Bülow's name. The German pianist was delighted, spoke of it as 'this splendid work' and played it in Boston, Massachusetts, in October 1875. Its first performance in Russia took place the following month, not in Moscow but in St. Petersburg.

The Petersburg Rubinstein (Anton) was also still capable of wounding Tchaikovsky's sensibilities. When the *String Quartet No. 2 in F major* was performed privately, to a select group, some months before the stormy scene over the concerto, it pleased everyone except Anton. He heard it with a lowering look, and then bitterly attacked it, saying it was not in the style of chamber music and pretending he could not understand it. These cutting remarks hurt Tchaikovsky, though in this instance he submissively made revisions, and did not turn at bay as he did against Nikolai.

When Tchaikovsky dedicated his *Six Pieces on One Theme* to Anton Rubinstein, he did not even receive an acknowledgement, and the great pianist never played one of them in public.

Tchaikovsky must be credited with much respect for justice and truth in finding as many occasions as he did to praise the merits of these extraordinary brothers, who never showed the like fair-mindedness in return.

It is hardly possible, on the facts, to assent to Kashkin's statement that Nikolai Rubinstein was 'purely an idealist' and was entirely above personal likes and dislikes. It may be so as far as conscious intention was concerned, but can he be acquitted of professional jealousy and bias? Tchaikovsky himself wrote to his patroness that 'Nikolai Rubinstein is not as much of a hero as he is often made out to be. He is a wonderfully gifted man, intelligent though poorly educated, energetic and clever. He is not small by nature but has become so because of the silly, servile admiration that surrounds him. . . . My relations with him are very strange. When he has drunk a little wine, he begins to be as sweet to me as possible, and accuses me of lack of feeling, lack of love for him. But normally he is very cold to me. He loves to make me feel that I am under obligation to him for everything. The truth is, he is a little afraid that I despise him. As I am not expansive, he sometimes imagines that I try secretly to get the position of director from him.' (Tchaikovsky adds that he does his best to make Rubinstein understand that he would rather be a beggar than the director of the Conservatory.)

The brothers differed a great deal in appearance and temperament, though both were fiery and opinionated.

Anton had a neck-length shock of dark hair, a broad nose, and a craggy, passion-worn face. Nikolai, short and stocky, was fair and curly-haired, with a weak chin, and had a dreamy, world-weary air when he was not thundering. The suggestion of the languid aristocrat, possibly cultivated, or possibly the result of the lack of sleep, as he would frequently gamble until dawn, was constantly belied by his verbal outbursts and by his displays of practical energy.

In his determination to secure a finer appreciation of Russian music in general and the Conservatory in particular, Nikolai Rubinstein took part in every social event worth mentioning in Moscow, and had contacts in many circles: business, official, artistic, aristocratic, and even scientific, to say nothing of bohemian and the demi-monde. He managed the Conservatory with skill and business acumen, he played and conducted and lectured and visited. He drank with truly Russian recklessness, he was a Don Juan among women, and night after night played for high stakes in the English Club.

His habitual generosity consorts well enough with his gambler's spirit of easy-come, easy-go. At a hard-luck story from a musician, especially a Russian one, he would empty his pockets.

When he was young, it was thought that Nikolai's genius was greater than that of Anton. He was a quicker learner, but it was Anton who devoted himself entirely to music and became the more famous executant. Nikolai chose a general education and went to the university. Moreover, he married a woman whose relations considered that playing in public was not a fit occupation for a gentleman, and to please her, he gave up doing so. But the differences between the musician and his in-laws became more and more serious, and the marriage quickly foundered, ending in divorce. So explosive a man cannot have been easy to live with. But he could not be expected to brook the philistine snobbery of his wife's family. Aristocrats were only aristocrats: the Rubinsteins were the Rubinsteins!

Such were the extraordinary men who presided over Tchaikovsky's career in the years of his making. It is a piece of dramatic irony that Nikolai Rubinstein himself unintentionally gave Tchaikovsky the means of his liberation, by securing for him as patroness one of the richest women in Russia, who was needing someone to adore.

Until that happened, Tchaikovsky was sometimes out of debt, but rarely. At times he lived very frugally. When he said, at the time of the opera contest, that he cared nothing about the money side of the matter, he was speaking the truth. Not only was he unmercenary, but he usually had little idea how much money he possessed, and he spent it or gave it away far too readily.

When von Bülow played his concerto in Boston, he sent a telegram to Tchaikovsky informing him that it was a brilliant success. The composer felt obliged to reply, for honour's and courtesy's sake, but he was so hard up at the time that the message took his last kopeck.

On the occasion when *The Snow Queen* had brought him some ready cash, he had promptly spent it on his summer tour, which took him to Germany, through Switzerland, to Milan and Lake Como, travelling much of the time with Jurgenson. His earliest surviving diaries date from that year and in them he confesses to homesickness not much more than a fortnight after setting out.

'What is more boring than a train trip and intrusive passengers?' he writes. 'Am bored . . . my heart sinks as I often think of Sasha and Modia.' And, 'How I love to be alone at times! I must confess that I remained in Breslau so as not to turn up at once to join the Jurgensons in Dresden. When alone, you are silent, you can meditate. . . .' Nevertheless he was pleased with Jurgenson's company, and they roamed the cities, sightseeing. In Dresden Tchaikovsky heard good performances of *The Magic Flute* and *La Juive* but his nerves were too bad to allow him to enjoy them and he could not sit out Halévy's opera.

He felt no better in Berne. 'On the advice of some Russian, we stayed at the Hotel de France, which was repulsive. Everything was vile, but the supper passed all expectations. It was putrid and disgusting.'

Parting from Jurgenson, he travelled alone and yearned for friends: 'Ran off to send a telegram and made a mess of it. Had supper. Strolled along the quay in futile hopes! Read the newspapers. Slept poorly. There was thunder and it was stifling.' He visited the castle of Chillon and went to a circus, but his longings were unappeased: 'My desires are excessive—but I have nothing.'

The glories of Swiss scenery were unsatisfactory, too. The mountains, it seems, were not made the same way as those at home.

'Experiencing all the impressions of a traveller, I still long for Russia with all my soul, and my heart sighs as I imagine its plains, meadows and woods. O my beloved country, you are a hundred times more striking and charming than these splendid, colossal mountains that are really nothing more than nature's petrified convulsions. In my country, you are calmly magnificent. But then—distance lends enchantment!'

Rejoining Jurgenson at Geneva, he writes, 'Am going unwillingly to Italy,' and sure enough, 'In Turin with a severe pain in my abdomen. I am taken to a disgusting *albergo* and receive a room with a bed three yards long. With difficulty get some castor oil. Sleep. . . .'

Thus the money and the time were spent; scarcely in riotous pleasures; and at length he returned with relief to his only solid happiness, hard work.

Tchaikovsky's opinions of his own productions at this period wavered between confidence and doubt. One moment he was sure that *The Oprichnik* was a fine achievement and he swore he would give up composing if it were rejected. But before its production in St. Petersburg, he wrote to his friends in Moscow advising them not to come over as there was 'nothing first rate' in it. The opera was warmly praised by Laroche, but Caesar Cui thought poorly of it: Tchaikovsky weighed the two critiques, and finally said that Cui's, in spite of vicious prejudice, was 'essentially a correct evaluation.'

When it was performed in Kiev, cheering crowds of students escorted Tchaikovsky from the theatre to his hotel. The ovation, he said, made him very happy. But soon afterwards, his only desire was to obliterate all memory of the work, by giving the public something new and better.

There was a brush with the imperial censorship over *The Oprichnik.* The censor forbade Ivan the Terrible to be impersonated on the stage, and objected to some verses of the libretto. This was not the last time the composer was in trouble in this way, though the Tsar could not have had a more patriotic subject than he.

The *Second Symphony in C minor* (the 'Little Russian'), had enjoyed considerable success at the start. A Russian folk song which Tchaikovsky heard a servant sing at Kamenka, called 'The Crane', provided the melodic basis for brilliant variations in the last movement. The composer was not entirely satisfied with this symphony, and revised it more than once, some few years after it was first performed. On the whole it is uncharacteristic of Tchaikovsky's genius, and is not much played today.

Tchaikovsky's *Third Symphony in D major* ('The Polish') was written in the summer of 1875. It was not, by the way, an expression of political sympathy for Poland: it merely ends with an allegro marked 'tempo di Polacca', a form of the polonaise.

No stability, no spiritual peace came with these years of achievement which gave birth to Tchaikovsky's first opera, first ballet, first tone poem, and three symphonies. His second nervous breakdown occurred just before he reached the age of thirty-five.

He began to send letters to Modest saying that life was intolerable and that he felt like committing suicide. Then in March came a repetition of what he had experienced nine years earlier. Once again he was utterly prostrated, feverish, and without hope. The doctor's advice, as usual, was rest, with a change of air, and he was again forbidden to touch the piano or attempt to write music.

As before, he was sufficiently frightened to obey, and until the cure was declared complete he did not look at the piano or put pen to paper. But he then revealed that he had conformed only to the letter. In his head, unwritten, was a complete new work, his *String Quartet in E flat minor*, which he was to dedicate to the memory of Ferdinand Laub, the violinist, recently dead. Tchaikovsky had the capacity to carry whole and elaborate compositions in his memory before he set them down, as Burns was able to retain his longest poems in his head for months before putting them on paper.

The Quartet was performed the following spring, at Nikolai Rubinstein's house. After it, Tchaikovsky told Modest he thought he was beginning to repeat himself, and feared that he had written himself out.

'Is it possible that my song is finished,' he asked, 'and that I have no further to go?'

CHAPTER VI

TCHAIKOVSKY AT BAYREUTH

ONCE a month for a whole year, Tchaikovsky's manservant would come to him and say, 'Piotr Ilyich, this is your day for sending to St. Petersburg.'

'Ah, thank you!'

The composer would go to his desk, take his music-paper, dip his pen and write a piece of music appropriate to the month. Then he would sand it, fold it, seal it in its envelope and give it to Sofronov, the servant, to post to a Petersburg musical magazine which had commissioned this series of a dozen pieces.

This amusingly illustrates how casual yet conscientious, how fluent and self-confident—as artist—Tchaikovsky had become. He did not take this small commitment too seriously, but he knew he would never be at a loss for the melody that would make a suitable miniature piano piece. The group, as published, has the title *The Seasons*, rather than *The Months*, to emphasise that it reflects the moods of nature.

After *Swan Lake*, which he completed rapidly in the spring of 1876 to earn money for a trip abroad, Tchaikovsky wrote little till the autumn. Instead, he became a listener and a reporter, attending the first Wagner festival at Bayreuth.

To this great event musical pilgrims had of course come in their thousands, to hear the first performance of *The Ring* in the presence of the German Emperor, in a theatre newly erected to enshrine the works of Wagner.

There was an element of comedy in Tchaikovsky's situation. His distaste for Wagner made him feel an alien in the atmosphere of the festival. Unfortunately, one of the staff of the Moscow Conservatory, Professor Karl Klindworth, chose to attach himself to Tchaikovsky, following wherever he went and pouring out praise of him and Wagner, in equal measure. All the Moscow musicians, and especially Tchaikovsky, were a little afraid of Klindworth.

Being embarrassed as to himself, and dissenting as to Wagner, Tchaikovsky thought it best to hold his tongue. But he did manage to speak to Laroche—out of earshot of Klindworth—and tell him that *The Ring* left him cold.

What he could not say to his companion he could put on paper, and did with gusto in letters, articles, and notes. One of his references to Wagner says, 'I cannot call that music which consists of kaleidoscopic, shifting phrases which succeed each other without a break and never come to a close—that is to say, never give the ear the least chance to rest upon musical form. Not a single broad round melody, nor yet one moment of repose for the singer! The latter must always pursue the orchestra, and be careful never to lose his note, which has no more importance in the score than some note for the fourth horn. But there is no doubt,' he adds, 'that Wagner is a wonderful symphonist.'

After the *Rheingold*, he wrote to Modest that he was charmed by the theatrical spectacle, but 'as music it is incredible nonsense' despite 'flashes of amazing beauty'.

He saw Wagner, serene in his carriage and being cheered as loudly as the emperor, and paid personal calls on both Wagner and Liszt, finding the latter 'nauseatingly' polite with a hint of condescension.

Tchaikovsky himself was recognised in the streets and was treated everywhere with deference. 'It would seem I am not so unknown in Western Europe as I had thought,' he wrote to his brother.

The total experience of Bayreuth repelled him: he did not share the general opinion of the quality of the work performed, he did not like the display of herd-emotion, and he found the conditions unpleasant: the famished crowds charging from place to place, climbing a shadeless hill in the hot sun to the theatre or hurtling down again in search of beer and sausages; the packed hotels and restaurants; the glitter, the tumult, and the continual strain on the attention. When the *Gotterdämmerung* ended he felt as though he had been 'set free from captivity,' he said, even though it might be epoch-making art.

All the Wagnerites went about seeking something—food! 'Throughout the whole festival, food was the chief interest of the public,' he said. 'The artistic performances took second place. Chops, baked potatoes and omelettes were discussed much more eagerly than Wagner's music.'

Tchaikovsky and Wagner being oil and water, these reactions to Bayreuth are not surprising. In a less generous nature than Tchaikovsky's such antipathy could be ascribed, in some measure at least, to the jealous dislike of a musical figure whose genius had diminished the glory of his contemporaries. But Tchaikovsky could be wiser than his critics and saw that another man's greatness in no way affected his own achievements. The world of music was a wide one and richer for the diverse gifts of those who peopled it.

No doubt it was galling to discover how powerful and arbitrary had become the cult of Wagnerism, and nowhere more so than in

England. To Shaw, the most explosive music critic of the late nineteenth century, Wagner was a Moses who had descended not from Mount Sinai, but from Parnassus, with a brand new decalogue: to hear was to obey. Tchaikovsky, however, as Shaw perceived, was not to be converted. Alas! he was neither 'philosophical' by Shavian definition, nor the creator of elaborate symbolic structures like the Wagnerian operas.

The Wagnerians were never able to shake Tchaikovsky's immense popularity with the English public. Love of his music took firm root in the composer's lifetime and its growth was phenomenal.

Russian music, it should be remembered, still had to fight the prejudice abroad that it was 'barbarian'. Tchaikovsky as late as 1888 encountered an amusing instance in Hamburg, where the chairman of the Philharmonic Society, Theodor Ave-Lallemant, a man over eighty, told him his percussion and noisy instrumentation were unbearable, but that he had the makings of 'a really good German composer'. Almost with tears in his eyes, the old man urged Tchaikovsky to leave his unenlightened homeland and settle in Germany, where classical conventions and the high cultural tradition would infallibly cure his faults. And this was a distinguished writer on music, the man to whom Tchaikovsky dedicated his *Fifth Symphony*.

Bernard Shaw's real attitude to Tchaikovsky is indicated by the fact that his favourite adjective is 'Byronic', used in a rather patronising way—'le Byron de nos jours', etc.

Shaw was present at a concert of the Philharmonic Society in London on June 1, 1893, at which Tchaikovsky conducted his own *Fourth Symphony* only five months before his death. Shaw in his criticism did not bother to identify the symphony by number or key, but merely said: 'Of Tchaikovsky's symphony, apart from its performance, I need only say it was highly characteristic of him. . . . The notablest merit of the symphony is its freedom from the frightful effeminacy of the romantic school.'

Shaw also attended the first London performance of the *Sixth Symphony*, the following year, and wrote: 'Tchaikovsky had a thoroughly Byronic power of being tragic, momentous, romantic about nothing at all. Like Childe Harold, who was more tragic when there was nothing whatever the matter with him than an ordinary Englishman is when he is going to be executed, Tchaikovsky could set the fateful drum rolling and make the trombones utter the sepulchral voice of destiny without any conceivable provocation.'

There we discern the authentic Shavian whipcrack, and see the bright dust fly. It does not bear examination, of course. How, in a symphony, is the composer supposed to show what is 'the matter with him', to *explain* the emotional mood of the work? Shaw the puritan liked a meaning, and a didactic one, writ plain with every work of art; and anyone not using the art of music for this transcendent purpose, but creating melody and harmony for their own sake, was an 'orchestral voluptuary', which is one of the things he called Tchaikovsky.

Havelock Ellis in his journal contrasts the feminine, yielding nature of Tchaikovsky's inner self with that of Beethoven, aggressive and muscular. The same life-challenge which inspired in Beethoven the spirit of conquest drew from Tchaikovsky, he says, 'the deep groan of utter despair.'

Havelock Ellis is here referring to the *Sixth Symphony*, which he calls 'the Homosexual Tragedy'. Although no professional music critic, he shows in this comment a deeper discernment than Shaw does.

When Shaw heard *Eugene Onegin* for the first time, his comment was curious: 'The music suggests a vain regret that Tchaikovsky's remarkable artistic judgment, culture, imagination, vivacity and self-respect as a musical workman should have been unaccompanied by an original musical force. . . . The opera, as a whole, is a dignified composition by a man of distinguished talent whose love of music led him to adopt the profession of composer. . . .'

He even referred to Tchaikovsky's operatic form as 'Balfian', although he added that it must not be inferred that Tchaikovsky's music was as 'common' as Balfe's.

Strange indeed are the historic shifts of taste. The First World War deflated the romantic movement, which Shavian arrows and the like had merely pricked. To the neo-classicists of the time, Tchaikovsky was scarcely mentionable, and when their hero Stravinsky came out with a defence of Tchaikovsky he was suspected of a *blague*.

But this, the opinion of a great musician, is worth hearing, for it states some fundamental truths.

In 1921 when the Russian Ballet was in London, Stravinsky wrote thus to Diaghilev: 'It gives me great happiness to know that you are producing that masterpiece *The Sleeping Beauty* by our great and beloved Tchaikovsky. . . . It is further a great satisfaction to me as a musician to see produced a work of so direct a character, at a time when so many people who are neither simple nor naïve nor spontaneous seek in their art simplicity, "poverty" and spontaneity. Tchaikovsky in his very nature possesses these three gifts to the fullest extent. That is why he never feared to let himself go, whereas the prudes, whether *raffinés* or academic, were shocked by the frank speech, free from artifice, of his music.

'Tchaikovsky possessed the power of melody, centre of gravity in every symphony, opera or ballet composed by him. It is absolutely indifferent to me that the quality of his melody was sometimes unequal. The fact is that he was a creator of melody, which is an extremely rare and precious gift. . . .

'Tchaikovsky's music, which does not appear specifically Russian to everybody, is often more profoundly Russian than music which has long since been awarded the facile label of Muscovite picturesqueness. This music is quite as Russian as Pushkin's verse or Glinka's song. Whilst not specifically cultivating in his art the "soul of the Russian peasant", Tchaikovsky drew unconsciously from the true popular sources of our race.'

Stravinsky's father, by the way, was one of the performers in *Vakoula the Smith*, and saw Tchaikovsky take a curtain-call in which hisses mingled with the applause.

Although that year, 1876, was one of nervous disturbance and comparative inactivity for Tchaikovsky, as well as such distracting events as the Bayreuth festival and visits to Vichy and Nuremberg, he had short spurts of intensive work, in one of which he composed, 'with love', the orchestral fantasy, *Francesca da Rimini*, suggested to him by Modest and based on Dante's account of the passion of Paolo and Francesca, in the Fifth Canto of the *Inferno*.

The same season also produced his popular *Slavonic March*, composed for a patriotic occasion—a concert in aid of wounded soldiers. At war with Turkey, Russia was the ally of Serbia, and Tchaikovsky was caught up in the Pan-Slav fervour and spoke of 'our beloved country upholding her honour'. Nikolai Rubinstein conducted the March and the occasion, of course, assured its success.

In this period of ebb and flow, another of Tchaikovsky's friendships had been ripening. It was with one of his students, Josef Josefovich Kotek, a generous, handsome young man who showed great promise as a violinist, and who won a Conservatory medal that spring. His attitude of simple adoration towards Tchaikovsky, which of course drew a warm response, was to have considerable importance very soon, when he became Tchaikovsky's courier and advocate at the house—one had almost said the court—of Mme. von Meck.

Having graduated, with some glory but without cash or prospects, Kotek looked about him for pupils, and thought that Nikolai Rubinstein might be able to help him to find some. Instead, Rubinstein introduced him to Mme. von Meck, who wished to employ a young household musician, to play duets with her and arrange transcriptions: music was her ruling passion. Kotek was engaged to fill the post; and about the same time the first links were established in the remarkable relationship between her and Tchaikovsky. When she sought information about Tchaikovsky, nobody could have been in a better position to provide it than Kotek.

The breakdown mentioned at the end of the previous chapter was of course psychologically connected with Tchaikovsky's homosexuality. It was followed by agonies of conscience, vain efforts to control the impulse which more than ever he hated and feared and condemned. In the late summer he told his brother he was passing through the most critical moment of his life, and declared that he had 'irrevocably' decided to get married.

In a further letter he said that should he lack courage to carry out this resolution, he would at any rate break his habits. Meanwhile he would seriously prepare himself, 'beginning from today', to marry—whom? 'someone or other!' But he promised Modest he would be cautious and move slowly towards his goal. He would obviously have to do so, since he had not yet picked a bride.

But it was quite true that he had absolutely made up his mind to marry, in spite of his friends' and relations' advice to the contrary; and he was to have plenty of that, from Modest, Sasha, and Rubinstein, to name only three. The decision had become almost an obsession by the time Tchaikovsky's friendship with Mme. von Meck began. If the friendship had begun sooner and reached a point of candour and privilege, his patroness too would have urged him not to marry. Would her persuasions have succeeded where the others failed? It is certainly possible, because she was more than a friend, she was able to be, with her wealth and position, a strong shield for him. The menacing face of the world was the reason for his desire to get married, as he made clear to Modest that autumn. He wrote, 'I want, through marriage or some other public bond with a woman, to shut the mouths of those contemptible creatures whose opinions I do not value but who have it in their power to cause sorrow to those dear to me . . .'

He had found by this time that his resolution to give up his habits 'at once, as one discards a glove' was impossible of fulfilment. 'I am far from possessing an iron will, and since writing to you I have already given way three times to my natural inclinations,' he wrote.

This was the torn and painful frame of mind in which Tchaikovsky faced the end of the year, its festivities and its demands. The most critical moment of his life was not just past, as he believed, but to come.

Nevertheless, the celebrated friendship, which was about to begin, was something for the other side of the account, bringing very positive values, for all its absurdities and exaggerations, and for all the mysterious collapse at its end.

The turn of the year brought an interesting encounter for Tchaikovsky. He had already met two of Russia's greatest writers, Dostoievsky and Turgenev; now he met the third, Count Leo Tolstoy. He had the greatest opinion of Tolstoy's genius and he was now able to pay it the tribute of his own. Tolstoy arrived in Moscow and himself made the approach; he was already familiar with some of Tchaikovsky's music and would like both to hear more and to meet the composer. Nikolai Rubinstein arranged a Conservatory concert in honour of Tolstoy, including in the programme the Andante Cantabile from Tchaikovsky's *First String Quartet in D major*. The performers played, said the composer, as they had never played before, and he saw Tolstoy, who was sitting beside him, moved to tears.

'Never in my life have I felt so flattered,' he wrote in his diary.

Tolstoy promised to send him some folk-songs from Yasnaya Polyana, and they talked at large. Tchaikovsky had heard Dostoievsky talk with more confidence than sense about music, and he now heard Tolstoy do the same thing. What really shocked Tchaikovsky was that Tolstoy failed to show in his conversation the greatness, the all-seeing human understanding to be found in his books. The composer was terribly afraid, beforehand, that this 'great searcher of hearts' would penetrate his secrets, even the most shameful, at a glance, and would then reveal his knowledge either by a delicate avoidance of 'the sorest spots', or if he lacked compassion would put his finger on the centre of the wound. Nothing happened. Tolstoy showed no interest in searching Tchaikovsky's heart or applying any scalpel (the surgical imagery is Tchaikovsky's own). He simply wanted to chat about music, and in this field he talked like a small man, not a great one.

These were Tchaikovsky's recollections in tranquillity, when the immediate impression of excitement and flattery had died away. Meanwhile, Tolstoy sent the songs, saying he was sure Tchaikovsky would make a wonderful treasure of them, but urging him to arrange them 'in the Mozart-Haydn style, not the artificial Beethoven-Berlioz style'. He threw in more compliments, and remarked how charming he had found Rubinstein, and saying he had never had so precious a reward for his literary labours as that musical evening in Moscow.

Tchaikovsky wrote back candidly that the folk-songs had been taken down by such an inexperienced hand that they bore merely traces of their original beauty, and they had been artificially forced into conventional rhythm. They could never be made into a publishable collection, without diffcult research and 'an exact transcription of the original songs as sung by the people', which would require high musical sensitivity and profound historical knowledge. (Such a standard of integrity in the matter of folk music was exceedingly rare in Tchaikovsky's time.)

But he thanked Tolstoy cordially and said, 'I cannot tell you how happy and proud I was that my music could touch and charm you.'

The friendship was not pursued, from either side: partly because beneath the cordialities there had been no living spark between them; partly because the vastly more significant bond with Mme. von Meck was beginning to establish itself, precluding the growth of any other new relationship for some time.

CHAPTER VII

THE TRANSCENDENTAL FRIENDSHIP

NIKOLAI RUBINSTEIN came to Tchaikovsky one winter's day in 1876 and asked him whether he would transcribe one of his works for piano and violin, as a paid commission for a woman who much admired his compositions: Mme. von Meck.

He accepted gratefully. It was, as we have emphasised, almost a point of honour with Tchaikovsky, as a professional musician, not to refuse commissioned work; and this job was pleasant, easy, and well paid. Rubinstein knew that he needed more money than his teaching salary and his rewards as composer amounted to; he was not a gambler or *bon vivant*, like Rubinstein himself, but he was generous and careless with money, and often ran into debt. He had borrowed a considerable sum from Shilovsky only a few months earlier. (It has been suggested, though without positive evidence, that he was being blackmailed by someone.)

Rubinstein told him that this would not be his last commission from Mme. von Meck: she had conceived a great enthusiasm for his music. How great, the maestro himself did not entirely realise, for she could not bring herself to tell him as frankly as she was later to write it to Tchaikovsky himself. To the composer she confessed that when she first heard *The Tempest* she was so utterly carried away by it that she lived in a state of delirium for several days.

This surpassed the tears of Tolstoy. Tchaikovsky had come upon the perfect auditor, that personification of an ideal public that every artist dreams of. Emotionally, the widow was an aeolian harp, attuned to his music above all other, quivering down to her musicianly finger-tips in response to it.

Artists are often embarrassed by the worship of people who have no understanding of what they are trying to do. But Mme. von Meck's adoration of Tchaikovsky was very knowledgeable. Her father was a violinist, she had a thorough musical education, and she played the piano with, at any rate, fervour. Her nature was as heavily charged with emotion as was Tchaikovsky's, though without his creative outlet. She really had a great deal in common with him—the same high nervous tension and liability to gusts of depression, the same shyness and compulsive tendency to run 'away from it all', combined with the same practicality and tenacity of will; the same sensitivity, the same unconquerable restlessness.

Nadejda Philaretovna von Meck, *née* Frolovskaya, was forty-five at the time of her friendship with Tchaikovsky: a tall, nervous but imperious woman, with a long melancholy face, a small thin mouth, and a mass of dark hair built up on her head like a coronet. Her father, whose violin playing first led her into the realms of music, was a landowner and a local judge. Her mother was a Potemkin, distantly connected with the famous lover of Catherine the Great. Hers was the comfortable upbringing of the Russian bourgeoisie.

At seventeen, Nadejda was married off to Karl George Otto von Meck, eldest son of a German Balt family, knights of Riga, who had ancient lineage but no money.

Nadejda's husband was an engineer in the Government service. He was poorly paid, and his thriftless family were living on him. Nadejda bore him twelve children, in the good old nineteenth century style, and during the coming of the first half-dozen they were very poor indeed. A young woman of spirit, she did not resent the poverty, nor the drudgery, nor the constant uprootings as her husband was transferred from one town to another: what she resented was the slavishness of the Government service, the base servitude of her husband's job, when all the time she believed he had the capacity to become a great man in his profession.

She begged him to resign, and follow his star. He exclaimed that they would starve. 'We can work,' she retorted. He resigned, the family lived on twenty kopeks a day, and Karl applied his engineering ability to the most rapidly expanding sector of industry, the railways.

Nadejda took over the business side and negotiated contracts; her husband planned great development schemes. He built the first railway from Moscow to Riazan and his sons extended it to the Urals.

When Karl died in his fifties, only a few months before Nadejda began to correspond with Tchaikovsky, she inherited great investments, houses, forests, agricultural land, and the only two privately owned railways in Russia. She sold one railway; the other, she continued to own, co-managing it with her eldest and favourite son, Vladimir, then twenty-four, a man of brains and character.

Nadejda was determined to be no merry widow. All her romantic feelings were sublimated into music and the arts, she had no intention of plunging into social gaiety, still less into the marriage market. She was afraid of fortune-hunters and had so much distaste for the physical side of marriage that she had a strong desire to become a recluse and avoid all further contact with men. She once wrote to Tchaikovsky that she thought it a pity that human beings could not be cultivated artificially, 'like fishes', and then there would be no need for the institution of marriage, 'and that would be a great relief'.

Such an attitude, in a woman of uncommon vigour, readily explains the great emotional pressures which her words and deeds constantly betrayed. As for her escapism, it is a little difficult to be a hermit and at the same time manage a railway and large estates, travel with a staff of servants, act foster-mother to a grandchild, rear a still-young family (her youngest child was only four), engage tutors and music-teachers, keep in touch with the musical life of the country through personal contact with its key figure, Rubinstein, attend every good concert and opera, maintain regal control over a network of relatives and dependants, and eagerly debate art, philosophy, and religion with her new friend. This was a very *engagée* recluse.

It may, however, be unwise to accept her remark about human reproduction quite at face value or as proof of frigidity, as has been assumed. One must consider the statement in its setting. Mme. von Meck was anxious to reassure Tchaikovsky that she was not playing the Widow Wadman and had no designs upon him; at the same time she wanted to sound out his own attitudes. Some allowance must also be made for the tone of the remark; it is a sort of civilised jesting, and rather daring for its period. Mme. von Meck was a freethinker, and emancipated in her fashion.

The friendship with Tchaikovsky began slowly: a mere trickle of rather formal letters for the first three months, then a growing spate. Her first few letters began 'Gracious Sir, Piotr Ilyich', while he addressed her correspondingly as 'Gracious Lady, Nadejda Philaretovna'. She thanked him for executing her commissions so promptly (this was Tchaikovsky the craftsman, who could carry out a bidden task at tremendous speed, and write a *Season* between breakfast and lunchtime if his servant jogged his memory). He thanked her for no less prompt payment, and said she rewarded him too lavishly for little work. But in these short letters, each made some advance towards more meaningful friendship. She told him that his music made her life easier and pleasanter to live, and that it would be unfitting to disclose to him the depth of ecstasy into which it could plunge her. He asked her to tell him *all* her thoughts, saying he felt deeply sympathetic to her, and added: 'Perhaps I know you better than you imagine'.

To this Mme. von Meck responded warmly, after a decent interval. Having confided to him a little more concerning the strength of feeling which his music engendered in her—sweeping her, she said, into a world of hope, insatiable yearning, joy and sadness—she now admitted that she was 'incapable of separating the musician from the man'; a very feminine way of putting matters, which might have made Tchaikovsky take fright, if it had not been coupled with the assurance that she was not seeking to meet him face to face.

'There was a time when I wanted to meet you,' she confessed. 'Now, the more I am charmed, the more I fear meeting.'

'I could not talk to you . . . I prefer to think about you at a distance, to hear you in your music. . . .'

She asked him for his photograph: he sent it, and she said it made her heart glow: she was now sure that in him she had found the unity of man and musician of which she had never ceased to dream, though she had suffered many disappointments in the quest. What composers, one wonders, had let her down? She does not say. If she had ever idealised her friend Rubinstein, his worldly dissipations may conceivably have disillusioned her. Not that she was naïve. She told Tchaikovsky, in her first really communicative letter, that 'a person who lives, like me, the life of a recluse, naturally grows to feel that what people call conventions, social laws, decency, are but sounds without meaning.' The remark is revealing and audacious. Mme. von Meck was not afraid of ideas, and liked to describe herself as a 'realist'—as, in her romantic way, she was. It was only in her own private life that she had settled for a sexless future; and after all, she had reached her middle forties and had had her share of child-bearing. She wanted to direct her still-abundant energy into other channels.

She was a woman of the world, to an extent that does not seem to be appreciated.

It has been assumed that Mme. von Meck never knew that Tchaikovsky was homosexual. Their correspondence gives no outright proof that she did know. But surely the view that she was ignorant of it is contrary to commonsense and probability.

Possibly Mme. von Meck not only knew the truth but would even have liked to discuss it in correspondence with Tchaikovsky: it was he who shied off from this region of fear and shame. Had he been bolder, he would pretty certainly have found an open mind and sympathetic heart at his disposal, a confidante to whom he could have told his troubles almost as freely as to Modest.

Her probing was delicate and determined; she did not force his confidence. While still on terms of comparative formality with the composer himself, she sifted two direct sources of information about him—Rubinstein and Kotek. Both knew him extremely well in their different ways, and the sophistication of the former could yield clues, as could the artless enthusiasm of the younger man.

Mme. von Meck told Tchaikovsky outright, in an early letter, that she had taken every opportunity to hear what was said about him, never allowing any channel of news to escape her. 'I have stored up every remark about you, every fragment of criticism,' she said. 'I must confess that just those things for which others blamed you were charms in my eyes. Everyone to his taste!'

This remark is ambiguous, maybe intentionally so. Some middle-aged matrons do develop a particularly soft spot for homosexuals, and offer them a protective tolerance and understanding which can be invaluable in a hard world. Mme. von Meck may have been offering something of the kind to Tchaikovsky, enticing him to be completely open with her, or at least assuring him obliquely that he need not fear that any facts about himself would alienate her sympathies.

He did not respond with any reference to his sexual nature, then or at any other time. But it is hardly possible that Mme. von Meck neither heard it from any other source ('storing up every remark') nor guessed it for herself and then sought a confirmation that would not be hard to obtain: Tchaikovsky himself is witness that there were 'contemptible creatures' gossiping about him. Moscow was whispering, and Mme. von Meck was listening.

The idea, accepted by some people, that she did not know the truth until the friendship had run its thirteen-year course, and was then shocked into dropping Tchaikovsky because of his homosexuality, seems scarcely feasible, and does less than justice to her intelligence, let alone her goodness of heart. If she had reacted in such a fashion, would she not have somehow conveyed her repugnance? There are other, more probable, explanations of the break, and Mme. von Meck was not at all the kind of person that such a reaction implies.

She felt a pang of jealousy when Tchaikovsky married, so much she later admitted. That fact by no means contradicts the view that she knew his nature. She was capable of a possessive love for him, though a bodiless one; his marriage was a double betrayal—of himself, and of her; a failure to appreciate the love she was offering, the only kind of woman's love he could take.

Mme. von Meck was also capable of angling, a little teasingly, as when she asked Tchaikovsky in a letter, 'Have you ever been in love?' and answered herself in the next breath, 'I think not: you love music too much to love a woman.' She went on to say she knew of one love in his life, 'but I think such love platonic'—a 'half-love' which she described as a thing of the imagination rather than the heart or the flesh.

This has been taken to refer to his long-past infatuation for Desirée Artôt. But was that what she meant? May she not again have been trying to let Tchaikovsky know that she understood, and that he could talk to her about his half-loves, if he would?

His reply was cautious though not untruthful. He answered as an artist. 'You ask if I have known non-platonic love. Yes and no. If the question were put a little differently: have I felt the happiness of fulfilled love, the answer would be no, no, no! I think the answer to your question is to be heard in my music. Ask whether I understand the power, the immense strength of that feeling and I can answer yes, yes, yes, reiterating that I have tried my best more than once to express in music the torment and delight of love. . . .'

Fulfilled love? no; the torments and delights? yes. Most homosexuals would be bound to answer in much that way. His answer carefully avoided any indication of the sex of those he loved. Mme. von Meck never elicited any more exact statement from him on the subject.

Tchaikovsky certainly assumed that his patroness did not know his secret, and that she would not have liked it if she had. A year after the great friendship began, he said in a letter to Anatol that not having heard from Mme. von Meck for some time, he began to imagine that she had found out about his homosexuality and wanted to break off all contact with him in consequence. He felt sure this had happened, until he received a letter from her, as kind and loving as ever.

These two, then, were drawn and held together by music, first, last and all the time; music chiefly in its aspect of a medium of the passions. In the second place, a non-corporeal love grew gradually and timidly between them. Thirdly, there was from the beginning the money relationship: she, the fantastically rich railway owner, anxious to take ever greater responsibility for his material welfare, lifting worldly cares from his shoulders to enable him to create music unhampered by them. But money was no more than a single strand in the cord. Each of them needed this friendship, needed it on its special *noli-me-tangere* terms.

Mme. von Meck's life resembles some terrible Victorian moral fable. After her husband's death, and her usefulness as mate, mother, and helpmeet in his pioneering work, she allowed herself to become insulated in her wealth, and in the little cell of despotism it created for her. Her desperate reaching out through music, through patronage of Tchaikovsky, proved to be in the end no more than a pathetic gesture. She could not save herself. She could not prevent herself from becoming eccentric, suspicious, guilt-ridden, frightened of losing her money, distrustful of those she loved, aware of her utter isolation; finally sinking, pulled under by the golden millstone. In the end she struck blindly at the object of her love, Tchaikovsky himself.

In preference to the moral thus indicated, a disciple of D. H. Lawrence might read the tale as showing the nemesis of a bloodless and bodiless love relation: a dangerously refined spirituality of emotion that damages the lovers and in the end destroys itself. Such a reading would surely be no less true.

Certainly the story has something about it which lifts it out of ordinary life, gives it a transcendental quality, and asks to be interpreted symbolically, one way or the other.

How the relationship must have thrilled with promise in its opening bars, in spring 1877, when he and she exchanged photographs, and Mme. von Meck declared, 'If I had happiness in my two hands, I should give it to you!'

At her behest, Tchaikovsky cobbled a Funeral March—since lost —out of themes from *The Oprichnik* which she said drove her distracted with their beauty.

She next asked for another melancholy piece on the lines of one she knew by Kohne, called *Reproach.* He replied that this would have to wait for enough time and the appropriate mood. She gracefully waived the suggestion and instead asked for a four-hand piano transcription of his *First Quartet.* He complied with alacrity, sent the transcription to be printed, and asked Mme. von Meck for the loan of 3,000 roubles! This was a large sum—a year's current salary; five times what his first year's salary had been as teacher at the Moscow Conservatory. He explained in a long letter both his need and his embarrassing impression that she had commissioned the *Reproach* solely out of a desire to help him.

He said he was afraid of falsity and insincerity in their dealings and in his work as a consequence of their money relations. He did not want to create work unworthy of him and thus give her 'base coin', just because he needed money—but he *did* need it. And he confessed that he, a man earning more than a comfortable living, had got so far into debt that it was poisoning his life and paralysing his impulse to work. He would like to put all his debts in the hands of one generous creditor, herself, and thus get out of the hands of the moneylenders. If she would lend him this large amount, he would repay her in three ways—by making such musical arrangements and transcriptions as she might wish for, by paying her the royalties earned by his operas, and by instalments out of his monthly salary.

He threw into this letter an irresistible inducement, an invitation to immortality: he was busy with a new symphony, his *Fourth*, and would like to dedicate it to her, because she would find in it an echo of her innermost feelings. But he was in such a state of worry and anxiety that he was making slow progress.

The terms of his appeal show how well, already, he understood the mentality of his patroness. The letter cannot be called artless: it was judicious: even its honesty was a little demonstrative. And this would be evident to Mme. von Meck: yet he rightly knew that she would be pleased. Already, an element of play, of make-believe by mutual consent, had appeared in their correspondence; and one remembers again Tchaikovsky's light-footed minuet with Desirée Artôt.

Mme. von Meck replied immediately, thanking him 'with all my heart' for his confidence: 'What I appreciate especially is that you have come straight to me, and I beg you always to do so, as to a close friend who loves you sincerely and deeply.' She sent him the money and told him not to worry about repaying her.

In his acknowledgement, he showed an honesty of a different brand, with a ring of his most characteristic self. He said he had known in his heart how she would respond to his letter, and when she did so he was ashamed. In spite of inventing excuses for himself, he knew he had been exploiting her kindness and delicacy. But her response was so full of sincere friendship that he believed he had done the right thing, after all, and nothing detracted from the simple fact of his gratitude.

And now they were both happy, and Tchaikovsky must have been freer from financial troubles than he had been for a long time.

The spring and the symphony advanced. Tchaikovsky began looking forward to his usual summer visit to Kamenka, and later to Essentuki in the Caucasus to take the waters. Mme. von Meck began planning her own vacation on her estate in the Ukraine and a trip abroad if Russia were not at war with Austria by then.

But before these summer relaxations came along, two major events happened to Tchaikovsky, one musical, one personal. The musical one was the inspiration for his opera *Eugene Onegin*. The other was the advent of his bride-to-be, and the curious interplay between this occurrence and the *Onegin* story.

Tchaikovsky hinted at both these things in a letter to Mme. von Meck in June. Concerning the opera he asked was it not 'a brave idea'? and added that he was going to stay with Konstantin Shilovsky, who was writing the libretto, so that he could put in some solid work on the score. All he said of the girl was that something was troubling him a great deal, and he would explain in his next letter what it was and how it would end.

He also disclosed that he had finished his symphony in outline, and hoped to orchestrate it in the late summer. If Mme. von Meck did not wish her name to appear on it, he would find some form of dedication that did not identify her, as he had learned that she did not as a rule accept dedications.

In the event, the *Fourth Symphony in F minor*, Opus 36, appeared with the dedication 'To my best friend'.

Tchaikovsky claimed, later, that there was not a bar of the symphony which did not spring from his heart, except for certain artificial connective passages in the first movement. He retained the highest regard for this work.

One may perhaps find in it signs of that recent nervous breakdown from which he had recovered, or of the tension set up by his wilful, persistent determination to marry. This is the only one of Tchaikovsky's symphonies of which he has revealed the content in so many words. It begins with a fanfare which announces the principal motif, and Tchaikovsky calls the introduction the essence of the whole work: like Beethoven's *Fifth*, its theme is Fate.

He speaks of the subject as 'that ominous power which prevents the craving for happiness from achieving its end. This power is overwhelming and unconquerable, and there is nothing for it but submission and vain lamentation.'

As in all Tchaikovsky's symphonies except the *Third*, the key signature of the *Fourth* is in the minor, chosen to express the sombre and melancholy. The lovely melody introduced by the oboes in the second movement seems the voice of regret for a past recalled with poignant clarity, and the mood is maintained in the dreamlike secondary subject, with the Fate motif intermittently recurring.

The third movement, the scherzo with pizzicato strings, is a brilliant adventure into fantasy. There is an odd notion held by some musicologists that it was inspired by the pizzicato in Delibes' *Sylvia*, which Tchaikovsky admired. But the parallel is scarcely discernible, and the probability is that Tchaikovsky would have openly avowed any such debt in his frankness about the content of the symphony. He never had the kind of vanity which would make him conceal such a thing, and he would not have failed to notice it.

With this symphony, we are in the presence of Tchaikovsky's mature genius. One interesting criticism made at the time, however, was put forward by Tannaev, his gifted pupil, the soloist of his *B flat Minor Concerto* when it was first performed in Moscow. It was that in every movement of the *Fourth Symphony* there were 'phrases which sound like ballet music'. He gave instances: the middle section of the andante, the trio of the scherzo and 'a kind of march' in the finale, and added:

'Hearing the symphony, my inner eye sees involuntarily our

prima ballerina, which puts me out of humour and spoils my pleasure in the many beauties of the work.'

Tchaikovsky's reply to Tannaev said, 'I have no idea what you consider "ballet music" or why you should object to it. Do you regard every melody in a lively dance-rhythm as "ballet music"? In that case how can you reconcile yourself to the majority of Beethoven's symphonies, for in them you will find similar melodies on every page. . . . I can never understand why ballet music should be used as a contemptuous epithet. The music of a ballet is not invariably bad, there are good works of this class—Delibes' *Sylvia* for instance.'

And Tchaikovsky could not foresee that Beethoven's symphonies, and his own, would be ballets a century later. (Massine's *Les Presages* is danced to the music of his *Fifth.*)

Tchaikovsky was still yearning for success in the theatre, still looking for the ideal operative theme. The inception of what was to be his most satisfactory opera, *Eugene Onegin*, looked deceptively like chance, but it quickly took on a very special significance in his life.

He attended in 1877 an evening party at the house of the soprano, Mme. Elizaveta Lavrovskaya, who had sung *None but the Lonely Heart* at the first concert of Tchaikovsky's compositions, six years before. Probably Tchaikovsky's own preoccupation with the search for a theme led the conversation to the question of what makes a good libretto. Much of the talk seemed silly chatter to him, however.

In the midst of it, Mme. Lavrovskaya suddenly said to him, 'What about *Eugene Onegin*?'

He had of course known the poem as a schoolboy, but he shrugged his shoulders at the bizarre suggestion. But afterwards he dined alone at a restaurant and the idea returned to him: it seemed much less ridiculous than when he first heard it. After dinner he spent the evening in search of Pushkin's work.

Before he went to bed that night he read the poem and was enchanted. He spent a sleepless night. By the morning he had worked out in his mind a sketch for a libretto. He gave it immediately to Shilovsky to work on, that same morning.

Tchaikovsky had a strong feeling for the modern as against the traditionally picturesque in opera. He wrote to Modest, when composing *Onegin*: 'You have no notion how crazy I am about this subject. How delightful to avoid commonplace Pharaohs, Ethiopian princesses, poisoned cups and all the rest of these dolls' tales! *Eugene Onegin* is full of poetry . . . I am in love with the image of Tatiana.' Echoing this a year later, he wrote to Tannaev, 'I want to handle human beings, not puppets.' He thought *Carmen* 'one of the most perfect operas of our day', and said, 'I want no kings, no tumultuous populace, no gods, no pompous marches, in short none of those things which are the attributes of "grand opera". I am looking for an intimate yet thrilling drama, based upon such a conflict of circumstance as I myself have experienced or witnessed, which is capable of touching me to the quick.'

By the time Tchaikovsky wrote the words 'I am in love with the image of Tatiana', he was already hypnotised by the image of Antonina Ivanovna Miliukova, his future wife, and a strange counterpoint between life and fiction had begun.

Antonina was a student of his at the Conservatory. She was a personable woman of twenty-eight, blonde, with a good figure and complexion, who both looked and behaved as if she were much younger than her years. She came of lower-middle class parents, and lived with her mother. Tchaikovsky, as her teacher, paid no special attention to this girl, ten years his junior, and devoid, apparently, of any talent.

Suddenly he received a letter from her—flattering, gushing. Tchaikovsky did not reply to his infatuated student. She wrote again. This time she succeeded in awakening his interest, and he sent her an answer: cautious, hardly encouraging. But soon he was asking her to tell him more about herself.

There are gaps in this early correspondence, but it had hardly begun before Antonina was telling Tchaikovsky that she was in love with him. It was an extraordinarily frank avowal, and a little earlier would certainly have driven him to take cover immediately. Now, for several reasons, he did not do so.

There were the hateful voices of scandal, which he had sworn he would silence by marriage, and there was his unappeased longing for a home that could be called a home, where he could relax in the loving care of a woman, such a woman as his mother, or his sister Sasha. Why, then, should he turn away from the approaches of Antonina, when they fell in so aptly with his intentions?

When Tchaikovsky first decided that marriage was the needful solution to his problems, he thought very little about the choice of a girl to marry: or at least, thought very unrealistically about it. The idea of looking round for a bride, making the social moves required, going through the romantic motions, dismayed him as much as it pleases young men of more normal temperament. What a godsend to be spared all that, to be courted instead of having to do the courting! Antonina's first great step to the conquest of Tchaikovsky, quite unconsciously the right one, was to confer on him the feminine role, by declaring her love and soliciting his favour.

Soon, she said, he would be leaving Moscow for the summer, and she herself did not expect to go on residing there. She would no longer be able to comfort herself with the thought that they were in the same city. 'But wherever I go, I shan't be able to forget you or stop loving you. What I like in you I shall not find in anyone else. In short, I don't want to look at any man but you. And yet a week ago I had to listen to the declaration of a man who has been in love with me almost since schooldays and has been faithful to me for five years . . . For a whole week I was in agony, not knowing whether or not to write to you. I see that my letters begin to annoy you.' But she begged him not to close their correspondence without meeting her once, alone.

Did he think her a fickle, infatuated girl, did he not believe in her sincerity? she asked. He had written to her describing some of his faults, as if wishing to put her off. But his faults meant nothing to her, she said: if he were perfect, perhaps she would be indifferent. No weakness of his could make her stop adoring him.

'I am dying with unhappiness and sorrow because I want so terribly to see you, to sit and talk with you. . . . This is not the love of a moment but a feeling that has been growing for a long time.'

And she pressed him to call and see her.

Tchaikovsky was not rash enough to go to her rooms, as she wished, but he consented to meet her and talk. His willingness to do so sent Antonina into ecstasies: she wrote that she had stayed at home all day, wandering from corner to corner of the room as if half-crazed, thinking of the moment when she would see him, imagining how she would throw her arms round his neck and kiss him. She hastened to add that in spite of this boldness she was a virtuous girl, and 'my first kiss will be for you and for nobody else in the world'.

Coming from any other woman, from, say, Vera Davidova, such words would have paralysed him with terror, and made him shun her forever. But in Antonina's letter they were counterbalanced by two extremely telling assertions, with which she instinctively broke down Tchaikovsky's psychological defences.

One was a warning not to try and disillusion her about himself, as it would be a sheer waste of time—in other words, that her love was great enough to accept *any* fact about him. Such acceptance was a necessity for him, if he was to have a marriage that would not be founded on a lie and a deception. Had he already hinted to her the problem of his sexual aberration? Had she heard it among the students? At any rate, it is established that he told her about it before they married, and she had the touching self-confidence to imagine she could change all that by the strength of her own passion, in the bridal-bed.

The other statement which overwhelmed Tchaikovsky was a threat of suicide. Whether she meant it or not, Antonina made Tchaikovsky believe her when she wrote, 'I cannot live without you, and so perhaps I shall soon put an end to myself. Let me look at you and kiss you so that I may carry that kiss into the other world. . . .'

She signed herself, 'Eternally yours'.

Antonina could not know she had Pushkin for her ally. In the *Onegin* story, then so strongly preoccupying Tchaikovsky, the simple girl Tatiana writes a love-letter in her moonlit bedroom to the bored young man of the world, Onegin, whom she has met only a few hours before. He regards her as just a little provincial day-dreamer, and tells her to discard her unreal infatuation for him. Years later he realises that he has wrecked both their lives.

The letter from Antonina, containing her first simple declaration of love seemed something more than a coincidence, arriving when it did. This was a striking instance of 'life imitating art', and art appearing to teach life a timely lesson. It came when Tchaikovsky was actually working on the letter scene, the second scene of the first act, of the opera. He was much stirred by the poem and the scene itself, quick to condemn the blind cruelty in Onegin's failure to recognise the girl's sweet nature and the tenderness of her first love.

He saw Antonina, and she wrote to him again afterwards, telling him what days she was in Moscow and apologising for having only one room of her own in which she could receive him. Again she declared she was madly unhappy apart from him, and ended, 'I kiss and embrace you ardently.'

Having seen her as well as read these passionate letters, Tchaikovsky was convinced that Antonina was truly in love with him. So she was, no doubt, with the qualification that she was less straightforward and more neurotic than he knew, and that she lived in a highly charged romantic haze.

At their meeting—to which he went 'as if fate had drawn me'—he tried to explain to her frankly that he felt no more than sympathy and gratitude for her love. He could not love her in return, as she loved him.

His words made not the least difference to her. She only repeated that she loved him with all her heart and could not live without him.

No sooner had he left her than Tchaikovsky began questioning his own motives. Why had he behaved so irresponsibly, why had he gone to see her if he did not wish to encourage her? Where was he leading the poor girl, or being led? How would this midsummer madness end?

He made some private inquiries about her, through a friend. The information produced, whatever it may have been, was rather a warning than an encouragement. But Tchaikovsky was now embarked on his fateful or wilful course, Tatiana and Onegin were pleading Antonina's case to him, and he was under the sway of his habits of chivalry and kindness. He also began to think of his eighty-two-year-old father and other relations who were longing for him to get married and found a family.

On a fine evening at the end of May or the beginning of June, Tchaikovsky went to see Antonina, as invited. Again he told her that he did not love her and that he could only be a devoted friend. The assertion made as little difference this time as before.

But, said he, she did not fully appreciate the flaws in his character. He was temperamental, irritable, liable to violent extremes of mood, difficult to live with. He was unsociable, timid, not fond of parties and fun. He was not even rich, but lived the insecure life that was the lot of artists, with the usual debts and anxieties.

It was then, probably, that with desperate honesty he forced himself to tell her the most painful of his secrets, which made it impossible for him to feel physical desire for her.

By all his statements, Antonina remained unshaken. Like the heroine of *Man and Superman*, she let her chosen lover 'go on talking', as though serene in the conviction that the life force, in the person of herself, could conquer him in the long run and use him as the instrument of nature's purposes. But with these two, Shaw's optimistic equation broke down, and the ending was not comedy but tragedy.

At length, Tchaikovsky found that he had nothing else to say against himself. He had done his utmost, as counsel for the prosecution of his character. There was only one thing left for him to say, and he said it.

'Will you be my wife?'

The answer, of course, was 'Yes'—without any qualification or hesitation. Tchaikovsky, bewildered, appalled at what he had done, yet convinced that Destiny had spoken, discovered that he was engaged.

Having accepted her ardent and frightening kiss, he hurried away to spend a month in the country and think matters over. He said he knew from experience that very often what was terrifying in prospect turned out to be bearable and all for the best, whereas what promised happiness was quite frequently a disappointment. By this rule of contraries, he hoped his marriage would be a success, even though his feeling towards his bride was little more than indifference. 'Let what is to be, be.'

On this unpropitious note, he began his marital meditations. Since he was careful not to pretend, or attempt to deceive Antonina, one cannot but admire her confidence and courage in pressing on to the fatal wedding.

Tchaikovsky and his wife, 1877

Tchaikovsky's brother Modeste

The brothers Nikolai and Anton Rubinstein

Balakirev

Rimsky-Korsakov

CHAPTER VIII

MARRIAGE MADE IN HELL

ABOUT the time that he proposed to Antonina and was accepted, Tchaikovsky made his first strange reference to the girl in his correspondence with Mme. von Meck, the remark about something troubling him.

She replied asking whether he considered himself her friend, pointing out that he had never used that term to her.

The composer did not immediately reply. Mme. von Meck, in accordance with her custom, then packed and departed for the Ukraine, to spend most of the summer at her great estate of Brailov. Weeks passed, with no letter from Tchaikovsky. It seemed as if the young friendship was waning already. In the heart of the country, out of touch with her Moscow sources of information, she had no idea what was happening to Tchaikovsky: how he was trying to make practical plans for his marriage, and at the same time working hard on *Onegin* at the Shilovsky estate; avoiding his fiancée, giving his heart to Tatiana, her fictional counterpart; trying to be realistic and to conquer his inner panic; putting the finishing touches to the *Fourth Symphony* and worrying about money matters and where he would make his new home.

His brother Anatol was the first of his relations to detect something strange in his letters and to accuse him of having something to hide.

Tchaikovsky admitted it at once. He wrote saying yes, it was true he had a secret: he had been engaged for the past month to a girl who was 'no longer very young', and was poor, but had one great virtue, that she was in love with him. He said he had at first planned to marry her in July without telling his family and then announce it afterwards, but had decided it would be wrong to wed without his father's blessing.

He thereupon invited Anatol to the wedding, and asked him to pass on a note to their father, seeking a benediction on the 'threshold of a new life'.

To all his relations he insisted that he was acting only after long and serious consideration, and that he was perfectly calm and knew what he was doing. One is reminded of his reassurances to Kashkin before his first appearance as a conductor. He told Anatol that a proof of his peace of mind and certitude was the fact that he had written two-thirds of *Onegin*. It did not really prove anything of the kind. Nothing short of a complete mental breakdown ever stopped Tchaikovsky writing music.

Ilya, his aged father, crossed himself and jumped in the air for joy when he heard that his beloved Petia was going to wed. He wrote delightedly to him and promised to go to the wedding if his son would tell him the time and place. He addressed a word to Antonina, too, calling her his heaven-sent daughter.

Tchaikovsky at length wrote to Mme. von Meck, only three days before the ceremony. He told her he had become engaged, 'to my own astonishment'. He gave her the story of Antonina's adoring letters, his foolish response, his sudden discovery that she loved him to distraction and his fear that she would commit suicide. He said he had had to face a painful choice: whether to marry her or risk her destruction. He frankly admitted to Mme. von Meck, as he had told the girl herself, that he was not in love, and declared that he was acting from a sense of duty. His conscience was clear.

The girl was 'rather attractive', had a blameless reputation, seemed to be kind and generous, earned her own living for the sake of independence, and was not above the average in education. As for himself, after having lived thirty-seven years with a hearty dislike of marriage, it was difficult to adjust himself to the role forced upon him by circumstances.

Changing the subject with obvious relief, he went on to write in praise of Pushkin, and then to discuss the dedication of his symphony. Giving his patroness the name of 'friend' which she had longed to hear, he proceeded to ask her for musical tasks to help him repay his material debt to her.

Only on the very eve of the wedding did Tchaikovsky write to tell his news to Sasha and Modest—two members of the family who knew too much about him to approve. He bravely told Modest that he believed that in time he might learn to love his wife.

Tchaikovsky tied the irrational knot with Antonina, in face of all bad omens and good advice, in July, at a Moscow church, and one of the witnesses was his former pupil Kotek: from some points of view a strange choice. However, Kotek's employer, Mme. von Meck, was many miles away.

The other witness was Anatol, who had the deepest misgivings about his brother's venture.

The wedding ceremony followed its elaborate course, and Tchaikovsky endured. But already, as he confessed afterwards, he was in agony. He always loved the poetry of the Orthodox Church ceremonial; the clouds of incense, the dramatic liturgy, the choral chants, the sense of 'losing oneself in eternal questions', and he remained a churchgoer though he no longer had any faith in the dogmas. But the overwhelming question now was not one in which he could lose himself. The service became for him a 'ghastly spiritual torture'. He looked at Anatol, saw that his brother was suffering in sympathy, and felt his anguish redoubled. At the same time, it was only his brother's presence that gave him the courage to go through with what he already felt to be a terrible deed.

For the bride, the ceremony was the crown of her dreams: she was marrying her master and teacher, the rising and gifted musician, the gentle and chivalrous man, who had admitted he was not a lover of women, and yet had chosen her to be his wife. How much she was assailed by doubts at that moment depends on how realistic and perceptive she was. Alas, everything seems to show she was enveloped in a rosy cloud of hope and self-deception.

The day went by, the agony continued for Tchaikovsky, under a thin social surface. In the evening, the couple left by train for St. Petersburg, on their way to see Tchaikovsky's father. The sense that he had done a grave wrong was incipient in Tchaikovsky, and the terror of spending the night with this woman, his bride, intensified as the hour grew later. When the train left the station, 'I was at the point of screaming, and my sobs were choking me,' he told Anatol later. But he was convinced that his wife understood nothing of all this. She looked happy and satisfied. She had agreed to his stipulations about their relationship, doubtless with the belief that in bed, all would turn out well. She could have no idea of the horror with which he contemplated an act which was *unnatural* to him, against the very grain of his nature, however natural it might be to his bride.

He made light conversation with her all the way to Klin, 'to earn' as he put it, 'the right to recline in the dark alone with myself afterwards, in my own seat'.

Poor Antonina soon had incontrovertible proof that she was not sexually irresistible, though her illusion survived as regards other men. Soon after his marriage, Tchaikovsky was telling Anatol that he had 'arranged matters' so that his wife would be content to fondle and take care of him, would not bother him and would allow him to retain his full freedom; all that was required was that they should be patient and get used to each other. He does not seem to have had much appreciation of the inadequacy of what he was offering her. He added that he was glad she was not bright, as a clever woman would have scared him to death.

Antonina blindly obeyed his every wish: she certainly had every intention of making a success of the marriage if it were possible. She even made Tchaikovsky feel that he was getting used to his situation, and that an affectionate relationship was possible in the absence of a passionate one. But within a week after the marriage he confided to Modest that physically his wife was 'absolutely repulsive' to him.

Returning to Moscow with Antonina, Tchaikovsky found awaiting him a letter from Mme. von Meck, answering his intimation that he was getting married. It was cordial and dignified, and, in congratulating him, and wishing him every happiness, she wrote, 'You are good and you will be happy.' Marriage was always a gamble, but it would have been a sin for him, a man with a heart of gold, not to share his treasures, she said. It was not until much later that Mme. von Meck confessed to experiencing other feelings than these on hearing of his marriage. But in this poised letter she again made what seems an invitation to bolder confidences. She hoped that in his new life, 'or under any circumstances, you will not forget that you have in me a deeply loyal friend, and will, regardless of all the fabrications and errors of public opinion, always see in me a soul devoted and true to you. Will you write me everything about yourself, frankly—everything?'

Thus, not without subtlety, she indicated her own forebodings and her readiness to understand and help when things went wrong.

He wrote back, a desperate, excited letter. The wedding expenses had swallowed up the money he had had from his patroness; they had hoped to retrieve the situation by the sale of a forest which his wife had inherited from her father, but the transaction had fallen through; now they had nothing to live on, they could not afford to take a flat or furnish it, he could not make his intended trip to the watering-place of Essentuki.

'Yet I need to go away—far away,' he wrote—'to be alone, to rest, to think things over, to have treatment, and lastly to work.'

He said he did not know what was happening to him, whether he was happy or unhappy, what he would do: only that he was in an abnormal, nervous state, unable to work and in need of help. Would Mme. von Meck send him another thousand roubles? He would tell her, later, the story of what he had lived through in the past few days.

Doubtless Tchaikovsky counted the days when he might expect a reply to his frantic appeal. The full realisation that he was trapped made death, in his worst hours, appear the only exit. Almost immediately after his marriage he longed terribly to die. But death would not come to him and he would not, could not go to meet it. He could not deal so fearful a blow to his father, his brothers, and other people who loved him. Besides, in spite of his misery he loved life, his music, his future fame; he still had much work to do!

The thought of death was shockingly reinforced by news of the sudden passing of one of his close friends, Vladimir Adamov, a schoolfellow and later a colleague at the Ministry of Justice.

Tchaikovsky told his wife, truthfully enough, that his health was bad and he must seek treatment. She persuaded him to visit his mother-in-law, whom he instantly disliked. Nor could he endure the rest of the family. They seemed to him violently quarrelsome, narrow-minded, and full of silly ideas. Every hour made Antonina more intolerable to him: simple friendship with her was out of the question.

Tchaikovsky began trying to escape from his sorrows by drinking. Wine made him dizzy but gave him only moments of forgetfulness. His best comfort at that period was Kotek, a truly devoted friend who understood what was happening. They talked together a great deal.

At last Mme. von Meck's letter arrived and the money for which he had asked. 'Go to the Caucasus and go quickly,' she said. For Tchaikovsky it was as if he had been freed from prison. He arranged future lodgings in Moscow and prepared to depart. When he had actually escaped from his wife's presence, he felt 'as if I had awakened from a terrifying, painful nightmare, or rather from a long illness'.

He believed, or tried to believe, that after a rest cure, he might return to Moscow and see his wife with different eyes: he might yet find happiness with her, since he was sure of her sincere devotion to him and realised that she had many good qualities.

Tchaikovsky did not go to the Caucasus but to Kamenka, and he stopped at Kiev specially in order to write a long letter pouring out his heart to Mme. von Meck. In it he said firmly that his wife was not in any way to blame. A chain of circumstances which he could not explain to himself had suddenly confronted him with the alternatives of either marrying or jilting a decent girl whose love he had 'carelessly encouraged'. But once married, he realised that she was abhorrent to him, and he had the feeling that the best part of himself, including his music, had perished!

As it would be cruel and unfair to make his guiltless wife feel that he disliked her, he had to pretend. But a lifetime of such pretending would be the height of torture.

If Tchaikovsky had been capable of a normal marriage, if it had been simply a question of time and patience and of both parties working to make a living relationship, then Mme. von Meck's gift, the means of escape, would rank as a very immoral act. Her motives were not entirely pure, for from the beginning she had felt hostile towards Antonina and the marriage. But in fact, since no valid relationship was possible between the couple, the lifeline harmed no one; and it saved Tchaikovsky.

Antonina remained in Moscow, buying furniture for the flat they were to live in when her husband returned. He meanwhile found the old tranquil happiness at Kamenka, and was able before long to resume his work, orchestrating the *Fourth Symphony*. He was Uncle Petia again and happy to be in the presence of the children: he loved them all, but especially his six-year-old nephew Vladimir ('Bobyk') Davidov, who became the darling of his later years, and to whom the *Sixth Symphony* is dedicated.

Modest was there, too. Tchaikovsky played parts of the *Fourth* to him and he showed heartening enthusiasm. The composer became exhilarated with the technical pleasures of the scherzo, where he felt he had invented effects of real originality. He also worked on *Onegin* again.

Instead of going on to Essentuki, he had its waters in bottled form at Kamenka. This, too, made him feel better, he thought. Calming down, he began to feel ashamed of himself, and accused himself of moral weakness and cowardice. He determined to try again to maintain a fair, kind, and affectionate attitude to his wife, and to appreciate the good qualities which 'no doubt' she had.

But as the month at Kamenka drew to its close, and he knew he must return to Moscow and put his good resolutions into practice, his heart sank. His wife wrote to tell him that the home was almost ready: her cheerful letter only increased his depression. He began to lose faith in his opera: his vision of Tatiana's love and Onegin's folly had perhaps become a little tarnished in its contact with life. At any rate he now thought the opera was turning out undramatic, that the music lacked brilliance, and that the public would receive it apathetically.

He had planned to deviate from Pushkin and allow Tatiana to run away with Onegin. But he changed his mind, in response to the persuasions of the old lady Elizabeth Davidova. She pleaded the case much of one mellow night, in the very grotto where Pushkin had once sat.

The harvest was gathered in: even the bareness of the autumn fields deepened Tchaikovsky's sadness.

The inevitable return to Moscow approached, and from writing to Anatol that his bride 'does not frighten me, she is simply an annoyance', he descended in a few days to the point where he was telling the same brother, 'I am afraid'.

His greatest longing was to run away, still further, forever: but it was impossible, and he knew it.

Towards the end of September he took the train to Moscow. Antonina met him at the station and took him to the new flat. She showed him with pride the furniture she had bought, the curtains she had hung. He was able to admire it all sincerely.

Everything was clean, new, attractive, nicely arranged. 'And yet I look at it all with hatred and resentment,' he told Mme. von Meck. But he still hoped the 'black mood' would pass, that he would adjust himself to the new life and recover the desire to work.

The day after his return he put in an appearance at the Conservatory (it was not far from his flat) and taught as usual. His friends noticed an abnormal tension in his manner and a strange look in his eyes. But he put on a swagger and tried to appear carefree. The secret of his marriage was out, among the staff of the Conservatory at any rate, but he did not refer to it, nor did they. They waited for him to break the news.

After a few days he did so, in his own fashion. Some of his colleagues, Kashkin and others, received an invitation to supper from Jurgenson, to meet the composer and his wife. With great interest and excitement, they went along—and the evening was, superficially at any rate, a success. Antonina looked pleasing and well dressed and was eager to be agreeable. Her manner was engaging and modest, though she sometimes faltered conversationally when these cultured, clever friends of her husband's tried to draw her out a little. After all, she had looked up to them not long before as the great men of the Conservatory, when she was a particularly insignificant student. Several of them talked with her, and even though the conversation was light and of no importance Tchaikovsky exhibited an absurd worry lest she should let him or herself down. Whenever she paused or left a phrase unfinished, he rushed in to supply the word or offer an interpretation of what she said. Never for a moment did he allow her to talk to one of his colleagues while he conducted some other conversation: he hung around her, shepherding every social contact, in a way that was either patronising to her or touchingly considerate, according to how one looked at it. Kashkin rather resented his interference and thought it 'not quite natural'.

Tchaikovsky had his piano in the drawing-room of their home, which was very small, and he tried to work, but in vain: he found his wife's presence too pervasive, too inescapable in the confined space.

He was wounded to discover, so he said, that Antonina did not know a note of his music. It seems scarcely credible, since she had been his own pupil, and since she claimed that she had been in love with him for the past four years. She assured him that she was a good musician, yet she never went to the concerts of the Musical Society—where, incidentally, she could easily have met socially the object of her worship, as well as hearing his compositions.

She was even tactless enough to ask her husband what piano pieces by him could be obtained from his publishers.

It was this ignorance, more than anything else, that made him feel 'our life had run into a blind alley'.

He was shocked at what he characterised as the 'absolute emptiness' of her heart and head; knowing full well that he ought to have realised this before doing her the immeasurable wrong of making her his wife.

When she followed him from one room to another he called it 'torment'. When he could stand it no longer, he went out. But he was afraid to call on the people he knew for fear they would ask him embarrassing questions about his marriage. He felt compelled even to avoid the theatres, because there were so many people of his acquaintance who might be there, ready to buttonhole him at the first interval—or who, even if they did not speak to him, would be sure to spread the report that he was already going about alone. Such gossip would at once cancel out one of the assets which his marriage represented, and one of the motives for his marrying at all: it would allow a revival of the rumours which he felt to menace him. He spent hours walking the back streets, for the sake of solitude. His only contact with his fellows, except for the one party at Jurgenson's, was his daily attendance at the Conservatory, where he continued to teach.

A week or ten days after his return to Moscow, Tchaikovsky's sufferings brought him to breaking-point. He left the apartment after dark, made his way to a lonely spot on the banks of the Moscow River, and waded into the ice-cold water.

He had rehearsed to himself all the reasons why he could not commit suicide: the fear that such an act on his part would kill his old father and deeply wound his best-loved relations and friends, and that 'weakness' of his, the love of life. He advanced waist-deep: two or three more steps and he could end his troubles. But he did not take them. He stood still for a long time, believing that he would thus catch pneumonia, and could die without the opprobrium of self-slaughter.

The bitter autumn night dragged on. When he could no longer stand the cold, which was numbing his legs and those powerful, importunate glands and organs where his troubles had their root, he turned and limped back.

He walked into his home in his wet clothes and finding it impossible to tell his wife the truth, he said he had joined some men who were fishing and had fallen into the water. She may or may not have believed him. Kashkin alone heard the truth from him, and that was later.

Tchaikovsky waited for the expected fever to develop and braced his soul for death. Of course it did not come. He failed to show any signs of physical illness, but the psychological symptoms sharply increased. His hatred of his wife—though he continually told himself, 'She is not to blame'—became murderously intense. He experienced a desire to strangle her, and was terrified by it. Things could not go on much longer in this fashion. A few days, and they must have been days of suffering for Antonina as well as for Tchaikovsky, however obtuse she might be, brought him to the point of action. He thought out a simple stratagem: he sent a telegram to Anatol, who, obeying his instructions, wired him from St. Petersburg in the name of Eduard Napravnik, the Czech conductor, summoning him to that city.

Tchaikovsky took what purported to be Napravnik's message to the Conservatory, showed it to Kashkin, Rubinstein and others, and with signs of great agitation took leave of them and hurried away.

When he arrived at St. Petersburg, Anatol, who went to the station to meet his brother, did not recognise him.

Profoundly alarmed, Anatol took the haggard wreck of a man to a nearby hotel and sat with him in a private room there ready to hear any confession and to give any advice or comfort he could.

At last Tchaikovsky was in the presence of somebody with whom he need have no reticences, factual or emotional, and whose love and loyalty were unshakable. But the release was too much for him: it swept away all control, even reason itself, and the third nervous breakdown of his life detonated within him.

After an attack so terrible that Anatol would never afterwards describe it, Tchaikovsky collapsed unconscious.

Anatol sent for a doctor who for two days failed to bring his brother out of the coma. The doctor warned Anatol that there was little chance that the patient would live. If he did, he would probably be insane.

Nevertheless, Tchaikovsky was a sane man when he came round forty-eight hours after his fit. The doctor now said, however, that his only hope of complete recovery was a change of scene and of his way of living. This Anatol interpreted as meaning that Piotr must part from Antonina, and set about arranging this vital part of the business.

Anatol travelled to Moscow and went first of all to see Nikolai Rubinstein, to whom he told the essential facts. Rubinstein knew all that it was necessary to know about Tchaikovsky's character, and was so strongly of opinion that the marriage must be ended that he declared he would go with Anatol to see Antonina and put the case to her. He was afraid that Anatol's gentle and pliable nature would be no match for a determined woman.

They paid their visit, and Antonina served tea to them. Rubinstein told her bluntly that her husband had had a breakdown, and that the doctor said it was necessary for his health that the marriage should be terminated. She listened, astonishingly calm, and said if that was the case she would consent to everything they wished for her husband's sake.

In an aside to Anatol, when they were alone together for a moment, she said she could never have dreamed that the great Rubinstein would be drinking tea at her home that day!

A week after his attack, Tchaikovsky said he was returning to life. But afterwards he could remember little or nothing of his spell of convalescence in St. Petersburg, except that he had some further nervous attacks which were very distressing, and that he was visited by his father and brothers.

Nikolai Rubinstein arranged for the Russian Musical Society to vote financial help for Tchaikovsky for his great services to it and to the Conservatory. The official story as given out by Rubinstein and Anatol was simply that Tchaikovsky had been taken ill and had been sent abroad for his health, and it was added that his wife would follow as soon as it could be conveniently arranged.

Meanwhile Anatol had conducted Antonina to her mother and sent the two of them to Odessa, secretly.

In mid-October Tchaikovsky went to Berlin, then to Geneva, finally to Clarens on the lake of Geneva, and there settled down to recuperate in the Villa Richelieu, which he leased. Finding the money for this and making separate provision for his wife, proved difficult. Tchaikovsky wrote to Jurgenson asking for commissions, song-writing, transcriptions, anything. His brothers, having no more themselves to spare, had borrowed money from his sister to pay his fare to Switzerland. The rate of exchange was unfavourable and he consequently found life expensive at Clarens. Inevitably, he turned once again to the woman of seemingly inexhaustible wealth and generosity, Mme. von Meck, and wrote for a further loan. Before he received her response to this appeal the situation was a little ameliorated by a message from the Conservatory saying it had been decided to pay him immediately the remainder of his year's salary as a teacher. He suggested in reply that they might care to stage the first part of his new opera, *Eugene Onegin*.

Mme. von Meck had been travelling abroad. After a spell at Brailov she had visited Italy, and one of Tchaikovsky's *cris de coeur* had been addressed to her in Naples, but apparently missed her—she had moved on to Venice. From there she wrote to tell him she was prepared to provide enough money to allow him to spend several months abroad: this letter of hers, forwarded from Moscow, reached him in Clarens, and he realised that she had written it even before receiving his appeal for help.

She herself and her retinue had meanwhile returned to Moscow, expecting that he would be there. She was quickly given the official account, that he had been taken ill and had gone to Switzerland. She learned rather more than that: 'such horrors,' she said, that she was shocked and frightened. She sent her brother to make inquiries from Nikolai Rubinstein, and presently had a visit from Rubinstein himself. Meanwhile she had read Tchaikovsky's own outpouring on his sufferings and his plight. She quivered with sympathy and compassion for him. But there were two reasons why, when Rubinstein called on her, Mme. von Meck concealed the knowledge she had already extracted from Tchaikovsky's own letter: one, the hope of finding out more details over and above what the letter contained; the other, a desire to hide the warmth of the friendship between herself and her correspondent—especially from Rubinstein who had initiated it, and who would have been very surprised, perhaps none too agreeably, if he had known how many confidences and how much money had passed since then.

Mme. von Meck therefore pretended to Rubinstein that she had no more than a mere admiration for Tchaikovsky's musical talent and only a distant interest in what had happened to him. She played this role so well that Rubinstein actually made efforts to excite a warmer sympathy for Tchaikovsky. Mme. von Meck asked him why Tchaikovsky had gone abroad and for how long, as though knowing nothing of his breakdown. He told her everything she wanted to know.

Mme. von Meck now wrote candidly to Tchaikovsky saying that she had previously refrained from telling him what she really thought about his marriage for fear of giving gratuitous advice. She now felt free to assure him that he had done right, in escaping from lies and hypocrisies that were unworthy of him. In his position she would have done the same but even sooner. He had tried his best for another's sake and fought to the limit of his strength.

Once more Mme. von Meck seems to give a clear indication that she understands Tchaikovsky's sexual inversion when she tells him that a man of his kind might perish in such circumstances as his marriage but could never hope to adjust himself to them.

She rightly prophesies that he will rest, recover, compose again and look back on his suffering as a bad dream; and music will fill his life.

As for the material side of his existence, she reproaches him for torturing himself over it and beseeches him to leave all that to her; not to interfere while she takes care of his affairs. She claims it as a right of 'spiritual kinship', and says that he is so indispensable to her that 'it is not you I help, but myself'.

The climax of this splendidly generous letter was financial: it enclosed the first instalment, a double one, of an annual allowance, or pension, of 6,000 roubles. Instead of further loans she was prepared to pay him this income, indefinitely.

It is difficult to give a reliable modern valuation of the figure but one may point out that it was ten times what Tchaikovsky received in salary when he first went to Moscow; to him it represented comfort, freedom from the need to do anything except compose, ample means for foreign travel, complete security—a dream-like gift of liberty. He was overwhelmed by this munificence.

To his patroness he wrote, 'I doubt if the opportunity will ever come for me to prove my readiness to make any sacrifice for you. You will never be able to ask of me a great enough service. Therefore I have no recourse but to serve you through my music. From now on every note that comes from my pen will be yours.'

At Clarens, Tchaikovsky had also been cheered by letters from Rubinstein, promising to 'kill the fatted calf when the prodigal returns', showing keen interest in the new symphony and *Eugene Onegin*, encouraging him to take care of his health and fear nothing: 'You are too highly esteemed as a musician to be compromised by anything outside music'—an important reassurance in case Tchaikovsky might be dreading possible disclosures about the reason for his matrimonial disaster.

On the other hand, Tchaikovsky was beginning to find the Swiss rest cure unbearable: it was very quiet, grey, and sunless there, and the mountains seemed frightening and oppressive. He considered moving on to Italy, in the footsteps of Mme. von Meck.

His sister Sasha had meanwhile gone to Odessa to see his wife and mother-in-law, who were quarrelling. She took Antonina away to Kamenka and tried to 're-educate' her, as well as talking to her very seriously about the marriage and the problem of her future. Sasha wrote hopefully to Tchaikovsky that, in time, Antonina would make a good life companion for him. However, Sasha soon betrayed some bewilderment: the deserted bride seemed strangely little affected by the things that had happened. She had accepted the separation and her husband's alarming illness with something that looked like shallowness or indifference.

The effect of Sasha's kindly action on Tchaikovsky was merely to make him feel that she was wasting her time and that Kamenka, his favourite refuge, was closed to him until his wife left it. This was no very long wait, as it turned out: even the tolerant, peaceful Kamenka household could not stand very much of Antonina's ways and soon Sasha's husband was writing to Anatol asking him to take Antonina from them and deposit her with her mother in Moscow.

Anatol had also had a letter from Antonina herself: a rather extraordinary one telling him that an army officer had fallen in love with her in the course of a train journey.

Antonina has been rather too glibly called a nymphomaniac. It is doubtful whether this is just or accurate. The principal evidence, as far as her life before her marriage is concerned, is the word of Tchaikovsky, who says she was always talking about the countless men who had loved her, most of them generals, 'nephews of famous bankers', well-known actors, or members of the royal family. But consider the girl's situation: it is not surprising that she should try, in her naïve fashion, to advertise those attractions to which her husband appeared blind. Nor is there any reason to doubt the truth of her earlier declaration to him: 'My first kiss will be for you and for nobody else.' As for her life after the marriage broke down, the term nymphomania seems inappropriate to a promiscuity springing from wounded self-esteem and the frustrations of such a mock-marriage.

Antonina was temperamentally unstable, so much is clear. She bit her nails to the quick, and her fingers shed blood on the furniture. She chattered incessantly in an egotistic vein and she squabbled noisily with all her relations, especially her mother. But she is a figure of pathos, inadequately equipped in understanding or emotional strength for the whirlpool into which she had plunged: the impossible match with a genius at once torrential and abnormal, terrifying and terrified.

A new letter from her reached Anatol, who was at Clarens with his brother. She had suddenly changed her tone: no longer gentle, undemanding, demure, she now exhibited hurt pride, and struck back with all her might. She heaped reproaches on Tchaikovsky, saying that he had shamelessly deceived her. This he denied and strongly resented—'she is ill-natured and a liar,' he told Mme. von Meck. Nevertheless, he said, he had written to Antonina refusing to be involved in an argument, asking forgiveness for the wrong he had done her, offering to accept any decision she might make, promising financial support, but affirming once for all that he would never live with her—never.

He now came to the conclusion that not only had he never loved her, but she had never loved him, either; though he conceded that she sincerely believed herself in love with him. He thought that because she wished to marry him she mistook the wish for love. This argument, however, is suspect: it is only too probable that he found it easier to pardon his own conduct if he could believe that Antonina's love had not been 'real'. Only in this way could the now-painful analogy to Onegin's behaviour be blotted out!

Tchaikovsky, as he looked back from convalescence at the events leading up to his collapse, could hardly find his actions admirable. He had experienced hideous and cruel emotions, of which he had not thought himself capable. He had lost the last elements of self-control. He had been blind and mad, he said. He realised well enough that his wife had done her limited best to make the marriage succeed, and that if in the process she had simply driven him into wild hostility, she was to be pitied, not blamed.

In attempting to explain the tragedy to Mme. von Meck, Tchaikovsky conveyed the odd impression, perhaps unwittingly, that Antonina had refused to have children. Mme. von Meck wrote back that such women were heartless. It is debatable, however, whether she actually believed this. Tchaikovsky's attempts, in his letters to her, to justify himself, to repaint the picture of what had happened, to ensure the future of his relationship with Mme. von Meck herself, and at the same time to be truthful and just to his wife, are transparent in the extreme.

'I am no dreamer,' Mme. von Meck wrote: 'I am a realist.' As a realist, she understood and yet could forgive.

Tchaikovsky's marriage to Antonina was foredoomed: nothing could conceivably have made it succeed. The question inevitably arises: could a marriage with Mme. von Meck have been a success? It is like such fascinating questions as 'ought' Coleridge to have married Dorothy Wordsworth, the one woman of his own order of sensibility? Hard matters, but not beyond all conjecture.

Suppose the unique prohibition had been dropped from the friendship of Mme. von Meck and Tchaikovsky, and they had allowed themselves to meet face to face; to converse, however timidly at first; to come eventually to the point of questions and answers on personal matters: might they not have perceived the possibility of uniting their lives? Here was the woman who was capable of understanding the necessary limitations, and who might have been able to live contentedly on platonic terms, asking no more than music and chaste caresses: old enough to mother Tchaikovsky, refined enough to respect his sensitivity, rich enough to insulate him from the harsh world. She worshipped his music, which she—unlike Antonina—knew in minute detail, and considered it his *raison d'etre*, as he did himself. She was at the safe age when women of her day considered themselves ready for 'retirement', and she had completed her life as a wife and producer of children.

Although it was Mme. von Meck who first expressed the wish that they should never meet, she later showed signs of a possible weakening in the direction of greater intimacy; and now it was Tchaikovsky who rejected the advances. Thus, less than a year and a half after they began to correspond, Mme. von Meck proposed that they should use the intimate *thee-and-thou* form of speech instead of the *you* form. He replied that he lacked the courage for such a break with convention, and would have to force himself. She withdrew the suggestion. The following year, when he stayed at Brailov in her absence, her small daughter Milochka—to whom he was always sending kisses and expressions of love—was to be brought over to see him by the intermediary of the moment, Pakhulsky, a Polish violinist. But Tchaikovsky refused even this indirect contact, although, as he said, he loved the little girl in the photograph, and was fond of all children. To Mme. von Meck he explained his refusal thus: 'My relationship with you, exactly as it now stands, is my greatest happiness, and the rock on which my welfare rests. I do not want to change it even a little. All the charm, all the poetry of my friendship with you is based on the fact that you are so close to me, so infinitely dear to my heart, and yet in the ordinary sense of the word we are not acquainted. And this same condition of not meeting must extend to those most nearly related to you.'

In this mellifluous way, he let her know he was adamant; for he sensed that she was not. After his experience with Antonina, he was too badly scared ever to risk the physical proximity of an adoring woman again.

But if he had thought of Mme. von Meck as an alternative choice in the first place, and had never suffered the scars of his marriage to Antonina, it is surely possible that he might have married his patroness. Her wealth and social position could conceivably have been a barrier, but there was no great class difference: both were of the professional classes, not the aristocracy; and Tchaikovsky was proud of the status of artist, considering it as lofty as any possible to mankind. In this opinion Mme. von Meck was at one with him.

There remains the further question of whether the match could have been a success. There *are* such 'marriages' of homosexual and protectress, marriages of mutual convenience, marriages of true minds, whichever term one cares to apply. Some are at any rate long-lasting. These two were difficult people in their different ways, yet each had much that the other needed. In their eagerness to forge lasting links they 'married', symbolically and by proxy, so to speak, by arranging a match between Tchaikovsky's niece and Mme. von Meck's son, Nikolai. They wanted a bond of flesh, but not their own flesh! Even at the wedding of these young people, the two matchmakers did not meet.

Tchaikovsky, for all Mme. von Meck's expressions of humility and his conscious superiority in knowledge and gifts, was a little frightened of her. He said—and by way of a compliment, too—that he felt towards her as a short person feels towards a tall one.

But in fact what he was most afraid of was her passionate, feminine self, that might suddenly pounce. Two years after his marriage and breakdown, Mme. von Meck confided to him, 'I am jealous in the most unpardonable way, as a woman is jealous of the man she loves. Do you know that when you married, it was terribly hard for me, as if something had broken in my heart? Do you know what a wicked person I am? I rejoiced when you were unhappy with her. . . . I hated that woman because she did not make you happy. But I would have hated her a hundred times more if you had been happy with her. I thought she had robbed me of what should have been mine alone. . . .'

When Tchaikovsky answered this letter, he did not make any direct reference to her alarming confession. He said, 'I read your letter with gratitude and love too strong for expression in any medium but music. . . .'

In the matter of music itself, Mme. von Meck's perceptions were different from and coarser than his, and he knew it well enough, though he expressed himself with delicacy to her on the point. She was also imperious and a great business organiser, qualities that always aroused fear in him. He was not blind to her character, indeed he shows himself very acute on some aspects of it; as when analysing her opinions of religion, he says, 'Hating evil and falsehood, you have walled yourself within the narrow circle of your family as a defence against the spectacle of human degradation.' He adds, to make amends for this rapier-thrust: 'You do a great deal of good; your passionate love of art and nature makes doing good a necessity for a noble spirit such as yours.'

If they had met and married, the price of an enduring relationship would have been a series of compromises on many levels, supposing Tchaikovsky had been weak enough to pay that price. It is doubtful whether he would have done so: whatever his weaknesses, he cherished his freedom as an artist and was quick to protect it with all his might. One can imagine a graver, more damaging conflict than his actual marriage produced, and an even worse disaster at the end of it.

But one cannot rule out the possibility that Mme. von Meck may have cherished for years some half-suppressed hope that one day Tchaikovsky would break through the wall of glass between them, and invade her life; and that she ended their relationship when the dream eventually died. It is at any rate more probable than the conjecture that she suddenly, at long last, heard of his homosexuality and that the revelation shattered the friendship.

Whether she ever heard the full facts about his marriage is another question. It may well be that she did not.

The composer in 1880

Tchaikovsky's first grand piano

CHAPTER IX

RETURN TO LIFE

'I THINK I am *un homme fini*,' Tchaikovsky declared, after the breakdown of his marriage. Three splendidly fertile years of musical production followed this statement.

The first need was physical and mental recovery. He knew that this was possible only if the nightmare of his marriage could be banished. He had put his foot down as firmly as he was capable of doing, by telling his wife he would never live with her again; he now took the precaution of staying away from Russia as long as circumstances allowed. Anatol, who was acting as his nurse and showing the greatest understanding of his needs, acquiesced in this.

In the late autumn, four months after his wedding, Tchaikovsky was in Paris, seeking medical advice about his digestive troubles. He was always liable to stomach upsets, and before journeys, concerts, or excitements usually had an attack of nervous diarrhoea. Serious disturbances had followed his breakdown, and he wanted to see a particular French doctor who had always shown great sympathy towards him. Tchaikovsky said he liked doctors who regarded their patients as suffering human beings—'not as something that complains and must pay a certain fee'. He was unlucky: Dr. Saligoux did not practise in the winter months.

Another doctor whom he tried left him very distrustful and dissatisfied. He cut short the patient's account of his symptoms, made a disparaging remark about the Russian climate, and prescribed kaolin, curative waters, the thermal baths at Barèges, and a diet a great deal less rich than a Russian is used to.

Tchaikovsky scorned this reasonably sound advice, considered his trip to Paris completely wasted, and hurried on to Italy, wishing he had gone there in the first place.

Italy, of course, was another disappointment. He now upbraided himself for childishness in blaming the mountains for his unease in Clarens, thought himself horribly stupid for going to Florence, and dreaded the approaching day when Anatol would have to return to Russia. He did not want to be left alone in a strange land. But he did not want to go back, either. In St. Petersburg, he would have to see his father, whom he could not face, and who had not been told the truth about the wrecked marriage but was suspicious and displeased. In Moscow, Rubinstein and all his numerous friends and colleagues would want to ask questions. Kamenka was 'out of bounds' to him: it harboured his wife. He did not feel fit and strong enough yet to face his countrymen, he told Mme. von Meck, who thought it time for him to go home.

His patroness gave him advice on his health—including a warning against drinking tainted water, as though with foreknowledge of the danger which was eventually to lead to his death. Always wash grapes, she added, and take a little wine with lunch and dinner.

She also reported that a girl named Alexandra Batalina had married his colleague, Professor Hubert, '*par dépit amoureux*, because I hear she was in love with you!' Whether or not this piece of hearsay had any truth in it (the girl arranged many of Tchaikovsky's works for piano), he must have shuddered at the very thought.

The correspondence between Tchaikovsky and Mme. von Meck now turned on religion and philosophy, and in the course of it she answered his implied criticism of the wall of gold that protected her. 'You think,' she said, 'that the rich are never really put to the test. Let me remind you that the rich care even more than the poor do about what people say of them.' She added, 'You must remember that I have not always been wealthy; and sometimes I am afraid; but my creed sustains me, and I do not bow before injustice or or ridicule.'

Her creed, as she expounded it to him, was an idealistic materialism. Heaven and hell existed only on earth, she said, and she doubted whether a heaven above could offer such happiness as she experienced below from earthly kindness, truth, and goodness. This point of view did not conflict essentially with Tchaikovsky's own, but she carried the materialism too far when she described music as a purely physical pleasure. He disagreed vehemently: did she equate music with 'Yquem and salted cucumbers'? She deceived herself, he said: he knew she loved music as it should be loved, with the soul.

He conceded that a heaven of eternal delight was inconceivable—the charm of life was its light and shade, joy and grief, good and evil in conflict. (A strong-minded assertion for a man who had so recently been lacerated in the struggle.)

He added: 'Perhaps there will be no music in heaven: let us then live fully on this earth!'

The return of mental vigour and the will to live is evident in the tone of these letters. But he was not yet ready to go back to Russia. He found Venice more tolerable than other Italian cities, and there he was able to resume work on *Eugene Onegin*. The opera was still unfinished when Tchaikovsky left, accompanied by Anatol, for a brief visit to Vienna where they were to meet Kotek.

The young violinist was now studying with Joachim in Berlin, but took a few days' holiday to see Tchaikovsky. According to one account, Mme. von Meck had dismissed him for not being discreet about messages entrusted to him; but Tchaikovsky refers to him freely without embarrassment in letters to Mme. von Meck. They examined Brahms' *First Symphony* together, and Tchaikovsky did not like it.

The worst year of Tchaikovsky's life was coming to an end. The arrival of his manservant, Alexei Sofronov, to whom he was much attached, lifted the burden on Anatol and not long afterwards Tchaikovsky's brother departed for Moscow, taking part of *Eugene Onegin* with him.

At Nikolai Rubinstein's rooms, the first act of the new opera and part of the second act was played through by Tannaev to a group of Tchaikovsky's fellow-musicians, all eager to find out whether the crisis in his private life had damaged his talent and left him 'finished', as he himself feared. The music gave them wonderful reassurance. 'It took our breath away,' says Kashkin.

Tchaikovsky and his servant meanwhile went to Venice and he immediately began the task of orchestrating the *Fourth Symphony*. His confidence was flooding back—'this is my best composition,' he said—and he worked fast, as of old. Money was running through his fingers, as usual, and he got down to three lire before he was saved by another instalment of his pension from Mme. von Meck.

Anatol carried out his diplomatic mission of removing the reluctant Antonina from Kamenka, and reported his success by telegram to his brother. Sasha also wrote warmly to Tchaikovsky: her first-hand experience of Antonina had swung her over completely to his point of view!

'I am loved in Kamenka as before,' Tchaikovsky recorded happily.

Antonina had suggested that she might become a nurse (the war between Russia and Turkey was raging, and Rubinstein was crusading for the Red Cross): Anatol promised to do all he could to arrange this for her.

His spirits rising, Tchaikovsky began to want other companionship besides that of Sofronov, and thought of Modest, and Modest's pupil, Kolya Konradi, a deaf-and-dumb boy of nine years old. Tchaikovsky had first met him two years before and was captivated. Modest had given up a government post to become tutor to the boy, and had taken a special training course for the task, which he did devotedly; struggling at the same time to equip himself for his true vocation as a writer.

Kolya's father consented, in response to Piotr Tchaikovsky's invitation, to his son's being taken to Italy, but not to Venice, as he considered the Venetian climate too unhealthy. So once more Tchaikovsky uprooted himself and moved on, this time to San

Remo, on the Riviera, stopping to hear a couple of operas on the way—*Ruy Blas* in Milan, *L'Africaine* in Genoa; both badly done in his opinion.

The question of how to get an adequate performance of his own opera began to worry him. He denounced the 'tradition' of the opera-houses, which made it certain that ageing artists would portray his youthful hero and heroine, and that Pushkin's charming conceptions would be vulgarised by stage routines. He did not favour the star system. He would have liked to see his opera performed by a company with average abilities, but thoroughly trained and able to act as well as sing. The chorus should seem to be real people, taking part in the action, not a flock of sheep. The décor should be fitting and true to its period rather than grandiose. The conductor should be neither a machine nor a mere stickler for musical accuracy but a true director of the orchestra.

These conditions, and the unlikelihood of getting them in the theatre of his day, may have been in his mind when, later, he asked Nikolai Rubinstein to let *Onegin* be produced by the Conservatory pupils, in case it would not stand opera-house treatment.

But meanwhile a quarrel broke out between Tchaikovsky and Rubinstein.

As we have seen, Rubinstein behaved very well over Tchaikovsky's folly and its terrible consequences. He went to see Antonina and persuaded her to give up her husband; he raised money; he showed himself patient, forbearant, and encouraging to his illustrious subordinate. Possibly with the idea that new responsibilities would be the best medicine, he had arranged for Tchaikovsky to be the chief Russian representative at the great Paris Exhibition which was to open on New Year's day, 1878.

The proposition had been put to Tchaikovsky just after his breakdown, in a letter from the St. Petersburg Conservatory, but he had been in no state then to consider it. So he had failed to give a definite refusal; and now, with the Exhibition imminent he suddenly received notice of the appointment from the Russian Finance Ministry, along with a detailed inquiry as to his plans, what concerts he would organise, how many choral and how many instrumental events? He was to go to Paris immediately, and remain there eight months, at a salary of 1,000 francs a month.

This official document reached him in San Remo and shattered his recovered calm. The idea of being his country's musical ambassador, organising and entertaining, attending dinners and soirées, in the Babylonian French capital, with all the nations of the earth gathered there for the great international occasion: being expected to conduct, to be lionised, to handle temperamental celebrities, to make speeches, maybe: the prospect paralysed him with fear. He was a patriot, he wanted to help make Russia's music more widely known; he was grateful and loyal to Rubinstein; his health was better; his fame would be enlarged if he undertook the task. But the very though of it made him ill again.

He told Anatol that if he went to Paris in this capacity he would simply drink every day, from morning till night. He admitted that he already got into the habit of secret drinking, and could not live without it. 'Before I go to bed I drink several glasses of brandy, and during the day I drink a lot, too. . . . I am calm only when I am a bit tipsy.' He kept the brandy bottle always by him now, and the mere sight of it gave him pleasure. But he regarded these facts as evidence that he was still a sick man.

He was possibly exaggerating, and ready to say anything that would justify him in declining the Paris appointment. There is no reason to suppose that he ever became anything like an alcoholic. He used alcohol as a 'tranquilliser', to put the case in modern terms. He found the drunkenness of the Muscovites disgusting.

Eight years later, he wrote in his diary that it was 'simply impossible to live without the poison of alcohol', even though the abuse of it was to be condemned. 'Every evening I am drunk, and cannot live otherwise,' he said. Again, the term drunk is relative: Tchaikovsky no doubt went to bed with the sensation of being affected by drink, but there is no testimony that he appeared drunk to others.

Be that as it may, Tchaikovsky summoned up the courage to refuse the Paris appointment, feeling that it would require far greater courage, more than he possessed, to accept it. He was instantly warned by Karl Albrecht that Rubinstein, who was out of Moscow at the moment, would be extremely angry when he heard of his decision. He thereupon wrote to Rubinstein direct, saying humbly that he was unfit for the role.

Albrecht was right. Rubinstein returned in the new year from his Red Cross tour, read Tchaikovsky's letter and wrote a ferocious reply. In it, he accused Tchaikovsky of idling and malingering, pretending to be sick and lounging on the Riviera spending Mme. von Meck's money, forgetting his obligations to the Conservatory and to Rubinstein himself.

Tchaikovsky also suspected, from a bantering letter of Mme. von Meck's, that she had had a visit from Rubinstein and that he had tried to persuade her to stop sending money to Tchaikovsky on the ground that this only encouraged him to be lazy.

Angrily he wrote back to Rubinstein denying that he was either indolent or ungrateful. Such reproaches chilled his actual gratitude, he said. As to his illness, 'possibly it is true I am only "putting it on", but that is exactly the nature of my disease'. He was particularly incensed by Rubinstein's attitude to the von Meck friendship, and told him he was cruelly mistaken about it. Tchaikovsky was afraid that Rubinstein's words would upset Mme. von Meck very much, as she was anxious that nobody should share their secrets; and he warned Rubinstein not to let his insinuations about Mme. von Meck and her money go any further. 'I owe her not only life but the ability to continue to work, which is more precious to me than life,' he said.

He stood firmly by his decision not to lead the Paris delegation. Mme. von Meck endorsed his refusal, told him his duty to society was to compose, and said it was not worth his while to quarrel with Rubinstein—who, she added haughtily, could always be dropped if he became intolerable. The Conservatory would be the losers, not Tchaikovsky.

Rubinstein at length swallowed his annoyance, and decided to represent his country at the Paris Exhibition himself.

Meanwhile, Tchaikovsky turned over in his slowly settling mind the turmoil through which he had passed. On a night of gales that rattled the windows so that he could not sleep, he tried to assess his life, and to understand how he had got to the verge of the abyss. Whatever the lessons of the past he knew one thing clearly now: that he might still have a future, if his health did not let him down; for he was a long way from reaching the frontiers of his abilities.

He went to Milan to get a metronome, to mark the tempi of the *Fourth Symphony*. Working late into the night, he finished this work and sent it off to Rubinstein. He was indirectly helped by the death of King Victor Emmanuel, which led to the closing of the Italian theatres and thus deprived Tchaikovsky of distractions or excuses to put his task aside.

Once the symphony was completed, he allowed himself to relax with his brother and little Kolya, in outings and simple pleasures. One February day which had all the attributes of spring, the three made an excursion to Colla, climbing the olive-clad hills, the men on foot, the boy on a donkey which they hired for him. Tchaikovsky records that he himself walked ahead, and sitting down alone under the trees, experienced an indescribable moment of happiness, such as he had known in Russia when alone in country places. Solitude was an essential ingredient of it he said, and the solemn stillness of the woods induced an intense delight. (He could have said fervently, with Andrew Marvell:

> 'Two paradises 'twere in one
> To live in paradise *alone*!'

On the way home he came upon a place where masses of wild flowers grew and he picked some to send to Mme. von Meck. In the letter enclosing them, he wrote: 'May they remind you of the south, the sun, and the sea.'

He confided to her that he and Modest were equally fond of flowers, and often disputed hotly about the respective claims of different ones:

'To my mind, the queen of flowers is the lily-of-the-valley: I love it to distraction. . . . Modest is all for the violet. I certainly recognise that the violet is a dangerous rival to the lily-of-the-valley, and am very fond of it.' Mme. von Meck replied that she, too, adored flowers, but preferred trees: they were stronger.

The brothers took the deaf-and-dumb boy to art galleries, though Tchaikovsky himself had little appreciation of pictures. He enjoyed far more the scenery and sunshine, and began to feel in good physical trim again. His still-recent sufferings looked to him like a nightmare, in which someone merely resembling him and bearing his name had gone through a series of meaningless, disconnected but painful events. He had undergone a conflict between will and intelligence, and the only word to describe it fittingly was madness, he decided. Yes, he had been temporarily insane, and three people had saved him: his twin brothers, and Mme. von Meck. He owed them not only his life but his health and sanity, too.

Waiting anxiously for news that his symphony had arrived safely in Moscow, he resumed work on *Eugene Onegin*, and quickly finished and despatched that, too.

He was in a rosy mood after that, happy at what he had achieved, happy to feel well again, in the spring, conscious of the love of his friends, filled with hope once more.

He made an exuberant good resolution to compose some music every day of his life.

Mme. von Meck sent him more money, including a sum to ensure that the *Fourth Symphony* would be printed handsomely—he told Jurgenson that he did not want royalties on it or on *Onegin*. (This of course did not apply to performing rights.) In spite of the quarrel over the delegation to France, Rubinstein now wrote that he himself would conduct the symphony for its first performance very shortly. Tchaikovsky was pleased and reassured.

He left San Remo and went to Florence before the end of the month. It was there he awaited news of the way his symphony was received, and the news travelled slowly. Rubinstein and other colleagues sent him a telegram telling him it had been performed, but they were tactfully silent about the impression it created. The faithful Mme. von Meck, the person to whom the work was, in veiled terms, dedicated, sat alone in the balcony, and after the concert she too wired Tchaikovsky. Her message was no formal congratulation. She managed to convey, even by telegram, her genuine enthusiasm for the masterly and original work which Tchaikovsky so flatteringly called '*our* symphony'. In his heart he considered it the best thing he had ever done. But he wanted to know what the critics and the public thought of it, too. Weeks went by and he heard nothing more. Naturally enough he fretted.

The truth was that, as on so many previous occasions, the audience and the critics were cool to the new work. Mme. von Meck, pressed for the facts, softened them a little for him, telling him there was great applause and that there were calls for the composer: Rubinstein took the bow, in the composer's absence. But she added that the orchestra appeared under-rehearsed, and played worse than she had ever heard them.

In the middle of the following month—March—when Tchaikovsky, ever restless, had moved again, with his servant, his brother and the little boy, to Clarens, the town he had been so eager to leave, he was turning from anxiety to wrath. 'I am deeply chagrined, offended and amazed by the incomprehensible silence of all my friends concerning the symphony,' he wrote. He thought it would at least have interested them even if it failed to move them. The only opinion he had heard was that of a bassoon pupil, who was reported by Kotek to have found it pleasing! Mme. von Meck was able to add another favourable witness—Vladislav Pakhulsky, her future son-in-law, who though an admirer of Wagner had exclaimed on hearing Tchaikovsky's symphony, 'Where is Wagner now, and why do the rest of us even exist on the earth?'

Mme. von Meck asked Tchaikovsky various questions on his method of work and whether the symphony had a programme. Replying he described the amazing speed at which musical ideas germinated in him, taking on precise form, elaborating themselves; he told her how he 'became a lunatic', forgot everything, trembled from head to foot, and was wildly irritated when his somnambulistic state was interrupted by the ringing of a bell, the arrival of a servant or the need to attend to the day's business. If such a state of inspiration were to continue, an artist could not survive a day: his strings would snap, Tchaikovsky said. But there were spells of cold, calculated, technical labour too, relieving the tension.

Elsewhere he has described himself stamping up and down his room, biting his nails, smoking innumerable cigarettes as he wrestled with a theme.

As for the programme of the symphony, he expounded it in some detail to his patroness, with snatches of notation and such explanatory phrases as 'This is Fate, the inexorable force that prevents our hopes of happiness from being fulfilled . . .' and 'Oh, joy, at last the sweet and tender dream appears—some bright human image passes, beckoning . . .' and 'The Fourth Movement: If you truly find no joy within yourself, look for it in others. . . .'

There are several pages of such exposition. However, that was only for the sympathetic eye of Mme. von Meck. The composer told Tannaev, 'Of course my symphony is programme music—but it would be impossible to present the programme in words: it would seem ludicrous and cause only smiles.' He said he imagined in his simplicity that the main ideas would be obvious to anyone: the central thought, but not its musical form, being the same as in Beethoven's *Fifth.* If that had not been clear to the hearers, it only proved that he was no Beethoven, 'on which point I never had any doubt'.

He stated his emphatic opposition to purely abstract music: 'I wish no symphonic work to emanate from me that has nothing to express and is made up merely of harmonies and a purposeless pattern of rhythms and modulations.'

The completion of his symphony and opera left Tchaikovsky still glowing with musical ideas—expressed in the *G major Piano Sonata*, the *Violin Concerto in D major* which followed, *Twelve Piano Pieces of Moderate Difficulty*, a naval march published under a pseudonym, and a number of songs, settings of poems by Alexei Tolstoy, Lermontov and others.

The violin concerto, captivating, mellifluous, and the perfect union of soloist and orchestra, was inscribed to Leopold Auer, a famous violinist of his day, but to Tchaikovsky's chagrin he said it was impossible to play. Tchaikovsky retorted that he had made no attempt to conquer its difficulties, but such was Auer's authority that his judgment was sufficient to deter others and condemn the work to limbo.

Four or five years later, in a café in Rome, Tchaikovsky picked up a copy of the *Neue Freie Presse* and found there a criticism of his concerto, written by the Austrian critic, Eduard Hanslick: it had been performed by the Vienna Philharmonic, and the critic found fault with the soloist who was Adolf Brodsky, former professor at Moscow Conservatory. He at any rate did not find it unplayable, and to him the dedication was transferred. But even Brodsky is said to have taken two years to screw up his courage for the task!

Brodsky ultimately settled in England and became leader of the Hallé Orchestra, and Principal of the Royal College of Music in Manchester.

To return to those songs that followed the violin concerto during Tchaikovsky's Clarens period, two of them which survive are the magnificently sonorous *Don Juan's Serenade*, and the charming *Pimpinella*, which has its own romantic history, as follows:

On his first visit to Florence, with Anatol, Tchaikovsky joined a crowd round a street singer, a boy of only ten or eleven with a guitar, singing a tragic song in a wonderfully rich voice and with an almost professional mastery of style.

He could not forget the song or the singer. When he returned to Florence three months later, in Carnival time, he inquired among other street singers and they undertook to find the boy for him. They did so: Tchaikovsky wondered whether they were cheating him—was it the same child? 'You will know I am the same when I sing,' the boy said proudly. 'But first—a silver piece!'

The composer paid, the boy sang. 'I don't remember any folk song ever making such an impression on me,' Tchaikovsky wrote. 'I cried, I trembled, I was in ecstasy.' Then the boy sang a Florentine song that was new to Tchaikovsky's ears: 'about one Pimpinella: what does it mean? I don't know, but I will find out.' He sang it again, the next day and the next, and Tchaikovsky wrote it down to give it to the world. Tchaikovsky spared a sigh for the fate of the child, who was being exploited by his family, singing for money from morning till night; his voice already a little cracked, compared with its purity three months before. If he had been born into a rich family, he might have become a great singer. But as things were, in a little while his voice would be ruined forever. . . .

Early in the spring of 1878 Tchaikovsky revisited Kamenka, where he had not dared to go for many months. Antonina had left long ago, but he was harassed by the problem of his wife and her future.

News of her still filled him with hatred, and he admitted longing passionately for her death. He dubbed her an inoculation of the plague, a spectre destined to persecute him forever.

The persecution at the moment consisted of letters to him and his relations, her theme being that at heart, Tchaikovsky loved her, and that it was the interference of others that was preventing them from making a successful marriage.

Anatol went to Moscow to try and persuade her to agree to sue for a divorce. Mme. von Meck was ready and eager to provide money to enable Tchaikovsky to free himself from the unhappy Antonina. She offered 10,000 roubles for the purpose.

Into Tchaikovsky's letters had crept the old touch of anxiety and dread. From other sources, Mme. von Meck heard that he had stopped working and that he was getting thin. She acted audaciously and decisively. He must leave Kamenka, she said, and come to her great Ukrainian estate of Brailov. The nightingales were singing over the river. He would be her guest . . . but of course she herself would not be there. He could be quite alone, and could leave when the time came for her to go there for her summer visit.

This was the first of a series of fantastic visits in which Mme. von Meck played phantom hostess to Tchaikovsky, in the Ukraine, in Moscow, and in Florence.

The experience of going to Brailov was very like that of Beauty in the fairy-tale when she goes to the estate of the Beast and is served by magic in the empty palace.

Tchaikovsky was much excited as he travelled through the blossoming countryside, relieved for a time of his burdens. Another traveller, who seemed to know the neighbourhood, told him that Brailov belonged to a banker named Meck and brought its owner 700,000 roubles a year.

Alighting from the train at Shmerinka, Tchaikovsky inquired whether any horses had been sent for him. A Russian servant of the von Meck household, with the French name of Marcel, came forward and led him to a splendid carriage. He was not only exceedingly attentive and deferential to Tchaikovsky, but was so much better dressed than he that the visitor felt embarrassed.

They drove to the house and Tchaikovsky saw that it was truly palatial: there was a number of separate suites of rooms; one huge wing, like a hotel, had a long corridor with ever-ready guest rooms opening off both sides. Tchaikovsky's luxurious suite was on the first floor, but he had the freedom of the house: the music-room, Mme. von Meck's study, wherever he cared to go. The garden was filled with lilac and roses. On his arrival Marcel showed him into the dining-room: a big silver samovar was steaming there, and as alternative there was a pot of coffee over a spirit flame, and a dish of eggs and bread and butter. Marcel had received orders from the absent mistress of the house and obeyed them: he neither tried to converse, nor yet stood obsequiously behind the chair of the guest, but merely served him and then went away.

Marcel asked Tchaikovsky what timetable would suit him. He replied that he would like a midday meal at one o'clock, tea at nine, and a cold supper. Everything was arranged precisely as he wished. The food and wines were exquisite.

He strolled around, looked at the pictures on the walls, tried the grand piano and the harmonium in the music-room and then went out into the garden, which he saw was large and well kept, but lacked shade. When he wanted to go for a drive he had only to order the carriage. The Brailov estate stretched away to forest and hill: there were 12,000 acres of it. He would enjoy many long walks there by sunlight and moonlight.

He began composing again as his mind eased.

Tchaikovsky began his day with coffee, early in the morning. Then he strolled in the garden and sometimes slipped out through a small wooden door, and jumped a ditch to reach a deserted monastery. The paths were overgrown, the oriole and the nightingale sang in the thickets, and there was no sign that human beings had set foot there for many years.

Tchaikovsky was content to sit there for hours at a time, meditating in his own fashion where the monks had meditated, listening to the bird-song and then returning, refreshed in spirit, to the music-room, to work on the little violin pieces which he was to leave behind as a gift for Mme. von Meck: *Souvenir d'un cher lieu.*

Suddenly the news came that Antonina had consented to divorce him (though she was later to change her mind). He was so happy and excited that he ran about the garden for an hour and a half, leaping and singing, till he wore himself out.

On Mme. von Meck's advice, he ended his Ukraine holiday at once, although he had been there only a fortnight, and went back to Moscow to see the officials concerned with divorce proceedings and hustle the case through before his wife changed her mind. This proved impossible, however, as she had gone into hiding.

Tchaikovsky was shocked to find what a maze of bribery and lying he would have to thread to obtain his freedom, and was baffled by his wife's disappearance. He left the city and went to one of the Davidov estates, south of Kamenka.

Jurgenson eventually found Antonina, but she now refused to give Tchaikovsky his freedom. The divorce was a plot by Rubinstein, Anatol, and Sasha, she said. She would talk to nobody but her husband.

When Jurgenson tried to persuade her to change her mind again, and commence proceedings, accusing Tchaikovsky of adultery, she refused, and in dangerous terms. If there was any attempt to assert that he had committed adultery, she would swear in court that he was innocent of it, she threatened.

Tchaikovsky gave up hope of cutting the legal knot, in these circumstances. He could not afford a scandal. The only thing to do was somehow to prevent her from molesting him.

He wrote to Mme. von Meck saying the sum she had offered would not be needed. One third of it would do: Antonina had said that for 3,000 roubles she would leave Moscow.

The thought of his wife produced in him a mad, sick hatred, which could lead to crime, he said. He could not trust himself. At nine o'clock every evening a terrible sleepiness came over him, which had to be fought, otherwise he had a night of 'heart cramps', nightmares, and pains.

It was merely a matter of nerves, he knew well enough. There were no remedies except work, will-power, and a glass of wine. He applied all three.

The Antonina question was pushed temporarily into the background, and Tchaikovsky, growing tranquil again, recovered the power to work. He began to plan a liturgy (St. John Chrysostom) for mixed choir, and a new opera on Schiller's *Maid of Orleans*.

Autumn swallowed him up in work, as usual, but he had come to dislike teaching so intensely that he now looked upon the Conservatory as 'a fetid jail'.

Rubinstein had, of course, returned from Paris as the envoy of Russian music in the West. He had not stinted his audiences of Tchaikovsky's music and had given them *The Tempest*, many of his minor compositions, and two performances of the *Piano Concerto in B flat minor* with, he said, tremendous success. Vanished was the rancour he had displayed on the occasion of Tchaikovsky's refusal to accept the Paris assignment, and he had many kind things to say to him both privately and also in an after-dinner speech, when he said the Conservatory was fortunate to possess so distinguished a composer as Tchaikovsky. Amid all this warmth and wine Tchaikovsky found his hand being wrung repeatedly, by people whose tears were freely flowing. 'A thoroughly repugnant comedy,' was his comment afterwards.

But undeniably, Tchaikovsky now had an international name, and his new works were awaited with excitement in his own country, though often slighted when actually heard in all their disconcerting newness. Tolstoy wrote to Turgenev inquiring about the opera *Eugene Onegin* which he heard that Tchaikovsky had written, and was told in reply that the piano score had been received in Paris: it was remarkable music, but the libretto was not good. Turgenev added that he had 'gaped' on being told by an English professor of music at Cambridge that Tchaikovsky was the outstanding musician of the day. He failed to name this very discerning Englishman.

Tchaikovsky himself considered that it was thanks to von Bülow that he was better known in England and America than elsewhere.

He paid the second of his visits to a house of Mme. von Meck's—this time to her Moscow home on the Boulevard Rojdstevensky, but stayed only a couple of hours. She had invited him to live there in her absence, but he was afraid of gossip, and declined. He enjoyed wandering through the many rooms. Here, in this quiet place, his fears fell away and for the passing hour he was no longer beset by the feeling of persecution that had troubled him since his return to Moscow. He halted before a picture of a wintry road: it recalled his first symphony, *Winter Day Dreams*, and carried his mind back over the years. Mme. von Meck's bedroom, into which he looked, was smaller than the one he had seen at Brailov, but had the same austere appearance. There were two pianos in the house, a Bechstein and a Steinway, and Tchaikovsky played both of them.

They were beautiful instruments, and with a Deben organ, incomparably the finest of Mme. von Meck's possessions there.

If Tchaikovsky, as he left the house, thought how strange it was to have come upon all the living signs of a muted friendship, the desk at which Mme. von Meck wrote her earnest and loving letters, the pianos which sang his music to her, the portraits of herself and her children, and all the many emblems of her pervasive presence, he must have realised that he had come as near to her as he ever would. Nearer, surely, than when he looked into her eyes in Florence and at Brailov in those accidental meetings which all their studied caution could not avoid.

CHAPTER X

THREE DEATHS

A CHANCE incident on a railway journey decided Tchaikovsky to give up teaching at the Conservatory. He was going to St. Petersburg, in the nervous state which journeys always induced, and, to calm himself as well as to escape the attention of others, he opened a newspaper. It contained a vituperative attack on the morals and internal politics of the Conservatory. Corruption and chicanery, it alleged, were entrenched in Moscow's academy of music. He himself was exonerated from any intrigue, being, it was said, too preoccupied with his art; which was true. (Mme. von Meck herself had a poor opinion of the morals of the Conservatory; she had heard of students seduced by their professors, and said she would not send a *son* of hers there, let alone a daughter!)

The article upset him, and while his thoughts were still full of it he overheard a conversation among his fellow-passengers, who did not recognise him. They exchanged gossip about the musical world and at length discussed Tchaikovsky himself, his marriage, his 'attacks of insanity'. He learned that he was 'not violent', but incurable all the same.

He changed compartments, and was recognised by the people among whom he now took his seat. They asked him personal questions with such effrontery that he would have done anything to escape.

Tchaikovsky felt that in this experience he had seen both Moscow life and the ugly side of human relations through a magnifying glass. He feared that if he plunged back into his work at the Conservatory as of old, his disgust would turn into a general hatred of mankind and would poison his life and his music.

On the positive side, the spread of his fame, his consciousness of having much work still in him to do, and the knowledge that Mme. von Meck and her millions were behind him, were three factors encouraging him to give up everything except composing and conducting.

In St. Petersburg he talked to the new Principal of the Conservatory there, Karl Davidov (unrelated to the Davidovs of Kamenka), successor to Anton Rubinstein, who had retired. Davidov expressed astonishment that for twelve years Tchaikovsky had been putting in twenty-six hours' teaching a week, and that it had never occurred to Nikolai Rubinstein to lighten this burden for the sake of the composer's own creative work, to save him from exhaustion.

Davidov pleaded with him to return to St. Petersburg, and to teach at the Conservatory where he had been a student. He offered him twice his Moscow salary for only four hours' teaching a week in advanced theory to a few chosen pupils, and said the lectures need not be given within the walls of the Conservatory. The terms of this offer make it clear what lustre now attached to Tchaikovsky's name, even in St. Petersburg, the citadel of the nationalist composers.

He decided to turn it down, partly because it would hurt Rubinstein's feelings too much, partly because it was freedom he wanted, and he had no more wish to live in St. Petersburg than in Moscow. But the conversation opened his eyes. Only now did he understand how very little Rubinstein and the other directors of the Moscow Conservatory had appreciated his needs as composer.

Tchaikovsky, for very good reasons, wanted Mme. von Meck's opinion and he wrote to her explaining that he might give up teaching altogether. She was in Paris, hearing his work being performed at the Exhibition. His letter missed her, and followed her to Italy, where she received it weeks later. When she did reply, it was with whole-hearted encouragement. 'Of course leave the Conservatory!' she said. 'I have thought for a long time that it was absurd for a person of your brains, training and talent to be at the mercy of a despotic, unscrupulous man who is your inferior in every way.'

She even proposed the romantic idea that she and Tchaikovsky should both settle on the shores of Lake Como—a few miles apart!

Armed with her approval, Tchaikovsky went to Rubinstein who received him in extremely friendly fashion, asking why he was so gloomy, where he had been hiding himself and whether he was ill. He invited him to 'be frank'.

Had Tchaikovsky been of tougher fibre he would have known how to respond to Rubinstein's prompting, but it was a situation he was unfitted by nature to deal with. Instead of explaining the very valid reasons for his resignation, he became confused by the thought that he was showing ingratitude to someone who had done so much for him. He lost control and began talking wildly of his absolute hatred for the Conservatory and the work that was expected of him there. He could stand it no longer.

The Thunder-hurler allowed Tchaikovsky to talk himself out, and then calmly said he would accept his decision, though naturally with regret.

Tchaikovsky was puzzled, even disappointed—was he then so dispensable? Probably Rubinstein, witnessing an outburst which must have reminded him of Tchaikovsky's dangerous breakdown of a year ago, decided it would be unwise to thwart him. Shrewd as ever, and not devoid of affection for Tchaikovsky, he saw it would be best to cut his losses.

He merely told Tchaikovsky that his departure would be a blow to the prestige of the Conservatory, and they ought to arrange matters as quietly as possible. Tchaikovsky agreed to go to St. Petersburg and write from there to say that his health prevented his returning.

Hubert and Tannaev took over his piano and harmony classes, and the break was smoothly made. Tchaikovsky was toasted at a little farewell dinner-party by those in the know, Rubinstein, Albrecht, Jurgenson, Kashkin, and Tannaev. The next day he went to St. Petersburg, and soon afterwards to Kamenka.

Already at Brailov he had begun sketching out his *Suite No. 1 in D major*, and now resumed work on it. Unfortunately during his many journeyings at this time he lost the manuscript and did not recover it until months later, when he had given up hope of ever seeing it again. In any case, the new opera, *The Maid of Orleans*, was soon demanding his whole attention. When the *Suite* did turn up he put it aside for future consideration.

Mme. von Meck was in Florence, where she occupied the splendid Villa Oppenheim overlooking the city. Her retinue there included a German governess for her children, four Russian maids, three Italian servants, as well as cooks, butlers, footmen, coachmen and others. It occurred to her to invite Tchaikovsky to Florence for a new variant of her game of phantom hostess. She rented a five-roomed villa for him, a quarter of a mile from her own, provided a grand piano for him and arranged the furnishings herself.

Tchaikovsky had just recovered from a nervous attack in which he thought he was dying. It was brought on by a wolf-hunt in which his brother-in-law insisted on his taking part, and he became so ill that he had to postpone his departure from Kamenka for twenty-four hours. When he did leave his journey was a misery: he had toothache, and a mental unease that grew as the train rattled along. For no particular reason, he began to suspect that this time Mme. von Meck intended to trap him into meeting her. The two houses were too close together. He could never rest if he were living in fear of encountering his soul's affinity in the flesh.

Pakhulsky, her musician, met him at the station and took him to the lovely house he was to occupy. The rooms were glowing with flowers, and on the writing-table was a letter from Mme. von Meck, welcoming him and putting his mind at rest. She told him what joy it was to her to breathe the same air as he, to admire the same scenery; she offered him books, carriages, any imaginable service. At the same time she tactfully informed him which way she took her morning walk and at what time—between eleven and noon—so that he could avoid meeting her.

Tchaikovsky relaxed. He enjoyed the wonderful peace of the place. In the stillness of the night he seemed to hear the earth intoning a deep bass note in its flight through space.

In the evenings Mme. von Meck drove to where she could see a light in the window of the room in which Tchaikovsky sat working on the score of *The Maid of Orleans*. At midnight they wrote to each other. Mme. von Meck, having chosen Tchaikovsky's house, was anxious for him to see the Villa Oppenheim. She would not of course be there when he called and this could be easily arranged. Tchaikovsky gently declined. He would not go, he said, until she had left Florence.

One day the inevitable accident happened: Tchaikovsky walked out of his house into the Italian sunshine and as he often did, strolled along so preoccupied that he was hardly aware of the road he was taking. Nor did he hear the belled approach of a carriage until a landau and pair drew level. Then he turned his head and saw it was Mme. von Meck out driving with a married daughter. His bow was acknowledged and the carriage passed on.

Tchaikovsky and his patroness also saw one another at the opera, but exchanged no sign, although the game of make-believe touched new heights in their letters. That night he wrote to tell her how happy her presence at the opera had made him. He knew she had been ill the day before and it meant she was well again. Mme. von Meck replied: 'How I love you and how happy I am to have seen you. Rising in the morning, my first thought is of you and all day I am conscious of your presence.'

After a fortnight of this romantic hide-and-not-seek, which would surely have appealed to the courtiers of Versailles, Mme. von Meck moved to Vienna. The new year, 1879, began, and Tchaikovsky went to Paris. There, 'living like a hermit', he finished his opera and attacked the problems of the *Suite* again.

The hermit found time for some theatre- and concert-going, however, and one day slipped into one of the Concerts du Chatelet, where the great conductor Edouard Colonne was giving his *Tempest*. He thought the orchestra seemed unenthusiastic like the audience. At the end there was faint applause, with two or three hisses, which provoked 'Oh, Oh's' of protest from the rest of the hearers. The composer sent a note of appreciation to Colonne, remarking modestly that the hissing did not surprise him: the composition 'is diffuse and lacks proportion'.

In early spring he returned to Moscow when *Eugene Onegin* was staged at the Maly Theatre. Tchaikovsky was content with the way the Conservatory singers handled the work, but Modest considered the performance was amateurish.

It was a brilliant first night. The staff of the Conservatory fêted Tchaikovsky and presented a laurel wreath to him. A complimentary supper at the Hermitage followed the fall of the curtain, when Tchaikovsky had taken his many calls. Even Anton Rubinstein was there, though he said not a word about the opera. Homeric drinking and gaiety went on until four in the morning. None of this adulation turned Tchaikovsky's head, or dimmed his clearsightedness.

'I noticed no particular enthusiasm in the audience,' he said. It was himself and not the opera or its performers who received the ovation, he observed; and that was not what he desired.

The new type of libretto, the deviation from accepted grand opera style, had to win its way in the world, and the first audiences to hear *Eugene Onegin* found it too unconventional. Anton Rubinstein dismissed the opera as trivial, and only came round to admiring it years afterwards. The critics, too, gave it a half-hearted welcome.

Tchaikovsky returned to St. Petersburg, and there he began to be harried by Antonina again. No longer elusive, no longer content with writing letters, she suddenly turned up and made pathetic efforts to break through the barriers her husband had erected against her.

She haunted the street where he lodged, called at the house when he was out, and one day he found her waiting for him when he came home.

Unknown to her, his brother Anatol was listening in the next room to the outpourings with which she greeted Tchaikovsky. Nothing her wretched husband could say would change her belief that fundamentally they still loved each other. Sooner or later they would be reconciled, she said, and their marriage would begin again. Tchaikovsky was terrified by this declaration. He tried hard to make Antonina understand how great was the necessity for a divorce but she would not hear of it. She talked excitably of love for two hours, attempting in ingenuous fashion to talk her way into her husband's heart. At last, Anatol entered the room together with Modest, who had meanwhile turned up. She greeted them with a show of affection and appeared calmer—Tchaikovsky having offered her a hundred roubles for a trip to Moscow; which she accepted. When she left them, Tchaikovsky thought he had succeeded in buying peace. But it was a very brief respite.

A week later his wife actually moved into an apartment in the same house, just above the one Tchaikovsky shared with Anatol. She pretended that this was a mere coincidence, and assured her husband that she was not trying to run after him. In a note she said, 'In imagination I kiss you many times,' adding wryly, 'I know you don't like kissing very much if it's in reality.'

Modest said she was not human, but was the sole specimen of a unique species. But Modest himself belonged to the homosexual species, and looked with little sympathy on the rejected girl and her plight.

Tchaikovsky, who had reached a stage where he said the very sight of her handwriting made him feel physically ill, certainly could not stand living in the same house with her. She was foolish to have attempted this desperate manoeuvre: it merely drove him away. He fled to Moscow. She followed him there, burst in upon him at his home and stayed an hour, reproaching and pleading. He could think of nothing to do except offer her more money. He fled again the next day to Kamenka.

She did not dare follow him to Sasha's home—but she could write a host of letters with maddening insistence on a theme that obsessed her and permitted of no variation. From Kamenka Tchaikovsky retreated to the sanctuary of Brailov, offered by Mme. von Meck, during another of her absences. He wrote to Anatol saying that thoughts of 'the reptile', as he called the importunate Antonina, spoiled Brailov for him, this time.

Nevertheless, he remained there for three weeks, and then went back to Kamenka to allow Mme. von Meck to return to her estate: their trains passed in the night, and even stood in the same station for a few minutes, but they shielded themselves and continued their separate journeys.

It occurred to Mme. von Meck, a little later, to reproduce the Florentine arrangement at Brailov, and Tchaikovsky was invited to stay at Simaki, a farmhouse two miles from her home. He arrived in August and again found everything provided for his needs and wishes. Nothing was forgotten. Mme. von Meck's servants awaited him, and on his desk lay the pens and paper for his work. It was arranged that Pakhulsky, who was to visit Tchaikovsky for lessons, should tell him where Mme. von Meck intended to drive or walk each day and the precise hour.

One afternoon, however, Tchaikovsky left for a drive an hour earlier than he had intended and their carriages met; so did their eyes. They bowed to one another, as they had done in Florence, and drove on. Mme. von Meck had Milochka, her little daughter, with her, a fact which particularly embarrassed Tchaikovsky, as he had refused to allow Pakhulsky to bring the child to the farmhouse. He immediately wrote to Mme. von Meck saying, 'For God's sake forgive me for miscalculating the time so carelessly.' His patroness replied that she was delighted to have met him on the road, and that as for Milochka, 'she is well able to keep a secret. When we got home she put her arms around Pakhulsky's neck and whispered that we had met you, not daring to say it aloud, though there was no one else in the room but myself.'

Milochka—she was seven—must have been a very puzzled child. When her governess asked her why they no longer went near the old farmhouse, the little girl had to run away to avoid telling a lie. Her mother had told her that Tchaikovsky must not be disturbed because he was 'composing beautiful music'; but she was devoured with curiosity and she understood only that there was a great secret which must not be given away.

One day, by careful prearrangement, Tchaikovsky revisited Brailov itself and explored all the rooms of Mme. von Meck's house while she and her family were out; he afterwards wrote a note admiring the new furniture she had acquired. Another day he hid in a summer-house among dark trees on the bank of the stream watching fireworks and boats bedecked with lanterns and flowers—festivities to celebrate the name-day of Mme. von Meck's little son Alexander; and his hostess passed very close to him without knowing it.

The strange pair, Tchaikovsky and his patroness, continued to express their adoration on paper, without stint: 'My beloved!' 'How I love you!' 'The thought that I might outlive you is unbearable!' 'You are so utterly dear to me!'—their verbal caresses were endless, tireless. They discussed by letter which of Tchaikovsky's nieces could be matched off with Nikolai, Mme. von Meck's son. They thought at first of Natasha; in the end they succeeded in arranging such a marriage, but between Nikolai and another niece, Anna Davidova. 'A suitable choice without the futile entanglements of passion,' was the desideratum, according to Mme. von Meck.

The Ukrainian holiday came to an end: with further exchanges of gratitude and love, Tchaikovsky and his hostess parted again. He went to Moscow, she to Paris. She had obtained his consent to her subsidising a performance of his *Fourth Symphony* there under the baton of Colonne.

Although he had conducted a performance of *The Tempest* when it was hissed, Colonne believed in Tchaikovsky's music and was anxious to give more of it. But a symphony: that was a big undertaking. However, he agreed to do the *Fourth* when Pakhulsky saw him on Mme. von Meck's behalf and conveyed her offer to defray all expenses.

Later there were times when Mme. von Meck, unknown to Tchaikovsky, paid Colonne to play Tchaikovsky's music for herself alone, or herself and her grandson, in a darkened theatre in Paris: the gesture of a Caliph.

Russia was listening to much more of Tchaikovsky's music, both orchestral and vocal. *Vakoula the Smith* was revived and so, too, was *The Oprichnik*, from which the censor's ban had been removed. Chaliapin, then unknown outside Russia, was in the cast. The composer no longer had any love for either work; *Vakoula* he now thought was full of grave mistakes and written like a symphony. *Swan Lake*, the *First String Quartet*, the *Piano Sonata* superbly played by Nikolai Rubinstein all found appreciative audiences. The *Fourth Symphony* was badly received in Paris, but French audiences showed great enthusiasm for Tchaikovsky's *Third Quartet* and *Melancholy Serenade*. The *Piano Concerto* was successfully played in New York, where the *First Suite* was no less successful. Germany and Hungary also heard Tchaikovsky's music about the same time. The Marinsky Theatre in St. Petersburg agreed to stage his *Maid of Orleans*. And the Grand Duke Constantine stopped his carriage in the street to invite Tchaikovsky to sail round the world with him in a battleship!

At Nikolai Rubinstein's insistence, Tchaikovsky composed for a patriotic exhibition the *1812 Overture*, which he thought of small value and later excluded from performance in Berlin. He liked better his recently completed *Italian Caprice*, which was an immediate success. His *Liturgy* was also performed, much to his satisfaction. Though he remained self-critical, Tchaikovsky must have had a godlike sense of his own fertility, with so much and such diverse music of his being played in so many cities.

Mme. von Meck had a new household musician, a Frenchman whom she referred to patronisingly as 'our little Bussy'. He was none other than Claude Debussy, and his first published work was a piano transcription of parts of *Swan Lake*, done at the behest of Mme. von Meck.

In the midst of his glory, Tchaikovsky was still in poor health—both he and Mme. von Meck were suffering from blinding headaches—and he was still being hunted by Antonina. Now he was afflicted, in different ways, by three deaths.

The first was that of his father, at the age of eighty-five, which occurred when Tchaikovsky was in Rome. Anatol wrote to tell him the details of his father's passing and he wept as he read them. But learning that his father had realised he was dying and had remained courageous and cheerful, Tchaikovsky himself became calmer and thought with resignation of the human lot. He said of his father, 'he was a good man, and truly pure in heart'. Three months later he went to St. Petersburg and visited the grave.

The second death was not a personal loss but the assassination of the Tsar, Alexander II, in the spring of 1881. Tchaikovsky was again in Rome when he heard this news. He felt miserable at being abroad at such a time, among people talking of the beauties of Sorrento, instead of among his own countrymen, talking of the nihilist bombs outside the Winter Palace and demonstrating for or against the new Tsar.

Alexander II had started his reign with liberal policies but had become harsher as he grew more frightened of the explosive social forces in the country. Three years before the murder, Tchaikovsky had observed to Mme. von Meck that to stop and think about the condition of Russia was enough to make anyone afraid. The government appeared panic-striken and confused, he said, and was exiling people by the thousand, while the indifferent masses watched this going on without making any protest.

The cruelties of autocracy were repugnant to him, and for all his conventional loyalty he had no personal affection for Tsar Alexander. When Nikolai Rubinstein suggested his writing a piece of music for the Tsar's jubilee, Tchaikovsky remarked that he had an antipathy towards that 'eminent personage'. It was sympathy rather with the Russian people, the sense of national solidarity, that moved him when the Little Father of All the Russias was killed.

Neither this death nor his own father's weighed with him like the one which occurred very soon afterwards: that of Nikolai Rubinstein.

Intestinal tuberculosis felled the tyrannical genius to whom, when all was said and done, Russia and Tchaikovsky owed so much. His death was like the cessation of some great force of nature.

He died in Paris at the age of forty-five. Tchaikovsky was in Nice, on his way home from Rome after hearing of the Tsar's death, when he received a telegram from Jurgenson saying that Rubinstein was gravely ill. He wired back for further details and waited for a reply. When it came it said Rubinstein's condition was now beyond hope, and another telegram followed very soon afterwards saying he was dead.

Three hours before his death, hardly able to move or speak, Rubinstein ordered oysters, ate them, and declared that he enjoyed them. It was the last flourish of a grandiloquent personality: he had suffered agonies in his last weeks, and looked emaciated and almost out of recognition when Tchaikovsky saw him lying-in-state in the Russian church in Paris.

Tchaikovsky saw the coffin start on its railway journey back to Russia.

'I am crushed with grief,' he wrote. 'My God, my God, how terrible are such moments in our lives.'

He had felt no deep affection for Rubinstein as a person, and they had battled often enough over ideas and principles. But he respected Rubinstein's musical abilities and other gifts, and was grateful to him for many wonderful performances of his works.

He was disgusted at Anton's behaviour when the latter arrived in Paris. It seemed to Tchaikovsky that instead of grief he betrayed a callous satisfaction at having his famous brother out of the way. Tchaikovsky decided not to accompany Anton to Russia for the funeral: they had both attended a memorial service in Paris, at which Turgenev and Massenet were among the mourners. But he followed a few days later.

The first person to whom Rubinstein's post as head of the Moscow Conservatory was offered was, naturally, Tchaikovsky. He declined it. Yet he had heard that Mme. von Meck had been losing big sums of money and he knew that if her support were withdrawn from him he would have to go back to teaching. He wrote and asked her to tell him candidly how things stood. She replied that his pension was a trifle compared with the scale of her financial setback, and she would continue to pay it as usual.

'I will not give up the right to take care of you,' she said.

But the news of her losses was 'far from cheering', as Tchaikovsky commented to his brother.

Shadows of death, great and small, filled that sad year for Tchaikovsky. He had made friends with a forester in the midst of the woods near Kamenka, whose cottage he passed on his daily walks when he was staying with his sister. One of the forester's large family, a little girl of four, was his particular favourite. Shy at first, she soon grew confident with him, and would caress him and prattle to him, with great tenderness. A letter from his brother-in-law, reaching him in Rome, told him that she and another of the forester's children had died of diphtheria.

Tchaikovsky's personal and public tribute to Nikolai Rubinstein was his *Trio in A minor* for piano, violin, and cello: 'dedicated to the memory of a great artist'.

The combination of instruments was one he had formerly disliked but which he now treated as a challenge to his skill in making it acceptable.

In the emotional aftermath of death's harvesting, Tchaikovsky began thinking about religion once more. The question of life after death preoccupied him: he could not believe in it, but longed to do so, and thought that if faith would come to him it would make him happy. Three or four years earlier, he had told Mme. von Meck that he found the idea of eternal life neither credible nor desirable, except in the pantheistic view of the eternity of nature. He refused to believe in eternal pain, and thought eternal bliss a wearisome idea. On the other hand the thought of never seeing dearly loved and now dead friends again was terrible to him.

At that time he was thinking of his mother: he said he could never reconcile himself to the thought that she 'actually *is not*, that I shall never have any chance of telling her how, after twenty-three years of separation, she is as dear to me as ever'. He went on, 'I am made up of contradictions, and have reached a mature age without resting on anything positive, either through religion or philosophy. . . . I should have gone mad but for music.'

After Rubinstein's death, Tchaikovsky prayed much and fervently for God's love, for peace of mind, for light in his darkness, for forgiveness of his sins. He wept and assured himself that he knew God must exist, even though he could not conceive where or how. He determined to try and live the Christian life and obey God's will.

One of the musical results of this devout period was a resolve to restore the ancient chants of Russian Orthodox ritual. This intention led to a dull job—editing the works of Dmitri Bortniansky, an arranger of Church music. He undertook the commission from Jurgenson, though condemning the work he was handling as rubbishy. He did it partly out of piety, partly for money, having squandered all he possessed on people who came to him with hard-luck stories. Mme. von Meck was annoyed at his labours. She sent him more money and asked him in future to be good enough to come to her in his need, not to turn to Jurgenson. The editing was a waste of his time and talents, and that was something which always made her angry.

The consolations of religion were one thing; Tchaikovsky's relations with the ecclesiastical authorities were quite another.

'All my efforts to work for Russian church music have met with persecution,' he said, adding that he was helpless to fight against this: 'ranged against me are influential people who persistently keep any ray of light from penetrating that sphere of ignorance and gloom.'

The church certainly showed little appreciation of his sincere efforts to improve the quality of its music, both by composing for it and by reviving and purifying the old chants. His own *Liturgy* had been confiscated by the director of the Imperial Chapel, who claimed an ancient right of veto over performance or publication of any religious work. The director, however, was sued and defeated at law by Jurgenson, who also won another case establishing a lay publisher's right to print church music: two small skirmishes in the general fight of that period for the freedom of the arts in Russia.

Then, when a concert-hall performance of the *Liturgy* was given, the clergy were angry, accusing Tchaikovsky—to whom a laurel-leaf harp had been presented—of what modern Russia would call a 'cult of personality'. The Bishop of Moscow wrote a venomous article in the newspaper *Rus*, spiced with a touch of gratuitous anti-semitism: let the faithful beware, he said: the next step might be the holy Mass by Rosenblum or Rosenthal, and there might be hisses instead of applause.

The same Bishop refused to allow Tchaikovsky's *Liturgy* to be performed at Nikolai Rubinstein's funeral.

Tchaikovsky, at Kamenka, was now distracted by the troubles of his eldest niece, Tatiana, who had been 'crossed in love' and had taken to morphine. He played duets with her and read to her, but was unable to be of any real help, and was depressed by the realisation of his failure.

This beautiful, wayward girl had been engaged to a man of aristocratic family, who behaved badly to her. Later, in 1883, she had a son by the music-teacher whom her parents employed. Modest took her to Paris to avert scandal, and she had the child there, leaving it to be reared by a French couple. Tchaikovsky was in Paris at the time and knew all about the matter: he was wrongly believed by some people to be the child's father! Tatiana died in 1886, at the age of twenty-four, and her little boy, Georges, was adopted by Nikolai, the eldest of the Tchaikovsky brothers.

In February 1882 Anatol, who had been Tchaikovsky's sick-nurse, confidant, agent, and lawyer to him during the worst period of his troubles, took a wife. Tchaikovsky congratulated him not without a sigh of envy. He said that only a wife could satisfy a certain kind of yearning for tenderness and consolation and that he himself had to confess to moments of 'insane craving for the caress of a woman's touch'. He realised, he said, that he had never experienced what he imagined Anatol to be feeling.

It was the era of change which every man has to encounter and endure in middle age, when 'marriage and death and division make barren our lives'. Tchaikovsky found it hard.

CHAPTER XI

THE HERMIT OF KLIN

IT was Jurgenson, as publisher turned detective, who freed Tchaikovsky from one of his greatest burdens: fear of Antonina. He knew that although little had been heard of her for some time, her husband's dread of her still preyed upon him. Jurgenson went quietly to work on his own, and traced her movements from one town to another, ascertained with whom she had stayed and at what dates.

Finally he wrote to Tchaikovsky, in the spring of 1881, saying he now possessed proof that Antonina was living in Moscow with a lover. She had had a child by this man, whose name was Bolkov, and had put it in an orphanage. (Later, she had other children.) If Tchaikovsky chose to sue for divorce, citing Bolkov as co-respondent, he would probably get it, easily enough.

This was a startling new situation to be considered. Tchaikovsky had given up hope of divorce when Antonina frightened him by saying she would deny that he had ever committed adultery and would bring up his 'filthy vices'. Now he had to ask himself afresh whether he should try to get the marriage dissolved.

His sole reason for wanting a divorce had been to end her legal rights and her nerve-racking pursuit of him. It was not a financial question: he had paid her debts, allowed her a steady monthly income, and gave her various additional lump sums when she demanded them. He did not begrudge any of this. He merely wanted a weapon of defence, and this Jurgenson had now provided.

He never began divorce proceedings. Such things as litigation were alien to his nature, and he would have shrunk from a court ordeal, even if he had not also had the secret fear that his wife might have a hysterical outburst and blacken his name. The facts unearthed by Jurgenson gave Tchaikovsky the assurance he wanted above all—'now she will leave me in peace,' he said. Divorce might have been of benefit to her, enabling her to marry; it had no value for him, since he would never again want to attempt a marriage, however much he might sometimes sigh for a woman's tenderness.

Antonina did not register her children in Tchaikovsky's name, as she could legally have done, a fact for which his family were thankful. She wrote occasional meandering letters to Tchaikovsky. He continued to pay for her keep, right up to his death, in spite of the knowledge that she lived with another man.

There was no real malice in Antonina, for all her obsessed pursuit of Tchaikovsky. Quite possibly she was already a little unbalanced at the time they first met and thus her abortive romance, and subsequent affairs, in which she may have endured certain brutal experiences, were not of themselves decisive for what happened to her ultimately. She became more noticeably the victim of delusions and three years after Tchaikovsky's death was shut up in an asylum in St. Petersburg, where she lived on for another twenty-one years. She died in 1917, the year of the Revolution, aged sixty-eight.

At the time of Jurgenson's discovery, Tchaikovsky's life was full of work and distraction, but appears to have become a little arid, humanly and emotionally. His principal attachments were to a brother, a manservant and a child.

Modest was still the person to whom he turned most readily for affection and understanding.

It is hard to assess Tchaikovsky's attachment to Alexei Sofronov, his servant. It has, of course, been suggested that it was a love relation and in some sense that may be true; on the other hand, master–servant relations were paternal and personal in the Russia of that day: no mere matter of paying wages and giving orders: they had the old feudal quality and—paradoxically—because the social gap was so immense and unquestionable, a warm familiarity was possible without endangering the position of either party. Such relationships scarcely exist today and our imagination does not find it easy to conjure them up. Alexei, by the by, was a happily married man until his wife's death from consumption.

He was called up for military service in December 1880, and Tchaikovsky went to see him in barracks. He was already grieving at losing him and seeing him roughing it brought on a fearful nervous attack. Tchaikovsky wrote very emotionally to Modest, saying he lacked words to express his sorrow. When Alexei was taken ill around this time, Tchaikovsky visited him almost daily in hospital. It was a happy day for Tchaikovsky when Alexei was out of the army again, four years later, and back in his service for life.

The child whom Tchaikovsky loved, 'Bobyk' Davidov, his nephew, grew up even more neurotic than himself, and eventually ended his own life. He was a youth of much charm and he had sufficient musical taste and talent to be able to share his uncle's interests and to play duets with him, even at an early age.

Tchaikovsky saw the boy only occasionally, chiefly on visits to Kamenka. Despite many professional and social demands on him Tchaikovsky's life was lonely. He was starved of the kind of warmth and friendship that he had shared with the poet Apukhtin, or with Adamov, in student years, or a little later with Laroche, to whom he wrote some 4,000 letters.

But for Laroche and Kashkin, too, he had no more than ordinary cordiality in his middle age; barely that, sometimes. In 1878 they visited him together in Moscow, and he wrote to Mme. von Meck afterwards: 'People have just left me whose society was once pleasant to me. Why was I so annoyed that I could not hide it, and both remarked on it several times?'

There was always the disembodied friendship with Mme. von Meck—his letters to her total more than 770; but Tchaikovsky had nobody at hand, day by day, to talk with in slippers, of matters great and small. There was no equally lively mind with whom he could exchange impressions of the passing show of life, and rarely anybody to sit down with him at the piano and go through the score of the latest work of interest. No wife to be his helpmeet; no home worth the name. Constant movement was his lot from one city to another, from town to country; a ceaseless stream of important people to see him, endless business dealings to fill in the spaces between his actual spells of composing—theatre business, publishing business, concert business. Everything but friendship, marriage, or love.

A gap, a void existed in the centre of Tchaikovsky's life. As for sexual satisfaction, any that he experienced in the years of his fame must have been wretchedly furtive and brief: there is no sign of any constant, passionate relationship that might have drawn on his rich capacity for unselfish love. His existence appears sterile except in one way, the one way that matters to a selfish posterity, his music. One cannot wonder that in spite of success he was so restless and so often melancholy.

Sometimes Tchaikovsky took upon himself the patronage of young talents. When staying at Kamenka he discovered that the daughter of the local priest had musical gifts, and he obtained a place for her at the Conservatory. He also sent to Moscow the son of a counting-house employee, to study art, being convinced that the boy had such promise that it would be cruel not to give him the opportunity. But he found that the cost of maintaining his protégé was far more than he had expected. He therefore wrote to Mme. von Meck, begging her to find the student accommodation in some corner of her house—a box-room, a bed, a cupboard, and a table; adding 'perhaps your servants would look after him, and give him a little advice?'

Mme. von Meck complied. The young man never fulfilled Tchaikovsky's opinion of him, but he made good use of his studies and became a drawing-master at an academy.

Not all Tchaikovsky's ewe-lambs turned out so well. A young man whom he persuaded Jurgenson to employ, on the grounds that he was very clever but was in miserable circumstances and longing for a 'wider sphere', was found to be nervous and peculiar, and gave no end of trouble. But more, much more, anxiety came Tchaikovsky's way from his efforts to help one Tkachenko, who wrote to him in 1879.

This man was a railway guard of twenty-three. Tchaikovsky, who had, of course, never heard of him, received an intelligent and affecting letter containing the 'curious proposal' that the composer should take him as his servant and pay him in music lessons. He had no knowledge of music, but all too easily convinced Tchaikovsky that he had a real love of it. The composer wrote back in a friendly tone saying frankly that he considered twenty-three too old to begin to study music (a rather surprising judgment). The correspondence apparently went beyond this question, but presently lapsed for nine months. Then in December 1880, Tchaikovsky received another letter well calculated to shatter his equanimity: Tkachenko enclosed all Tchaikovsky's letters, saying that he did not want them to fall into 'strange hands' after his death, which was imminent. He bade Tchaikovsky goodbye, and said he was about to commit suicide.

Tchaikovsky noticed that the postmark was Voronezh, and telegraphed to a friend of Anatol's in that town, asking him to go to the local police. Tkachenko was found before he had done anything desperate, but was in a terrible condition, according to Anatol's friend.

Inevitably, Tchaikovsky now sent money to the young man and invited him to Moscow. First impressions were sympathetic. His sufferings, Tchaikovsky told Mme. von Meck, came from 'the internal conflict between his aspirations and stern reality'.

Nervous, 'morbidly modest', and the possessor of strange views, he seemed to have an interesting mind but a broken spirit. His eagerness to become a musician was so great that Tchaikovsky relented and found him a place at the Conservatory, where he began to study with the greatest enthusiasm.

Only two months after he was saved from suicide, Tkachenko took the first bite at the hand that fed him. He asked for an interview to discuss 'important business' with Tchaikovsky. This consisted of asserting that he had come to the conclusion he was not being kept for his own sake but to confer on Tchaikovsky the reputation of a benefactor. He was not disposed to be the *victim* of Tchaikovsky's desire for popularity!

Tchaikovsky, according to his own account, replied coldly, telling the young man not to trouble about the motives of his patron, who was indifferent to his gratitude, and advising him to apply himself to his work. 'He is mentally and morally deranged,' Tchaikovsky wrote.

Nevertheless, they must have corresponded further, as three years later Tkachenko again sent back all Tchaikovsky's letters in a parcel, obviously intending to create the same impression as before—that he was on the verge of suicide. At first Tchaikovsky was worried lest it might be so. But on reflection he decided it was unlikely; and he was correct. After a few days he received a scornfully phrased letter from the young man, asking for money and not mentioning the parcel of letters.

'He is a man to be pitied,' Tchaikovsky said. They had no further dealings.

Tchaikovsky's sense of homelessness and of the frailty of all things was sharpened by the news that Mme. von Meck had sold Brailov.

She took this drastic action from necessity, not caprice. Her fortunes had declined, she had to raise money somehow, and the huge Ukrainian estate was an extravagance. In spite of the large sum it was reputed to bring in every year, Brailov lost money, to such an extent that Tchaikovsky was convinced that its owner was being cheated, and offered to ask his brother-in-law, Davidov, to go over from Kamenka and question Mme. von Meck's steward. She declined the offer, and in 1881 sold Brailov for nearly one and a half million roubles, which she considered only half its value. She told Tchaikovsky they must both forget the great estate, 'imagine it as occupied by strangers'.

So Mme. von Meck's material splendours were that much diminished; the chief setting for the game of let's pretend was gone, and with it the farmhouse of Simaki, where Tchaikovsky had stayed.

Well, they had always proclaimed the spirituality of their relationship: the crack in the golden wall should mean nothing. All the same Mme. von Meck's wealth had spelt security to Tchaikovsky, since she had asserted the right to 'take care of him'. The loss of Brailov was a portent. It dispelled the illusion that her wealth was limitless.

The *Maid of Orleans* had been produced at the Marinsky Theatre in February 1881, after endless troubles, and another farcical brush with the Russian censorship. The censors had ordered that no cross should be permitted on the stage—which meant excising even the scene in which a soldier gives Joan a cross of two sticks when she goes to the stake. Another ruling, presumably to protect the dignity of the Church, was that the Archbishop should not be called an Archbishop, but 'a pilgrim'! Tchaikovsky was furious. 'How stupid it is!' he said. 'Who could believe that such orders could come from an institution that supervises every printed thing in Russia, and should therefore consist of educated men? But there is nothing to be done: I have had to comply.'

However, after further thought about this absurdity, he persuaded the censorship to allow him to call the Archbishop a Cardinal instead of a pilgrim: the Orthodox Church, which has no Cardinals, was thereby cleared of any unflattering imputation!

When he was finishing the work, Tchaikovsky believed that at last he had written an opera which fulfilled all the exacting conditions of this medium. Like a gambler in reckless mood, he declared that if he was wrong again, and this opera failed, he would never write another.

The *Maid of Orleans* did fail, but Tchaikovsky did not give up writing for the stage—even when its successor, *Mazeppa*, had no better welcome.

After the troubles with the censor over the *Maid of Orleans* there was a conflict with the directors of the theatre: cuts and alterations were demanded, and some of the singers did not like their roles or each other. The newspapers took it upon themselves to forecast disaster, a prophecy which may have contributed to its own fulfilment. There was also an unpleasant press insinuation that the composer had an interested motive in dedicating the opera to the man who conducted it, his friend Napravnik, and this, though absurd, was hurtful to Tchaikovsky.

The first-night audience treated Tchaikovsky as the star, and gave him twenty-four curtain calls. The critics trounced the opera, and the Marinsky Theatre dropped it from the repertoire. He dropped it from his mind. By the summer of the following year he was already composing *Mazeppa*—while reading the proofs of his ten-volume edition of Bortniansky.

Among Tchaikovsky's interesting encounters around this time was his meeting with seventy-year-old Franz Liszt in Rome, when the old man was honoured at a birthday concert of his works in December 1881. The Italians' display of enthusiasm was touching, Tchaikovsky said, but the performance was poor and the music shallow.

It was his first contact with Liszt since that occasion, five years before, when they had met in Bayreuth. He regarded Liszt as 'an old hypocrite', who could not be relied upon for sincere criticism, but only for flattery.

Tchaikovsky worked slowly on *Mazeppa* and without his usual mad fervour and sense of inspiration. Other works of his were meanwhile being well received. Tannaev played the *Piano Concerto in G major* at a concert in Moscow and Anton Rubinstein conducted a performance of the *Serenade for Strings*. Rubinstein, usually

The Tchaikovsky Museum at Klin

The drawing-room in the museum

Tchaikovsky in 1891, photographed during his only visit to New York

silent about Tchaikovsky's music, said this work was his best composition—a typical Rubinstein judgment! In Prague the *Maid of Orleans* was given a hearing.

How firmly Tchaikovsky was now established as *a*, or even *the*, national composer is shown by the fact that he was officially commissioned to write both a *Coronation March* and a cantata, *Moscow*, for the coronation of the Tsar. He was in Paris when he finished the cantata. To his consternation it went astray in the post, but turned up in time for the performance.

Tchaikovsky had by then returned to Russia, but he was not present when his works were played. Alexander III showed his appreciation of these works by sending a diamond ring to Tchaikovsky, who pawned it as promptly as he had sold the gold and turquoise studs given him by the previous ruler. He managed to lose both the pawn-ticket and the money, almost immediately.

These actions are like a text-book illustration of Freud's psychopathology of everyday life. Two years earlier Tchaikovsky, finding himself in desperate money difficulties, had written to the Tsar asking for help, although he regretted the act as soon as his servant had posted the letter, and he told none of his friends what he had done. The Tsar sent him 3,000 roubles as a gift. The *Coronation March* was the outcome of his 'mingled feeling of shame and gratitude', says his brother. Tchaikovsky told Jurgenson the story, under pledge of secrecy, when declining payment for the *March*.

The underlying motive for his first pawning the ring and then losing the proceeds is obvious, and is probably also the reason for his not going to hear his work performed.

A cloud hung around Tchaikovsky's head all the time that he was composing *Mazeppa*. Never had any important work given him so much trouble. 'Perhaps it is the decadence of my powers—or have I become more severe in self-judgment?' he wondered. He felt that he was a changed man since the days when he could write music as the fish swims, as the bird flies, by the laws of nature, feeling no strain or uncertainty.

This view of his former self was nevertheless an illusion, as has been sufficiently demonstrated: his first symphony was born in strain and anguish, to look no further.

In *Mazeppa*, Tchaikovsky chose to adhere to Pushkin's picture of a cunning freebooter, rather than feed the popular appetite with heroics about the legendary chieftain tied to a horse and borne from Poland to the Ukraine. For this opera the skies were threatening all the way: delays and difficulties in the composing of it, trouble over the amount of royalties: a squabble with Jurgenson, whom Tchaikovsky accused of exploiting him: refusal at first of the percentage he demanded from the state theatres, though this was eventually paid; a production in Moscow that, though lavish, seemed to him bad. Yet Tchaikovsky had the rare and flattering experience of having this same new opera staged by two different companies, in the principal theatres of Moscow and St. Petersburg, within a week of each other.

He was in a state of fear and almost hysteria when *Mazeppa* was played at the Bolshoi, before the glittering audience which his name now sufficed to ensure. Again, as for the *Maid of Orleans*, he himself was cheered and applauded and recalled to the stage many times. But he no longer believed in his opera and, sickened by this idolatry, he fled in panic from Moscow the next day, as if he himself were tied to a wild horse. Tchaikovsky missed, of course, the first performance of his *Second Orchestral Suite*—completed when his composing 'fever' returned, as it did when he had finished *Mazeppa*. He had played a piano transcription of it to a few of his friends and they had listened with genuine pleasure. The same was true of the public performance, but when a clamorous audience called for him he was in the train on the way to Smolensk, en route for Berlin and Paris.

Mazeppa, once the first-night ecstasies and excesses had blown away, was manifestly another operatic failure. This was perceived in both cities, Moscow and St. Petersburg. Jurgenson wrote to the composer, breaking through the web of kindly lies woven by his friends, and told him it had gone down badly in the northern capital: Tchaikovsky himself ought to have been there, to give it a fillip by his presence. This candid letter struck Tchaikovsky like a thunderbolt, he said. At his age, 'when one has nothing more to hope from the future' (he was forty-three), a small failure could seem like a great fiasco. He knew that if he could have overcome his nerves and forced himself to go to St. Petersburg to please the first-nighters, he would probably have returned crowned with laurels.

After some desultory theatre-going in France, Tchaikovsky returned to St. Petersburg to be presented to the Tsar, who was giving his patronage to *Onegin*, and was to confer a decoration on its composer. The ceremony took place at the palace of Gatchina, and the honour consisted of the Order of St. Vladimir, Fourth Class. Tchaikovsky calmed his nerves with bromides for this trying occasion. He found the Tsar charming and the Tsarina bewitching: the monarch's manner was extremely friendly and sympathetic. It was not to remain so.

In January 1884, Tchaikovsky and Mme. von Meck became 'united' by the marriage of Anna Davidova and Nikolai von Meck in St. Petersburg. Tchaikovsky was there, but Mme. von Meck stayed away to avoid the tabooed encounter. The two had planned this match when the young couple had scarcely even heard of each other. Natasha, their first nominee, had other ideas; Anna proved more pliable.

Spring came and Tchaikovsky went to Kamenka. He and his manservant occupied a small house on the estate, but he ate with the Davidov family at the big house. There were many relations there, old and young. Sasha had become a sick woman. There were dull, sad days: due, Tchaikovsky thought, to the presence of Vera, who seemed to be still hopelessly in love with him. He was irritated by her attentions and bored by her chatter and began to avoid her when she suggested they should take a walk together.

He alternated between bouts of composing and wondering whether he was played out; between cheerful horseplay with the children and bursts of unreasonable anger, caused in part by dyspepsia; between Bible-reading and losing at cards.

The struggle with his homosexual impulses finds expression in his diary: 'There was much Z: O, what a monster I am!' . . . 'I was extremely irritable and angry, not on account of the game, but Z was torturing me!' . . . 'Z torments me unusually today!' and 'Was very tortured not by the sensation Z itself but by the fact that it is in me.'

The happiest hours of this holiday were spent with Sasha's son who led his uncle into some undignified pastimes, such as walking on stilts, leaping games, and roof-climbing. 'Ran around the pole, the game of "giant's stride" with Alesha (Sofronov) and Bobyk—he will finally drive me simply crazy with his indescribable fascination,' says one entry. 'Picked lilies-of-the-valley with Bobyk' . . . 'Sat on the roof with Bobyk—where would I not climb for the sake of that angel!' . . . 'Was about to sit down to work after tea, but Bobyk lured me away with his stilts. Following a despairing day, clouds suddenly began to gather; however nothing or almost nothing happened. Went out several times looking for Bobyk. As soon as I do not work or walk (and that is also work for me) I begin to crave Bobyk and get lonely without him. Frightful, how I love him.'

Tchaikovsky played quadrilles on themes given him by the young boy, read Gogol to him, watched him build with blocks, talked with him about school. Best of all were their *moments musicaux*: 'played duets with my darling, the incomparable, enchanting, ideal Bobyk, to his immense enjoyment.'

Bobyk fell off the stilts and broke the skin of his knee: his anxious uncle sent for the doctor. Bobyk tumbled off a horse: Tchaikovsky furiously blamed another boy, the 'intolerable' Mitya, whose clowning he said was responsible.

Sometimes Bobyk visited him at his house on the estate, and Tchaikovsky was happy to put his work aside for the boy's company. He writes: 'was inseparable for about two hours in the afternoon from my marvellous, incomparable Bobyk; at first he lounged about on the porch, on the bench, and was fascinatingly relaxed; and chattered about my works. . . . Then he sat in my room and made me play.'

During the spring holiday Tchaikovsky had the first idea for his *Fantasy for Piano and Orchestra*, and 'sowed the seeds', as he put it, of his *Third Suite for Orchestra*. He made great strides with it before he left Kamenka that summer and thought very highly of it. He played endless games of three-handed whist but became steadily more bored in the process: he was embarrassed if he won and annoyed if he lost. As usual, he walked a great deal. He also took English lessons and read music-proofs, and kept up his enormous correspondence. He was restless, unwell, and impatient of disorder or any interference with his set habits. Once more, he thought about acquiring an estate of his own. A particular one was discussed, but proved too dear. The idea was prompted by the fact that Sasha's husband was helping the newly married Nikolai von Meck to buy a home.

On the eve of his birthday, Tchaikovsky sat down an hour before midnight and passed judgment on himself:

'Eleven o'clock. Soon I shall be forty-four years old. How long I have lived and—truthfully, without false modesty—how little accomplished! Even in my present occupation there is nothing, I swear, that is *perfect* and *exemplary*. I am still searching, doubting, wavering. And in other things? I read nothing, know nothing. I spend no end of precious time on whist: I am sure that my health will not benefit from it. Today I was so angry, so exasperated, that in another moment I imagine I would have created an ugly scene and done harm. I was angry a good deal today, in fact, and the time of calm, quiet living, unperturbed by anything, is over. There is much excitement; much that goes against me; much that a madman of my age cannot endure with indifference.

'Yes, it is time to live *in my own home* and *in my own way*.'

Still, when June came on, Tchaikovsky noted: 'a strange thing: am terribly reluctant to go away from here. I think it's all on account of Bobyk.' The boy had become a substitute son for him.

That year Tchaikovsky, despite protestations about wanting to forget the past and caring little for auld acquaintance, gave time and help to two friends of former days, now both sick men. One was Laroche, to whom he read aloud, and at whose dictation he took down a long critique on Mozart: he thought Laroche's mind decidedly impaired, though he staunchly maintained that there was still no better musical critic in Russia. The other afflicted friend was Kotek, now twenty-nine, who was consumptive. Tchaikovsky went to Switzerland to see him, and arranged to make him an allowance for his requirements. This commitment did not last long, as the young man died little more than a month later.

Modest Tchaikovsky was now becoming established as a dramatist and in an enjoyable reversal of roles the composer went as guest to the first night of one of his brother's works in Moscow: a play entitled *Lizaveta Nikolaievna.* He had had that pleasure before, when Modest's comedy *The Benefactor* was staged in St. Petersburg. Modest was later the librettist of Tchaikovsky's *Queen of Spades* and *Iolanthe,* as well as of operas by Arensky, Rachmaninoff and others.

A month later, Modest went to the first performance of his brother's *Third Suite,* and recorded that it was a great triumph for the composer. Hans von Bülow, touring Russia, conducted, the interpretation was masterly, and Tchaikovsky himself felt that for once the whole audience was carried away. 'Such moments are the finest ornaments of an artist's life,' he said. A fortnight earlier, correcting the parts, he had had to shut himself up for days with the work, and did it with anger and resentment; but all the labour was paid for by the marvellous success which crowned it.

A new honour came to Tchaikovsky—he was elected to the directorate of the Musical Society. Once installed, he set about securing the appointment of Tannaev as head of the Moscow Conservatory—Nikolai Rubinstein's old post. He threatened to resign if it was given to anybody else; and Tannaev was appointed, filling the position for five years.

With middle age, majestic achievement, and the world's acclaim, Tchaikovsky became no more emotionally stable and no more worldly minded than he had ever been. He had an innate, unconscious personal dignity, unaltered by age or circumstance; he never became smug or self-satisfied. He still had his nervous crises and his terrors, though no longer to the point of breakdown, and still had the same resilience, which enabled him to come up for a fresh attack on a problem like operatic form, immediately after a defeat.

Underneath the surface of his mind, and it was a civilised and fascinating surface, was the old dissatisfaction, the constant unhappiness; even, in Modest's opinion, a secret despair, which made it impossible for him to settle contentedly anywhere, much as he longed to do so. But at least it was the romantic despair that makes music of its sorrow, not the dull despair of the realist that can make nothing at all.

Fighting within him against the unconquerable restlessness was the strong desire to have a house in the country, to live alone and at peace with his music. The impulse was very much akin to that of Yeats when he acquired his famous tower at Thoor Ballylee to end his days in—and used it for only a few summers, though he lived a score of years longer. The poet too wanted to settle but was driven to wander, although he had by no means the unquiet spirit of Tchaikovsky.

Tchaikovsky did not dream of towers, but wanted a small house, not too new, with a garden, rather than an estate. It must be detached, and not one of a row. He would like it to be close to a stream, a forest—and a railway station, for he knew he would often want to get quickly to the city.

Mme. von Meck was sympathetic to his wishes, but being herself a businesswoman and knowing Tchaikovsky's character, she advised him to be a tenant, not a landlord: property-owning was very troublesome, she said.

He followed this advice, and at the beginning of 1886 he rented the house he had been looking for. It was at Maidanovo near Klin, a district which had the desired streams and woods, and good train services to Moscow and St. Petersburg. He agreed to pay a thousand roubles a year for the house. The village, on the Sestra River, was pleasant though new houses were springing up thereabouts. He left it to Alexei to engage servants and prepare the place for his coming, and apparently he never saw the inside of the house or its furnishings until he moved in. He relied on Alexei's assurances that it was splendidly appointed, and was surprised to find that Alexei's taste differed from his own. However, in spite of its vulgarity, he placidly accepted it, and grew quite house-proud, in his own way.

Tchaikovsky had a dog named Top and taught it tricks. He strolled in his frozen garden and looked through drooping pince-nez at the glittering woodlands. He wrote in his diary, after asking God's blessing on him in his new home: 'How much there is yet to be done! how much to be read! how much to learn! I am terribly reluctant to die as yet, even though at times I imagine that I have lived, O so long.'

On his gate he placed a notice announcing that he was not at home to visitors except on Mondays and Thursdays between three and five in the afternoon. 'Please do not ring.'

In this fashion began the legend of 'the Hermit of Klin'.

CHAPTER XII

THE LAUREL YEARS

IN his new-found solitude Tchaikovsky worked on two compositions: his symphony *Manfred*, always very much neglected, and his opera *The Sorceress*, even more so.

The programme for *Manfred* had been offered to Tchaikovsky more than three years before by Balakirev, to whom he owed the idea for *Romeo and Juliet*; but he had dismissed it as uninspiring to him. The programme had existed much longer than that, as Balakirev had given it to Berlioz in 1868 and he, too, had turned it down. Meanwhile Balakirev had become something of a hermit himself, but from motives of religious mysticism, not for Tchaikovsky's reasons.

It is a curious chain of events: Balakirev emerged from his retirement, sought out Tchaikovsky, and produced the *Manfred* scheme which had lain unwanted for years. Tchaikovsky, consciously, rejected it but must have unconsciously accepted it and brooded on it in secret. Then Tchaikovsky went into his own kind of retreat, and wrote the massive *Manfred* symphony. He found it uniquely absorbing—'sometimes it wears me out completely'. It cost him, he said, a whole year of his life.

Before becoming wholly engaged on the new symphony and opera, he extensively revised *Vakoula the Smith* and retitled it *Cherevichki*, or *The Little Shoes*: it was later renamed once more, becoming *Oxana's Caprices*. In its revised form it had quite a long survival, having risen, as he put it, from the river of oblivion. He discarded whole scenes, wrote new ones to replace them, and afterwards had to seek the permission of the original librettist, Polonsky, for these alterations, before publishing the score. By the late spring he was in Moscow discussing a production, and the new director of the opera-house, Vsevolozhsky, promised that it would be staged with the utmost magnificence, with faithful reconstructions of imperial palace interiors.

At Maidanovo, Tchaikovsky meanwhile began to take an interest in the life of the village. He consulted the local priest about the founding of a school and pledged the necessary finance if authority could be obtained for such an undertaking. The priest wrote to the Government and secured permission and Tchaikovsky supported the school with an annual contribution for the rest of his life. He attended the opening and occasionally looked in to see the children at their work. It would perhaps be unkind to connect this piece of philanthropy with the fact that Tchaikovsky was so persecuted and pestered for money by the lawless, unschooled boys of the neighbourhood that he was sometimes afraid to go walking. There were men and women beggars too, of all ages, and the word had doubtless gone round among them that the rich musician at the manor-house was soft, and would seldom refuse to give money.

'Walked to the river,' says one entry in his diary, 'through Praslovo (on the side, being afraid of the boys).'

Sometimes it was all fun and laughter, with the children dancing attendance on him and Tchaikovsky gaily scattering his small change like giving crumbs to the birds, in buying himself the needful peace for a walk in which he could work out some new musical theme. But the bigger and rougher boys could turn into birds of prey if their demands were not met, and in his defeated, dispirited moods they were more than he could stand.

The countryside gave him infinite pleasure. He had always said that nothing made him happier than country solitude. On a typical day of his life at Maidanovo, Tchaikovsky would rise between seven and eight in the morning and spend part of the morning at the piano, working over the notes of the previous day or starting some fresh composition. Then he would turn to the correcting of proofs.

He kept a regular timetable. Lunch was at one o'clock sharp, and after it a two-hour walk. Boys might scare him but the weather did not, however bad it might be. He was annoyed with himself if he arrived home even a few minutes before the two hours were up; he believed fervently in the value of the walking habit for his health.

On these walks Tchaikovsky always carried a notebook, and as his eyes took pleasure in the familiar but ever-changing pattern of fields, trees, and skies, his inner ear was listening to his own new-born music. As musical ideas and constructions evolved in him, he made rapid notes.

After his first breakdown twenty years earlier, he had ceased to work at night. He would spend the lonely evenings playing the piano or reading. When there was no visitor he would sometimes play patience.

As for his meals, there was no shortage of wine in Tchaikovsky's house, but he was reputed to be indifferent about the quantity of the food and the quality of the cooking. When he had guests, he is said to have sent compliments to the cook while his friends, who were still hungry, exchanged indignant glances!

Bedtime for Tchaikovsky was eleven o'clock, unless some rare guest induced him to stay up a little later. When Kashkin and Laroche came to see him, they would read aloud to one another.

Tchaikovsky's tastes in reading extended to history, philosophy, poetry and drama, as well as fiction. He learned enough English to read some of our classics in the original. These do not seem to have included Byron, in spite of his musical dealings with Byron's themes—*Don Juan*, *Mazeppa*, *Manfred*.

The works of Shakespeare, Dickens, Thackeray, and George Eliot came his way: he extolled their genius without allowing them to soften his hostile judgment of England and the English—because of Disraeli's skilful diplomacy at Russia's expense. He loved de Maupassant, but thought Zola obscene and abominable; it was the conventional opinion of the time. He always read, by his own admission, with 'feverish haste', as if afraid the book would be snatched from his hands, and the consequence was that although often much moved, he tended to forget what he had read as quickly as he had imbibed it. He admired Chekhov, who dedicated a volume of short stories to him and hoped to write a libretto for him, but of course never did. They met in 1889. 'A great man,' Chekhov said.

As a librettist Tchaikovsky treated his poets with scant respect, pulling the verses about on a procrustean bed to fit his musical requirements. His attitude is defensible; but he never in fact gave poetry its due, though he could weep and sigh over it: to him it was always an inferior art to his own: an effort to achieve music through the wrong medium, so to speak.

The libretto was really one of the drawbacks of opera to Tchaikovsky, a regrettable necessity. He felt much the same about symphonic programmes, in spite of the fact that so much of his work is in fact programme music.

From his Maidanovo solitude he wrote to Tannaev in June 1885 that he had made up his mind to compose *Manfred* after some hesitation, as his conscience insisted that he should fulfil a rash promise to Balakirev. 'It is a thousand times pleasanter to compose without any programme,' he said, and added the curious remark: 'When I write a programme symphony I always feel I am not paying in sterling coin but in worthless paper money.'

Balakirev, in proposing the subject to Tchaikovsky, said he could not write the symphony himself as the subject matter did not harmonise with his personal moods. He then struck his customary note of condescension: 'Your *Francesca* gave me the idea that you were capable of treating this subject brilliantly, providing you took great pains, subjected your work to stringent criticism, let your imagination fully ripen and did not hurry.'

He set out the programme, roughly that of Byron's poem, and

also laid down the key scheme for each movement—something he had not been so bold as to offer Berlioz fourteen years earlier. In the first movement, Manfred, wandering in the Alps under the burden of his sins and hopeless longings, is trying in vain to forget his lost love, Astarte. In the second he summons up a spirit—Byron's witch becomes a fairy here. The third movement depicts the simple free life of the mountain dwellers. The fourth movement is an orgy in the infernal palace of Arimanes. The shade of Astarte brings pardon to Manfred before he dies—a sentimentalising of Byron's poem, in which Manfred defies the fiends to destroy him and claims the right to be his own destroyer, dying unpardoned.

A long and difficult work, *Manfred* contains some of Tchaikovsky's finest symphonic writing, notably the pastoral music in the third movement. The symphony itself is scored for the largest orchestral assembly Tchaikovsky ever employed: three flutes (alternating with piccolo), two oboes, English horn, two clarinets, bass clarinet, three bassoons, four horns, two trumpets, two cornets, three trombones, tuba, three tympani, cymbals, bell, tambourines, triangle, bass drum, gong, two harps, and harmonium. The bell, which has a small but important role, 'should be of medium size and preferably not in the concert hall but in an adjacent room,' Tchaikovsky instructed.

When it was finished, the composer told his publisher that whatever the obstacles he was determined to see it brought out and performed without delay, as he regarded it as one of his very best works ('my best', he told his brother). He said candidly to Jurgenson: 'Even were *Manfred* a work of the greatest genius, it would still remain a symphony which on account of its unusual intricacy and difficulty would be played only once in ten years. This work therefore cannot bring any profit either to you or Mackar (his French publisher). On the other hand, I value it highly.'

A few hundred roubles would not compensate him for his labour, he said; but he knew Jurgenson was not rich, and he felt gratitude towards Mackar, who he knew could not have made much out of his works in France. He had therefore decided to claim nothing for *Manfred* from either of them. It is the kind of gesture that publishers scarcely expect from writers and composers; but it was characteristic of Tchaikovsky, and has the pleasant stamp of a less commercial age than ours.

Manfred was first performed in March 1866, and Tchaikovsky spent ten days in Moscow, attending both the rehearsals and the concert. The performance entirely satisfied him, but the audience did not, although they gave him an ovation. He thought their response to the music was unintelligent and chilly.

Press notices were terse and few, until *Manfred* was given in St.

Petersburg nine months later, when Cui praised it lavishly. The symphony also won a prize of 500 roubles given by an anonymous donor for the best new work of the season.

Tchaikovsky had seldom written a work which left him more exhausted: none perhaps since his first symphony. He said it would be played once or twice and then disappear, and his sad prediction came true. Kept in currency during his lifetime, *Manfred* not long afterwards drifted into that limbo of the respected but seldom-performed where so much great music lies. It was revived in Britain by the B.B.C. Symphony Orchestra in 1952.

He had his usual reaction against his creation, after admiring it above all the rest. Three years after he composed it he found everything about it except the first movement 'repulsive', and told the Grand Duke Constantine that he intended to throw away the last three movements and convert the work into a symphonic poem. Later he abandoned this plan and became reconciled to the composition. This was a normal pendulum-action in his feelings towards his later offspring. In his earlier days there was often simple repudiation without reconciliation.

One change in Tchaikovsky may be noted here: a change that roughly dates from his settling in the country as the Hermit of Klin. He had grown reserved about his work, no longer showed it to anyone before completion or discussed how it should be done. No longer surrounded daily by an intimate circle of musicians whose opinions he valued, he 'strove with none, for none was worth his strife', and sought nobody's encouragement. *Manfred* is a case in point. What he had undertaken he did, and with much toil; he kept Mme. von Meck and others informed of his progress; but it was no longer a question of culling advice. He stood alone.

No sooner was the first performance of *Manfred* over than the restless Hermit was off on his travels again. The excuse was a visit to his brother Hippolyte, in the Caucasus. He went to Tiflis, then by sea to Trebizond, on to Constantinople and thence to Marseilles. He was stalked on the voyage by some oddities and bores—a Frenchman who made him read a treatise on a complicated piano he had invented, a Turk whose boots squeaked 'mercilessly', and an Englishman who pestered him to know which of Tosti's songs he liked best. (He might justifiably have replied: '*Good-bye!*')

Tchaikovsky was aroused at 2 a.m. to watch Etna in eruption, and again at 5 a.m. to stand on the captain's bridge and see the sunrise.

He had chosen a ship which did not touch Italy because cholera was raging in Naples, otherwise he would have traversed Italy by train to make for Paris, where friends and admirers awaited him: Fauré, whom he particularly liked, Marmontel, Lalo, Ambroise Thomas, Delibes and others. His happiest hour in Paris was breakfast with Pauline Viardot-Garcia, the famous mezzo-soprano, who had been Desirée Artôt's teacher, and reputed to be Turgenev's mistress. Tchaikovsky said that though seventy, she looked only forty. Actually she was a sprightly sixty-five. She possessed the original score of Mozart's *Don Giovanni*, which her husband had acquired cheaply and by chance thirty years before. To handle it was for Tchaikovsky a moment of communion with the godhead of music: 'I felt as though I had pressed Mozart's hand.'

More surprising to him than the warmth of his welcome in Paris was what occurred in Tiflis. He found there a devoted interpreter of his music, Ippolitov-Ivanov, director of the music-school and conductor of the local orchestra, an authority on Caucasian and Georgian music, who had arranged a concert of his works in honour of his visit. It proved as great a triumph as any gaudy night of Moscow or Petersburg. A supper and presentation ceremony followed the performance, and Tchaikovsky was crowned with a silver wreath and laden with silver gifts. 'There were endless cheers. I had never experienced anything like it before,' he said. It revealed to him what to that very moment he had doubted—that the great mass public of Russia had begun to know his work and to love it. At last, at last, he could believe it.

The trip had its longeurs and its excitements. One day Tchaikovsky confided to his diary that he had fallen completely in love with a young princess and afterwards got drunk with a German consul. Another day he was captivated by a young Russian officer who inspired 'an unusual feeling', but who was over-demonstrative. There was a good deal of whist playing, sight-seeing, heavy eating, and leisurely drinking: there were operas and headaches, jokes and arguments, a visit to the circus, parties, 'everlasting cotillions'; and a send-off from Tiflis by an enormous crowd, who threw flowers into Tchaikovsky's carriage as the train pulled out. So crammed and yet so spacious a time it seems, in retrospect.

There may have been more than a mere momentary attraction for the young artillery officer Verinovsky, whose display of affection embarrassed Tchaikovsky. Back at Maidanovo in July, the composer learned that Verinovsky, having failed a military examination, had shot himself. He wept violently and thrust aside his work. He felt physically ill. That evening a fortunate chance brought his old friend Kashkin to the door. They drank together, and Kashkin's calm cheerfulness drew him back from the pit of gloom that was always waiting to engulf him.

In these years, so much nearer the end of his life than he or anyone else could possibly have guessed, he reflected a great deal on the lessons of fame, death, and the frailty of material things.

To his cousin, Anna Merkling, he wrote that he had no wish to die, and indeed wanted to live to a ripe age, sixty or seventy, if he were still sound in mind and body, but he would not like to have his youth back and go through life again. 'Once is enough!' he said.

'No one feels more keenly the emptiness and brevity of life, but I do not wish to be young again. . . .'

One ought not to fear death, he added, but he was not sufficiently religious to regard it as the beginning of a new life, nor philosophical enough to be satisfied with the prospect of annihilation. 'I envy no one so much as the religious man.' The fervour of a few years earlier, which followed the deaths of Rubinstein and of Tchaikovsky's father, had guttered down to this.

On the question of fame, and the impossibility of knowing what works would endure, Tchaikovsky meditated earnestly. A story concerning Brahms made him laugh: when these questions were being discussed, Brahms remarked, 'Yes, immortality is a fine thing —if one only knew how long it would last!'

Mme. von Meck was curious to hear what fame meant to Tchaikovsky and for a reply she received a remarkable outburst. He began calmly enough reasoning that the artist could not help but wish his product to be widely known and loved; fame in this sense being the aim of all that was most serious in his work. But, he went on with a rising note of consternation, 'when I begin to reflect that with an increasing audience will come also an increase of interest in my personality, in the more intimate sense; that there will be inquisitive people among the public who will tear aside the curtain behind which I have striven to conceal my private life: then I am filled with fear and disgust, so that I half wish to keep silence for ever, in order to be left in peace'. He protested that his conscience was clear, but it was sad and terrible that someone might try to force open the inner world of his thoughts and feelings, 'which all my life I have guarded so carefully from outsiders'.

Words like these must send a guilty shiver down the spine of a biographer, for what is he doing but tearing down that same curtain? The only defence is that men of genius belong to mankind, that no earthly fault can stain their quality, that they deserve too well of us to be curtained with false delicacy, and that 'when all treasures are tried, Truth is the best'.

But this dread of unveiling, of which he speaks with so much freedom and feeling to Mme. von Meck, was, intermittently, very strong in Tchaikovsky and had one regrettable result nearly twelve years after he had written as he did. In his country home, one day in 1891, he experienced, according to Modest, an onrush of panic at the thought that he might suddenly drop dead, without time to put his affairs in order. In this moment of alarm, he gathered and burned his secret diaries. This may have been the whole explanation, unless his action was also prompted by some new episode in his secret life which he was afraid might become known to all.

For twenty years he had committed details of his thoughts and activities to his notebooks. Those that remain after the bonfire are of the greatest interest and paint a very human picture of him. The destruction of the rest of them seems a deplorable burnt offering of truth on the altar of respectability, almost as bad as the destruction of Byron's letters and Turner's 'improper' drawings. The obvious difference is that those were the acts of others, not of the artists themselves, while Tchaikovsky sentenced his own writings to death. One may concede that he had a perfect right to do so; and can only sigh that he thought it necessary. It is not unlikely that associated with this fear of scandal was a strong desire to protect, too, the reputation of others.

Since the diaries he did not destroy contain many tell-tale turns of phrase, eloquent to even the most unsophisticated reader, Tchaikovsky cannot have imagined, if he thought about it rationally, that posterity would never learn of his inversion. His name was from time to time 'breathed upon'; and there were consequences, such as an otherwise inexplicable change of attitude on the part of the Tsar. Tchaikovsky was surprised and gratified at his sovereign's cordiality around the time of the coronation, and he had been able to ask for and receive money from him when in need. But he was no less surprised at the difference when he was again received in 1888 at the height of his own fame. The Tsar was formally polite but now all personal warmth had gone. To Tchaikovsky's kind of sensibility the coldness was disconcerting. Nor was it a passing mood or caprice. Two years later, the court patronised the first performance of the *Sleeping Beauty*. The Tsar's cool comment, 'very charming', and his failure to show any sign of enthusiasm set the note for the audience as a whole, and the ballet was given a tepid send-off. Tchaikovsky wrote, 'His Majesty treated me in a most offhand manner—God be with him.'

The likeliest cause for the Tsar's change from personal benevolence to reluctant patronage of the man who had become his subjects' favourite composer, is some whiff of brimstone from his private life.

Tchaikovsky's health in the late eighteen-eighties was far from good. He had liver trouble (he admitted he was drinking rather heavily) and tried after the fashion of the time to remedy it by taking the waters, rather than by temperance. He was still liable to nerve torments, indigestion, bouts of weakness and sometimes vomiting, and he also suffered increasingly from eye-strain. But his life remained as full, and he as exhaustingly active, as ever.

He achieved an important self-conquest in 1887 when he took up the conductor's baton again for the launching of the revised version of his opera *The Little Shoes*. A cloud of troubles gathered: the prima donna fell ill and a substitute had to be found just in time for the first night; news that his beautiful niece Tatiana Davidova, the morphine addict, had dropped dead at a masked ball in St. Petersburg dejected him. He had fierce nervous headaches and suffered so severely that before the first rehearsal he decided more than once to abandon the attempt to conduct. But when the time came, he forced himself to the music-stand, made a little speech to the musicians, and 'began very bravely to brandish the stick'. He was warmly praised. Soon afterwards he conducted no less successfully on the concert platform—after an attack of hysterics.

The Sorceress, produced in the autumn of that year, was no spell-binder with its audiences and the St. Petersburg critics fell upon it with malice and ill-will, according to the composer.

Writing it off as a failure, he was soon on his travels again, now conducting his own works with confidence and success in Prague, Paris, London.

Most of the London critics were cordial to him on this visit of March 1888. He was dissatisfied with the acoustics of the St. James's Hall, where his works were performed—'something was lacking,' he said.

London musicians were as a matter of fact very proud of the acoustics of this imposing and uncomfortable hall. It no longer exists, but it was at the time the greatest concert hall in the country, and had splendid artistic associations. But possibly there crept in some vagrant sounds from the cellarage: for directly under the platform where Tchaikovsky conducted there was a smaller hall occupied by the Christy Minstrels.

The St. James's Hall was built in 1858 on the site now occupied by the Piccadilly Hotel. The estimated cost of £23,000 shot up to £70,000 because the builders ran into a forgotten quicksand, and enormous quantities of concrete had to be poured in. Most of the money was provided by Tom Chappell, head of the music publishing firm, and St. James's had nearly half a century of glory. Its main hall seated 2,500 people, there were two smaller halls and various banquet rooms. But rivals sprang up, the Albert Hall in 1871 and the Queen's in 1893, and the St. James's was pulled down in 1905.

Most of Tchaikovsky's notes on his first London visit are gloomy: he had toothache and felt generally out of sorts, the fire smoked, he could not find the lavatory at his hotel, he was pestered in the

Strand, he slept badly at night and was drowsy or bored by day. He was pleased with his conducting, however, and recorded that the *Serenade for Strings* was a big success, the Theme and Variations from the *Third Suite* less so. Next day he ate 'unwisely' at Gatti's, in consequence of which he stayed an extra twenty-four hours in London, and saw Coquelin, whom he thought marvellous.

A year later he went to London again: a happier trip, but with the weather living up to its continental reputation. He crossed on 'the marvellous steamship *Folkestone*', but his travelling companion, a pianist protégé named Vasya Sapelnikov, aged twenty, was sea-sick. They had a pleasant reception on their arrival; then 'playful talk. Rain. Strolling.' That evening they went to the home of Francesco Berger, secretary of the Philharmonic Society. The diary entry closes: 'Home. Drunkenness in private.'

Next day: 'Rehearsal. *Extraordinary fog*, like night. I lunched alone. Strolled during darkness and rain. Home. Dinner with Vasya. We strolled along the Strand.'

Tchaikovsky was perturbed to find the musicians 'very cold' at rehearsal, yet all went well at the concert. He conducted his *First Suite* and *First Piano Concerto*, with Sapelnikov as soloist. Vasya, he wrote, 'had a huge success. A lot of people came to the artist's room.' No word as to his own reception.

He left for Paris the next day: 'Kissed sleeping Vasya and departed.' Never since Kotek's day had he cared for anyone so much as he did for the gentle Sapelnikov.

Tchaikovsky had changed homes again, moving to Frolovskoye—no great distance, but deeper in the woods and the solitude. The new house was a plain bungalow: again he allowed his man-servant to furnish and prepare it in his absence. He began gardening enthusiastically, and said that the fear of frost, which might kill his seedlings, kept him awake at night.

But a rather worse worry now beset him once more: fear of musical sterility. 'Have I utterly written myself out?' he asked Modest.

A fortnight later he was writing the *Fifth Symphony*.

He started it with difficulty, continued doubtfully, and completed it in four months—with no stronger conviction than that he had not wholly failed. When Tannaev rhapsodised about it, the composer was as surprised as he was delighted.

In the same four summer months he had also written his *Hamlet* Overture, in fulfilment of a promise to the French actor Lucien Guitry (father of Sacha Guitry) who wanted to play the role and had urged him to write the incidental music.

How could Tchaikovsky have failed to realise what he had achieved in the *Fifth*? One is driven back to the concept of the

Tchaikovsky was twelve days dead when Eduard Napravnik conducted the second performance in St. Petersburg of the Sixth Symphony on November 18th, 1893

One of the last photographs taken of the composer

'creative sleep' out of which comes art born in the depths of being. Yet it is a symphony without impenetrable mysteries. The magic is in the melodies and in that orchestral writing, especially for the strings, which no one has ever been able to emulate.

As the classicists used the minuet and gavotte dance rhythms, Tchaikovsky used the contemporary waltz, which he loved, even in sombre passages of symphonic writing. Here, in the *Fifth*, the third movement, in waltz time, is based on *Pimpinella*, the song that was sung to him by the little boy in the streets of Florence.

The leading motif, the Motto theme, announced by the clarinet, recurs in the climax of every movement, even of the third, while in the last Tchaikovsky gathers together all the themes of the symphony; for this work is cyclic, carrying over from movement to movement, instead of observing the classic separation of its parts.

No more need be said about its popularity than that it is one of the half-dozen best known orchestral works in the world.

It was first performed in St. Petersburg and soon afterwards in Prague. Tchaikovsky himself conducted and his *Second Piano Concerto* was also on the programme. He came to the conclusion that the symphony did not really please the public. He himself was certain that his *Fourth* was very much better than the *Fifth*, whih was steadily sinking in his esteem. He even accused himself of insincerity in it, and an excess of colour. Once again he asked 'Am I played out?' And already he was at work on the ballet music for the *Sleeping Beauty*, to a scenario proffered by Ivan Alexandrovich Vsevolozhsky, director of the Russian Imperial theatres.

It was based on Charles Perrault's version of the old fairy-tale. The later version of the title, *The Sleeping Princess*, was given it by Diaghilev when he staged it in London, because he was told that otherwise an unsophisticated section of the English public would think it was a pantomime!

It was only in the last three years of his life, according to Edward Evans, that Tchaikovsky was really recognised as a true master of ballet music. Ten years passed between *Swan Lake* and the proposal that he should compose the *Sleeping Beauty*.

He wrote it in a few weeks, and it was staged, with Petipa's choreography, at the Marinsky Theatre, St. Petersburg, in January 1890. He was promptly asked for another—*Casse Noisette*, on a story by Hoffman, 'The Nutcracker and the King of Mice'. Strangely enough, Tchaikovsky did not care for the idea. But he accepted the commission, completing it in 1892. He thought this enchanting music 'infinitely worse than its predecessors'. Its main interest for him seems to have been the opportunity to introduce the newly invented celesta. He had come across the instrument in Paris, and had asked Jurgenson to import one with due secrecy for fear Rimsky-Korsakov or Glazounov should steal a march on him.

In these years of high fame Tchaikovsky became entangled in the nets of a person whom he designates simply, 'Herr N.', but whose name was actually Dmitri Friedrich and who was merely a pioneer specimen of a modern type—the resourceful publicity agent. Their encounter was a rich bit of comedy, because neither could understand the other's attitude. It is all the more diverting seen through Tchaikovsky's own innocent eyes.

From the first he was confused by the fact that 'Herr N.' called himself a Russian, without qualification, but spoke the language very badly. It was agreed that he should arrange a concert tour for Tchaikovsky, taking in Leipzig, Dresden, Hamburg, Prague, and Copenhagen. Presently the composer discovered that the itinerary was being looped round to take in a succession of small German provincial towns. He refused to carry out this plan, saying that his works would have to be performed by inadequate orchestras in those places, and that he was in any case unknown to the public there. The agent reluctantly yielded.

Tchaikovsky was to meet 'Herr N.' in Berlin at the end of December 1887, and warned him in advance that he wanted a minimum of fuss. 'Herr N.' interpreted, and capitalised, this in his own fashion. He printed and distributed in Berlin a circular announcing that Tchaikovsky would be arriving and saying that he was a very modest man who wished the welcome to be of a friendly and intimate kind. Music-lovers, artists, and fellow-Russians were invited to a breakfast at a well-known restaurant to meet the composer.

Proud of this effort, the agent sent a copy to Tchaikovsky. He wired angrily from St. Petersburg that he would have nothing to do with such an event.

'Herr N.' had also sent his circular to the newspapers, and one of them made hay with it, putting sarcastic query-marks in parentheses after the words 'friends' and 'admirers'.

Tchaikovsky arrived in Berlin and booked in at a hotel, without contacting his agent or anyone else. With his morning tea the waiter brought the daily paper, and there Tchaikovsky found his modesty mocked and the reception plan ridiculed.

Cold with horror and indignation, he stalked out and went to the museum, trembling—he says—for fear of meeting 'Herr N.' or some of the 'numerous friends and admirers'. He imagined all Berlin to be laughing at him. He would have liked to murder 'Herr N.'

He failed to turn up at the breakfast, and did not let the agent know he had arrived until the next day. It was 'Herr N.'s' turn to be puzzled and hurt.

At the interview which at length took place, Tchaikovsky and 'Herr N.' got on surprisingly well together. But throughout their dealings there was a strange alternation of kind and 'hostile' acts on 'Herr N.'s' part, says Tchaikovsky. The hostile ones were undoubtedly 'Herr N.'s' excesses in the young art of personal publicity, new and frightful to the Hermit of Klin. Surely only an enemy could do such things to him? Yet 'Herr N.' seemed well disposed! Brooding on this paradox, Tchaikovsky could only conclude that he was dealing with a peculiarly unreliable sort of eccentric.

In the spring of 1888 Tchaikovsky wrote to Modest: 'I got rid of N. We parted in peace, but my purse was lighter by 500 marks in consequence. I do not regret it in the least. I would have given a great deal more to see the last of him.'

One can see 'Herr N.' shaking his head sadly over his impossible client, the famous man who hates the cultivation of his fame.

In this harvest-home of Tchaikovsky's life, with no winter but death to follow, he met his great musical contemporaries on equal terms: they were eager to see him and to pay homage. In Prague he met Dvorak, who afterwards wrote telling him that *Onegin* had entered his heart so deeply that he could never forget it: he felt transported to another world whenever he heard this wonderful creation.

In Berlin, Tchaikovsky met Desirée Artôt again and saw her every day during his short stay. It was at her house that he met Grieg, whom he described as a short, fragile-looking man with shoulders of unequal height, and the big blue eyes of a child. There was nothing about him to intimidate even a Tchaikovsky, and an immediate sympathy sprang up between them. Tchaikovsky was already very fond of Grieg's music: its northern melancholy, he said, went straight to the heart of a Russian.

He was surprised to notice the close resemblance between Grieg and Mme. Grieg, until he learned that they were cousins as well as husband and wife. They were equally warmhearted and sincere. Mme. Grieg was a singer of talent and a well-informed, cultivated woman, whose conversation disclosed considerable knowledge of Russian literature. But in spite of grey hair and erudition, the Griegs had a childlike air. When Tchaikovsky went with them to a concert in Leipzig, a woman pointed them out to her daughter and was heard to say, 'Look, dear, there is Tchaikovsky with his children.'

Tchaikovsky's meeting with Brahms was a *pas de deux* on thin ice. The trouble was that he had never been able to like or admire

Brahms's music, which he thought 'elevated' but unlovely; and this induced a feeling of constraint when they met. They were entirely polite: Brahms said cordially that he did not like the last movement of Tchaikovsky's *Fifth Symphony*, and Tchaikovsky stated that he was not very fond of Brahms's works, either.

'Brahms is rather a short man, but suggests a sort of amplitude, and possesses a very likeable appearance,' Tchaikovsky wrote afterwards. 'His fine head—almost that of an old man—recalls the type of a handsome, benign, elderly Russian priest. . . . Brahms's manner is very simple and free from vanity, his humour jovial; the few hours spent in his society left an agreeable impression upon me.'

Anton Rubinstein, meeting Brahms when he was a younger man, remarked that he did not know what to make of him: 'He is not graceful enough for the drawing-room, nor fiery enough for the concert-room, nor simple enough for the country, nor social enough for the town.'

Presumably he had ripened as the years increased his fame; Tchaikovsky found no fault with his manners. In his diary covering his visit to Leipzig at the end of December 1887, he wrote however: 'To Brodsky's. Meeting with Brahms, Grieg, Fritzsch, etc. Suffered greatly. Grieg and his wife awfully charming. Brahms' trio. My interference in the performance. . . . Slept abominably.'

The story behind this entry is elucidated by Brahms's biographer, Florence May. The host was Adolf Brodsky, the violinist, and it seems that Frau Brodsky, knowing Tchaikovsky's temperament—and possibly his lack of enthusiasm for Brahms's works—refrained from telling him that there would be other guests to dinner. Tchaikovsky arrived unexpectedly early: in the Brodsky music-room, Brahms's *C minor Trio* was being rehearsed. Frau Brodsky hastened to meet Tchaikovsky in the entrance hall and asked him to go into the music-room. He looked disconcerted, but Brodsky came out to persuade him and took him in to meet Brahms.

He sat down inquiring, 'Shall I disturb you?'

Brahms replied gruffly, 'Not in the least, but why listen? This is not at all interesting.'

Tchaikovsky listened nevertheless, but the rehearsal ended with further embarrassment. Tchaikovsky could not think of a single kind word to say about the trio. He was silent, and the room seemed to be filled with his disapproval.

Grieg and his wife then came in, unaware of the atmosphere, and their smiling ease went far to dissipate it. But not entirely; for when the party sat down to dinner Mme. Grieg herself, sitting between Brahms and Tchaikovsky, felt the electricity and sprang up exclaiming, 'I cannot sit between these two any longer, it makes me so nervous!'

Grieg rose and volunteered to take her place, saying he felt brave enough to do so.

Tchaikovsky's poor opinion of Brahms's music was of long standing. 'I find him dark, cold, pretentious and lacking real profundity,' he said, years before their first meeting; and often repeated the opinion with variations, seeming sometimes to make Brahms his symbol for all that he disliked in German music; all that he wished Russian music to challenge. His most generous remarks were in praise of Brahms's incorruptibility. To resist the temptation to write for the stage required, in Tchaikovsky's view, a heroic soul, such as he himself did not possess: 'only one such hero is alive today—Brahms.' He conceded that Brahms had never sunk below the highest ideals, but added: 'unfortunately, his creative gift is meagre, and unworthy of his aspirations.'

He met one formidable English Brahmsian with whom he got on very well indeed. It was at Brodsky's house in Leipzig, that same Christmas-time, when, as Tchaikovsky and the Brodsky family party were at the tea-table, a frisky setter bounded into the room. Everybody exclaimed, 'This means Miss Smyth will soon be here!'

A few minutes later, in she came—'a tall Englishwoman, not handsome, but having what people call an "expressive" or "intelligent" face,' says Tchaikovsky. He describes Ethel Smyth as one of the comparatively few women composers who can be taken seriously and the creator of several interesting and promising works. She had been in Leipzig some years, studying theory and composition. Presently she and Brodsky played one of her compositions, a violin sonata, and Tchaikovsky much admired it.

'No Englishwoman is without her originalities and eccentricities,' he remarks. Those of Miss Smyth were 'the beautiful dog which was quite inseparable from this lonely woman, and invariably announced her arrival . . . a passion for hunting, on account of which Miss Smyth occasionally returned to England for a time; and finally an almost passionate worship for the intangible musical genius of Brahms.'

Dame Ethel Smyth records that of all the composers she had known, Tchaikovsky was the most delightful: 'a polished, cultivated gentleman and man of the world', in contrast to 'the uncouth, almost brutal manners affected by many German musicians'. The relationship which sprang up between them would have ripened into close friendship if circumstances had favoured it, she says; for he was magnanimous enough to accept without resentment the fact that she had only qualified admiration for his own work.

He tried in vain to break down her Brahms-worship: arguing

by the hour, strumming passages of Brahms on the piano to prove to her that they were hideous; even pretending to believe that she must be under hypnotic influence, since her admiration for 'that awkward pedant' did not square with her otherwise sound musical instincts.

She agreed with him on one point: that her school neglected tone-colour. 'Not one of them can instrumentate,' said Tchaikovsky. 'What happens in ordinary conversation? If you have to do with really live people, listen to the inflections of their voices: there's instrumentation for you!'

Ethel Smyth says, 'I followed his advice on the spot, went to concerts with the sole object of studying orchestral effects, filled notebook after notebook with impressions, and ever since have been at least as much interested in sounds as in sense, considering the two indivisible.'

Around this time, Anton Rubinstein had completed fifty years on the concert platforms of Europe as the world's foremost pianist. A jubilee celebration was planned, and Tchaikovsky was the principal organiser. This was not an easy thing for him: pupil and admirer of Rubinstein though he was, he had been haughtily and sometimes hurtfully treated, or else simply avoided, by his former master. Remarking on this later to an old friend of his youth, Professor Anton Door, Tchaikovsky said, 'Do what I will, I can get no hold on him, he escapes me like an eel.' Professor Door laughed and advised him not to take the great man's ways to heart, explaining: 'Rubinstein, a distinctly lyrical temperament, has never had great success in dramatic music, and avoids everyone who has made a name for himself in this sphere. He cut Richard Wagner, and many others besides.'

However, Rubinstein was flattered by the jubilee tribute, and unbent, temporarily, when he learnt that Tchaikovsky had composed for the occasion a chorus of greeting and a piano impromptu.

The organising had its incidental pleasures, in the course of which Tchaikovsky, with something of the zest of years gone by, sat up late and drank deep with a brilliant company—Rimsky-Korsakov, Liadov, Glazounov.

It was, all in all, a mellow year, and the end of a great decade.

CHAPTER XIII

BETRAYAL

FRESH troubles were soon gathering. Tchaikovsky went to Florence in the new year—complaining, as usual, of homesickness the very day he left Russia—and before the end of the month he was searching the depths of his soul and finding nothing but utter boredom and desolation. Looking into his purse he found it equally empty. Modest wanted to join him but he had to reply that he could not afford to have him as an unpaying guest.

It is astonishing that Tchaikovsky could have found himself in these difficulties at the beginning of 1890, when he was on the crest of the wave. Mme. von Meck was still paying his comfortable pension, his works were being constantly performed in Russia and abroad, he had at last achieved success as a conductor and had toured in triumph in many lands, he was constantly turning out new work, and his publishers were garnering royalties for him. Still more reassuring, the benevolent Vsevolozhsky, of the Imperial theatres, had secured for him a Tsarist pension of 3,000 roubles a year for life.

Yet the fact remains that he had to approach the Musicians' Aid Fund for a loan. There is no obvious explanation of how he had managed to get into such a position, apart from his general style of generosity and improvidence. The upkeep of his home, his removals, and his drinking habits must have run away with a good deal of money, but the expenses of his constant travels are the most likely cause of the crisis.

He was still keeping his wife, and news of her in a letter from Jurgenson, reaching him in Florence, upset him violently. In spite of Tchaikovsky's allowance, which Jurgenson saw to it that she received regularly, she was appealing to well-known people for money. The idea of her causing scandal in this way was torture to Tchaikovsky. 'Like a madman all day. Slept badly. Did no work,' he recorded. He wrote a long reproachful letter to Antonina but never posted it.

A day went by and his mind was no longer filled with thoughts of the mischief Antonina might do him. They were pushed out by a burst of musical ideas for his latest opera, *The Queen of Spades*, on which he had been struggling without passion for nearly three weeks. Now he began to work more in his old way, sometimes 'madly inspired', sometimes bedevilled by considerable difficulties but able, nevertheless, to complete the opera in five months.

Pushkin's story of the young gambler who learns of an old woman said to possess the secret of an infallible winning sequence at cards, and who frightens her to death in trying to extort it from her, is one which Tchaikovsky could well understand: he had experienced the fascination of gambling and its insane extremes of hope and despair. In real life, moreover, he knew a woman who believed she had found an infallible 'system'—Mme. von Meck herself. A truly Russian gambler, she loved all games of chance, but especially roulette, which she played in Germany, Switzerland, Spain and other lands. She told Tchaikovsky in 1878 that after suffering losses at roulette, she had 'studied' the game until she knew how to win without fail, and thereupon recovered all she had lost.

Thus life again gave Tchaikovsky the substance to fill out the shadows of a libretto.

When Vsevolozhsky originally suggested the idea two years before, he had in mind another composer. Modest Tchaikovsky provided the libretto but the plan fell through, and it was then put up to Tchaikovsky, who was absorbed in the *Fifth Symphony*. *The Sorceress* had left the taste of failure in his mouth and he told his brother he would not again attempt an opera unless he found a subject that really set him on fire. He was not at all moved, he said, by the *Queen of Spades*.

The sequence is much the same as with *Manfred* and *Onegin*: Tchaikovsky's first reaction is hostile, but the idea germinates in the dark of his mind, then flowers into enthusiasm. When Vsevolozhsky sounded him again he found him amenable, and therefore urged him to try to complete the *Queen of Spades* in time for the next operatic season.

While composing the scene where the young officer points his pistol at the old Countess and she dies without naming the cards, Tchaikovsky became so emotionally absorbed that he lived in a state of terror for days. He wept when writing Herman's last aria. During this time he felt as if he were actually living in the eighteenth century, the period of his story. It seemed to him impossible that his audience should fail to share the emotions which had so overmastered him, and he was soon confiding to Modest that he really believed he had finally accomplished his masterpiece. There were passages of the piano score which he could not play without bursting into tears.

His confidence that the audiences would respond to his emotion was justified. The first to hear the piano score, among them Kashkin, were deeply impressed, the principal singer was moved to tears, and the first night audience in St. Petersburg, and soon afterwards in Kiev, were taken by storm. This work, at least, did not have to fight its way through any barrier into the public favour which it has ever since enjoyed.

Tchaikovsky wrote the *Queen of Spades* in Florence and the day he finished it he joined the crowds at the Piazzale to watch Buffalo Bill's Wild West show. A diary entry says: 'Unexpectedly 800 francs: from whom, I don't know. Buffalo Bill at lunch. . . .'

His next composition, commissioned, was the *Sextet for Strings*, which he enjoyed writing principally for the technical interest of mastering a form that was new to him. It pleased him so much that he began to transfer his affection to it from the opera, though not for long. After that came summer holidays, and Tchaikovsky looked in at Kamenka, which seemed to him a scene of melancholy decay. He also visited the home of Kolya Konradi, the deaf-and-dumb boy, now twenty-two, and took him on a tour to Kiev, Kharkov, and Tiflis, in the course of which they went to see Tchaikovsky's niece, Anna, and her husband, the son of Mme. von Meck.

In Tiflis that autumn Tchaikovsky conducted a concert of his works. He stayed with Anatol, and it was fortunate that this strong, reliable brother, who had been his prop when his marriage collapsed, was at hand at this time; for Tchaikovsky was to need all the sympathy and support he could get.

Resting and sightseeing after his concert, he was vulnerable, unbraced. Then he received a letter from Mme. von Meck: the last she was ever to write to him. The great friendship was shattered, and nothing remained but dust, bitterness, some shining fragments of memory.

Tchaikovsky scarcely realised the finality of it at first: he sensed it, indeed, but could not believe it. He did not give up trying to salvage something of the friendship until nearly nine months later. Even then, he could not understand it; he never did.

Mme. von Meck's letter said tersely that she had lost her great fortune and she would be unable to send Tchaikovsky any more money whatever from now on. She hoped that now she was poor she would not be entirely forgotten by him. She ended, 'Do not forget, and think of me sometimes': a strange, masochistic note, on which to close their long, spiritual intimacy, which had survived Tchaikovsky's marriage and breakdown and the many other vicissitudes of their two lives!

Tchaikovsky replied the same day. He began with the same endearments they had so often used—'My dear, sweet friend'—and, like a true friend, his first thought was for her, not for himself. It is a singularly delicate letter: he is careful not to say that the loss of her gifts and pension means nothing to him, but he strives at the same time to lessen any guilt or anxiety she may feel about withdrawing them. It would be false, he says, to pretend that so radical a change would make no difference in his budget, but she is not to feel the smallest sorrow on that account: his income has substantially increased in recent years and will probably do so even more. He is sorry for her: she is used to wealth, he cannot imagine her without it, and the thought of her suffering any privation grieves him.

He is sure that her financial loss is not her own fault, and wishes he knew whom to blame for it—but he has no right to pry into her family affairs, he hastily adds, and his indignation can be of no use to her.

'The last words of your letter ("do not forget, and think of me sometimes") hurt me a little, but I tell myself you cannot really have meant them.' The letter goes on: 'Do you think I remember you only when using your money? Can I forget even for an instant everything you have done for me and all that I owe you? Without exaggeration I can say that you saved me and that without your friendship and sympathy I should certainly have gone mad and perished.'

Fervently, Tchaikovsky assures her that he will remember her untill his last breath: a promise which he literally fulfilled, for hers was the name he repeated in his final delirium.

He says he is happy that in the moment when she can no longer share her wealth with him he can freely express his boundless, passionate thankfulness for all she has done for him, the extent of which he is sure from her letter that she herself fails to realise.

'With all the warmth in my heart I kiss your hands,' he writes, and ends: 'Forgive this hasty scrawl—I am too upset to write clearly.'

Tchaikovsky's letter, so loving, so full of courtesy and gentleness, would have brought a remorseful reply from women far less emotional than Mme. von Meck. But she did not answer it, and six months passed without any further communication from her household to Tchaikovsky, who had once been its sun and moon.

Meantime he travelled to Moscow, made some inquiries, and received the full weight of the blow.

Mme. von Meck had not lost her fortune. No privation threatened: she was still the owner of a railway and of great estates.

True, she had had financial losses nine or ten years before, when she had had to sell Brailov, but she had assured him then that his pension was a trifling matter in her huge budget and he could rest assured that she would not dock it. At that time she had not even mentioned her setback until he wrote to inquire, on hearing rumours in Moscow. There were no such rumours now.

She had made an excuse, she had told him a lie, she had cut off both support and correspondence without even giving him the true reason! These were terrible facts. What, then, had their friendship meant? If she could end it thus cruelly, had her heart ever been in it, or had he been merely her pet, her provider of musical satisfaction? Tchaikovsky may have imagined that time would answer such questions for him: he waited patiently for some explanation, but none ever came.

In spite of his reassurances to Mme. von Meck, he was worried at first about the loss of income, as he had found himself getting into a tight corner earlier in the year. He told Jurgenson he expected to have to cut down his scale of living and would probably have to find a salaried job in St. Petersburg, which would be very humiliating. It did not come to that, however, and he suffered no hardship. The *Queen of Spades* was a success, and ballet and opera commissions were awaiting him. The St. Petersburg Conservatory fêted him on the twenty-fifth anniversary of his professional debut in Moscow. He was booked for a new European tour and then for his first visit to America. He had declared not long before that he was going through a phase of exceptional love of life. This was because life was loving him: he had the consciousness of mature powers and the knowledge that an international public awaited his works with excitement and wanted to see him in person.

This may have had something to do with what he came to call Mme. von Meck's 'treason'. Like Nikolai Rubinstein long before, she may have resented his independence: Tchaikovsky was the world's musician now, not hers. But any such pique can have been only a single factor among others: it would be insufficient by itself to cause the sudden deathstroke to the friendship.

Tchaikovsky wrote to Pakhulsky, now her son-in-law, husband of her daughter Julia. He hoped through this channel to re-establish his correspondence with Mme. von Meck. But Pakhulsky politely put him off. He persisted. Pakhulsky at length wrote in June 1891 a letter that was clearly meant to be final, saying that Mme. von Meck was ill, nervously prostrate, weak, and could no longer write to him.

To this, Tchaikovsky said he would be the last person in the world to add to her suffering, but what was to stop them from communicating through intermediaries, to wit, her daughter and son-in-law? But she had apparently never even asked either of them to find out how his life was going: in short it seemed she had lost interest and become cold to him, and this was what wounded him profoundly. Above all, he had desired that the cessation of his pension should make no difference to their personal relationship. But alas, every connection was severed from the moment the payments ceased. This humiliated him terribly and made it a torment to think that he had ever accepted her money.

He even came to wish that Mme. von Meck had been speaking the truth and that she was really reduced to poverty, so that he could help her as she had helped him, and thus prove to her that *his* affections had been disinterested and sincere.

He re-read all her letters, and was convinced that no illness, no anxiety, no financial troubles could alter the feelings expressed in them. But the feelings had changed, that was evident; and now it seemed her state was such that he could not even tell her how this distressed him.

Perhaps it was because they never met that he had idealised her, he wrote. In such a person, half-divine, he could not imagine treachery, and it seemed to him that the earth would fall apart beneath him before she would change. 'But it has happened, and all my faith in people, all my trust in the world, has turned upside down. My peace is gone, and whatever happiness fate intended for me is poisoned.'

Pakhulsky returned the letter. Mme. von Meck was seriously ill in mind and body, he said. That was the sole cause of her indifference. He was sure that in her heart she still loved her old friends. But in her present condition he dared not even show her Tchaikovsky's letter.

Tchaikovsky gave up the fight, and wrote no more. He told Jurgenson that what he had believed to be an ideal relationship had turned out to be a 'meaningless farce', which filled him with disgust.

Jurgenson had proof, if any were needed, that Tchaikovsky's protestations of love and gratitude to Mme. von Meck had not been coined simply to please her; for he had a letter from Tchaikovsky a few years previously saying: 'She is my good genius; to her I owe all my prosperity and the ability to devote myself to my beloved work. Yet I have never seen her, never heard her voice. . . .'

The question remains: how *could* she have done it? What illness or anxiety could have made her so perfidious?

It is true that Mme. von Meck was ill: she was yet another victim of tuberculosis, which had killed a number of Tchaikovsky's friends, among them Nikolai Rubinstein and Kotek, and she died at the age of sixty-three, in 1894, only three months after Tchaikovsky himself. More to the point are the various references to her nerves, her fierce migraine attacks, her 'terrible nervous affliction', her sudden ageing. Modest had seen her and remarked, 'How queerly she dresses!' She was able to *afford* to be eccentric and despotic. Was she also a little mad? She was so insulated in her power and magnificence that it would perhaps be hard to tell! It was scarcely a proof of madness to have torn up the paper friendship with Tchaikovsky, any more than to have begun it; but there is no sane explanation for the break, however one looks at it. The enormous penalty of the pact by which they were pledged not to meet fell upon Tchaikovsky at the end, for he was forbidden by the rules to do the obvious thing—go and see Mme. von Meck and ask her to tell him what was the matter; to have it out, in short.

There have been many guesses concerning Mme. von Meck's motives—which, of course, are not explained by merely saying that she was not in her right mind, unless there is some auxiliary explanation of why her madness should take that form; why, for instance, she did not break with Pakhulsky, or with her family.

One theory is that somebody interested in her money had poisoned her mind against Tchaikovsky. Another is that she came to the conclusion that she was dying and decided to cloister herself with her family for her last days, breaking off all outside friendships. There is also the view, discussed earlier, that the unnatural bodilessness of the great friendship was bound to destroy it, with a kind of pernicious anaemia. Yet another suggestion is that Mme. von Meck's proud pleasure in Tchaikovsky's growing success turned into bitterness and envy as her own wealth and position seemed less secure and her health crumbled away.

The supposition already mentioned that Mme. von Meck had suddenly heard, after thirteen years, that Tchaikovsky was homosexual and that this decided her to end the friendship cannot be disproved, but there are many things that make it improbable; it would have to be assumed both that she did not know already, and that she could not accommodate the knowledge without revulsion.

The most original, and among the most feasible, of theories is that propounded by the authors of *Beloved Friend* (Catherine Drinker Bowen and Barbara von Meck, widow of Mme. von Meck's grandson). It is briefly this: that Mme. von Meck was a prey to a violent sense of guilt, brought on by the incurable illness of her handsome eldest son, Vladimir, and that she was accusing herself of neglecting him to devote herself to Tchaikovsky. We are not told what this slow, wasting disease was, but the once-brilliant Vladimir was decaying both in mind and in body. The suggestion is that Mme. von Meck, though she had not left her son materially in want, had given her thoughts and feelings to Tchaikovsky and now felt an intolerable sense of sin for having done so. 'In secret she had had this joy; she had told no one but Julia and Julia's husband.

Vladimir had not known. She had thrust her son from her and had set up a secret idol in his place, and thereby she had destroyed her son. . . .'

It is possible that some such irrational idea had taken possession of her mind. That would certainly account for her irrational break with Tchaikovsky; it may even be true that she had starved her son of love and given it all, in spiritualised form, to Tchaikovsky.

The trouble is, there is no proof of any of these excellent theories; no witness has recorded that Mme. von Meck murmured anything about guilt, no one has named a possible slanderer of Tchaikovsky, there is no medical witness to say that the great lady was unhinged. Why did she tell the lie about her finances? She could have said that she had heard things about him that she did not like (if she had); or told him she thought her life was ending and she was retreating from the world (if that was the case). If she had really been 'poisoned against' Tchaikovsky, would she have added the wish that he should think of her sometimes? In default of new evidence, the mystery remains; ingenuity can never solve it.

Mme. von Meck's defection was soon followed by another blow, the death of Tchaikovsky's sister Sasha. An attempt by Modest to suppress the news for a time, though well meant, worked out very badly.

Tchaikovsky was bound for America, in the spring of 1891. He went first to Berlin, where 'incognito' he heard some of his own works performed, and then to Paris, where he conducted the Colonne orchestra very successfully, and was, as he put it, the centre of Parisian attention for some days. Modest had already been in Paris a month. The meeting of the brothers lacked the usual warm-heartedness: there was almost a positive estrangement, for the first time in their lives. Tchaikovsky did not let his brother know the time of his arrival, and instead of his usual eagerness to spend the first possible hour with him, went to bed and left a message with the hotel staff that he did not wish to be aroused. When they did meet the next morning, Modest had the impression that his brother was not pleased to see him. Tchaikovsky merely said chillingly that he could not understand how Modest could care to stay away from Russia so long, when there was nothing to detain him!

After that, Modest saw little of him during the visit, and that little he did not like: he remembered afterwards only gloom or bitter laughter, the hectic flush of excitement, and the air of the great artist on tour, always occupied with visitors, in conference with Colonne or the publisher Mackar. Modest was made to feel *de trop*, and was hurt. The impression was mitigated on some evenings when Tchaikovsky relaxed, in the company of Sapelnikov,

Sophie Menter the pianist, and young Konius, a former pupil of his, now a violinist in Colonne's orchestra.

As soon as he was free of business, Tchaikovsky left his brother and went alone, sightseeing in Rouen. Then came a telegram telling Modest of Sasha's death, and he hurried to Rouen intending to break the news. But Tchaikovsky's mood somehow put him off: Modest decided it would not be good for him, excited as he was, to embark on the long voyage, among strangers, with the burden of such news. So he merely announced that he was returning to Russia, as though homesickness had stricken him at last.

But after he had gone Tchaikovsky decided to return to Paris before going to Le Havre, and in a reading-room near the Opera, he picked up a Russian newspaper and read what his brother had failed to tell him.

He 'ran out as though stung by a serpent'. It was very bitter to him, for he had loved Sasha deeply and constantly, and with profound reliance on her loyalty and understanding. Another of the few, the very few, women whom he trusted was gone from his life.

His first impulse was to cancel his New York trip and hurry back to Russia. He could do nothing for Sasha, but he was anxious about Bobyk, no longer a child (he was now twenty) but a highly strung creature, with little stamina of mind.

All the same, Tchaikovsky decided he must sail. He had made his commitments and he had his duty. Nothing, really, would be served by his rejoining his family for the funeral of Sasha, and he consoled himself where Bobyk was concerned with the reflection that 'at his age, we get over such blows easily': this from the man who still recorded in his diary the anniversary of his own mother's death, thirty-five years after it happened!

Money was another cogent reason why Tchaikovsky had to fulfil his engagements. He had already received a sum in advance which it would be difficult to repay, and he had paid his transatlantic fares, which he feared he would forfeit if he did not go the next day.

Fortunately he had sympathetic friends, including Sapelnikov, in Paris, and stayed overnight with them.

His voyage had an unpropitious start. A young man leapt overboard on the first day. Tchaikovsky was below when the siren sounded, the ship hove to and everyone rushed on deck. Emerging with the rest, Tchaikovsky saw a boat lowered, a life-belt thrown, in vain. The suicide, a second-class passenger, had scribbled some last words in his pocket-book and flung it down before he jumped. Tchaikovsky, the handiest person able to read German, was asked to translate the message, which said, 'I am innocent, the young man sobbed.'

Miseries multiplied: the weather was stormy, Tchaikovsky was seasick, homesick, sleepless, afraid. His wallet, containing nearly 500 francs, was stolen from his cabin—exactly the kind of incident to intensify his general sense of insecurity, as he walked the unsteady deck, thinking how betrayal or death put paid to love, and realising how far away was his homeland, and wondering how in such a world he could ever portray in music the Sugar Plum Fairy. . . .

The theft came back to his mind later, after one of his New York concerts, when a M. Buso, whom he had met on the voyage, forced his company upon him, staying a long time and wearing so sad an expression that Tchaikovsky felt obliged in the end to ask the reason. The visitor replied that he had been robbed of all his money in Central Park, and had come to ask for help. Tchaikovsky said he had no money to give him at the moment but might be able to do so at the end of the week; and so got rid of him. His suspicions were aroused because M. Buso had previously boasted that his father was rich. Were all his extravagant stories rubbish, Tchaikovsky asked in his diary, adding: 'I am beginning to wonder whether he didn't steal my wallet on the ship.'

He determined to discuss these suspicions with Morris Reno, President of the Music Hall (as the newly built Carnegie Hall was then called), one of the many hosts during his visit; after which there is no further mention of the matter. No doubt he came to see the futility of pursuing it, lacking evidence; or perhaps it was forgotten, drowned, in the dollars and bouquets and champagne that rained down all around him in lavish America.

The enthusiastic welcome for him when he came ashore from the *Brétagne* included the unwelcome information that he was booked to conduct in Baltimore and Philadelphia as well as New York, and so would have to stay in the United States longer than he had expected.

During the crossing, Tchaikovsky's identity had become known and he had at last consented to play for the passengers, after trying hard to say no. Thus even before reaching America he found himself drawn out of his melancholy solitude and into the committed world of fame again; and certainly he had nothing to complain of in American warmth and hospitality, as he admitted. But his diary for the day of his arrival, April 26, 1891, says that on the way to the hotel he kept up an unbelievably amiable and animated conversation, 'as though I were pleased with all that was happening', while his soul was filled with 'despair, and a desire to flee to the end of the world'.

There were reporters to meet him, and however much they knew of his musical reputation they evidently did not know much of his private life. He sat in a carriage alongside Reno's daughter Alice to drive from the harbour to the place where he was to stay, the Hotel Normandie, on Broadway, near the Metropolitan Opera House. The next day several newspapers stated that he had arrived with a young and pretty wife, and after that he was frequently asked by journalists whether his wife enjoyed being in New York.

In spite of himself, Tchaikovsky began to find pleasure in the very new New World around him. He had gone there at Walter Damrosch's invitation, principally to conduct at the inaugural concert of the Carnegie Hall. He found himself treated as a more important person in New York than in Moscow, and learned that some of his works which Russia neglected were frequently played in America. 'I am ten times as famous here as in Europe,' he wrote to Bobyk.

The handsome, beetle-browed Walter Damrosch was immensely taken with him, tried to make him promise to return the next year, and wanted to go to Russia and study under him. (Walter, son of the conductor and composer Leopold Damrosch and heir to his talents, was at this time twenty-nine.) Tchaikovsky diplomatically avoided a flat refusal.

He was the first great composer of the time to visit America. 'We all loved him from the first moment—my wife and I, the chorus, the orchestra, the employees of the hotel where he lived, and of course the public,' Walter Damrosch says in his autobiography, adding that he had never met a composer so gentle and modest. Although rehearsals and concerts tired Tchaikovsky to excess because he was never quite a professional conductor, he knew what he wanted, and got it: the atmosphere he exhaled was so sympathetic and 'love-compelling' that all the executants strove with double eagerness to carry out his intentions.

Damrosch and the other American musicians knew nothing of the sorrows and losses that were weighing on the spirits of their guest but they were aware of his haunting sadness: in spite of the success of his visit, says Damrosch, 'he was often swept by uncontrollable waves of melancholia and despondency'.

Tchaikovsky's bright eye was not dimmed by his sorrows, however. There was much to see: 'ridiculously colossal' buildings ('I refuse to understand how anyone can live on the thirteenth floor!'), Government treasury vaults with bags of gold and secret locks, trains with barber's shops on them, negro faces in the streets, and a socialist May Day demonstration on Broadway, with banners demanding an eight-hour day, which the conservative Tchaikovsky dismissed as 'buffoonery'.

He was taken to Washington, and to Niagara, where, to escape the self-accusation of cowardice, he descended in a lift and walked through the tunnel to stand below the falls, even though he found it a frightening experience, and had to wear distasteful protective clothes.

He met many kind people, the usual percentage of cranks and bores, and some persons of remarkable effrontery, such as a man who told him he *must* compose a fantasy on the folk-tune *The Red Sarafan*—'I will send you Thalberg's, please do one like his!'

His hosts took him to the studio of Napoleon Sarony, photographer, a little old man in a red cap who seemed to Tchaikovsky the most eccentric person he had ever seen, a caricature of Napoleon the Third. The photographer turned him about, this way and that, expounding a theory of 'the good side of the face' and entertained the sitter between poses by clowning and performing tricks. Tchaikovsky found him unusually likeable, 'in the American way'; and for all the clowning, he understood his art, for he produced a very fine photographic study of Tchaikovsky's head.

Carnegie Hall was not yet finished. The hammers of the builders and the rushing to and fro played havoc with rehearsals. The composer was displeased, too, with the way that the orchestra was spread across the huge stage: the tone was uneven and bad, the musicians seemed tired, and Tchaikovsky several times grew angrily inclined to walk out.

He was fascinated by the founder of the hall, Andrew Carnegie, whose looks, he said, amazingly resembled those of Ostrovsky. Carnegie sat opposite to him at an extravagant endless banquet given by the Renos, where the ices were served in boxes to which were attached little slates bearing finely-written excerpts from Tchaikovsky's music and a space for his autograph. Carnegie, whom Tchaikovsky described variously as possessor of thirty and forty million dollars, professed adoration of Moscow, and flattered and fêted its representative hugely. 'This amazing character,' said Tchaikovsky, 'who has risen in the course of years from a telegraph messenger to become one of America's wealthiest men, but has remained simple, modest and not in the least supercilious, inspires me with uncommon affection, probably because he is so much interested in me.' Throughout an evening at Carnegie's own home, he pleasantly embarrassed his guest—'He grasped my hands, declaring that I am the uncrowned but true king of music; embraced me (without kissing—here men never kiss), expressed my greatness by standing on tiptoe and raising his hands up high, and finally threw the entire company into raptures by demonstrating how I conduct. He did it so seriously, so well, so convincingly, that I myself was delighted.'

Tchaikovsky was more nervous about his conducting in America than he had been in Europe, and was afraid this would be detected by the audiences and critics. But it was not. His firm and confident manner was praised in the press.

Musically, the American visit was not of great interest. Tchaikovsky thought the New York Symphony Society's orchestra excellent, but the Lyceum Orchestra in Baltimore was inadequate and under-rehearsed, so that his *Third Suite* had to be dropped from the programme there and the *Serenade for Strings* substituted.

As for the Carnegie Hall festival, he conducted his *Coronation March* before five thousand people on the opening night (Damrosch conducting Beethoven and Berlioz): on the third day, his birthday, the *Third Suite*; and at his final appearance, choral works and the *First Piano Concerto*, with a splendid solo performance by Adele Aus der Ohe, whom he had coached in the nuances, as he had found her powerful, crisp playing rather coarse at first. He had the curious impression that the enthusiastic audience shouted 'Upwards, upwards!' as they waved their handkerchiefs.

Adele Aus der Ohe's career impressed him. A pupil of Liszt, she had arrived in America penniless but with an invitation to play with the Symphony Society. Her performance was a success and she went from city to city, accumulating in four years 120,000 dollars—'that's America!' he wrote.

America touched nothing deep in Tchaikovsky: at most it beguiled him from the ache of recent loss. It was less an experience than an interlude, and his heart was never in it. The tables were covered with roses. There were a hundred autographs to sign. Whisky with lemon and bitters was a novel and extraordinarily delicious drink. Then a chance heart-to-heart talk in his own tongue with a Russian woman, and suddenly his voice trembled, he burst into tears and ran into another room, burning with shame at his behaviour but unable to master himself. Nothing could assuage these pangs but his own people and his homeland. His diary quotes the words of Goethe which became Tchaikovsky's best-known song, *Nur wer die Sehnsucht kennt*, the very voice of the exile's anguish.

His sorrows, the advent of his fifty-first birthday, and certain remarks made about him in America, combined to make him think about his age and wonder whether he was growing prematurely old. The American press was partly responsible: he was disconcerted by the fact that the journalists were not content with writing about his music but described his manner and personal appearance, too, and one paper—the *New York Herald*—spoke of him as tall, interesting, grey-haired and 'getting on for sixty'.

Soon afterwards he made a mistake which mortified him and made him think his memory was failing. Sitting next to the conductor Gustav Dannreuther, Tchaikovsky talked to him for two hours ostensibly about his brother, Edward Dannreuther, while the other sat open-mouthed and mystified: Tchaikovsky was actually speaking of another pianist, Hartvigson. 'I must have seemed either crazy or a hopeless liar,' he says.

All the supper guests, Carnegie especially, were astonished when he told them he was just fifty-one. They said with transatlantic candour that they had thought him much older.

'Have I aged much in recent years? It's very possible. I feel that something within me is crushed,' he wrote. That night he had terror-dreams, in one of which he was tumbling down a long descent into the sea and saving himself only by clinging to a small projection of rock. He attributed his nightmare to the conversation about his age. He had not much fortitude for the senility he was never to be called upon to endure.

What happened next was a grotesquerie of bad luck. He was met in Washington by a compatriot, Botkin. Exuberantly they kissed—and out came a loose front tooth of Tchaikovsky's. He now sounded, as well as looked, like an old man. The whistling of his sibilants filled him with horror, and took away all the pleasure of speaking his own language again.

None too soon came the farewells, presentations, a final all-Tchaikovsky concert in the Metropolitan Opera House, with an ovation, a speech he did not understand, but which he acknowledged in French, and bouquets. One woman threw a gorgeous bouquet of roses which hit him full in the face. After hasty packing, hasty gulps of champagne, and a night drive to the piers, Tchaikovsky boarded the *Fürst Bismarck* for Hamburg, and promptly fell asleep. He assiduously dodged acquaintances on the ship and spent most of the first day in sleep.

Having put some solid hours of oblivion and silence between him and the hectic, arid American visit, Tchaikovsky began the next day to write music again: sketches for a future symphony. (Apparently one which he never finished, but which turned into his *Third Piano Concerto*.)

The crossing was rough, much of the time, but Tchaikovsky's spirits rose, his drooping appetite revived, and the dawns became more magnificent, as his longing for home neared fulfilment. Arriving at Hamburg, he had no difficulty in choosing a hotel. It was the Hotel St. Petersburg.

CHAPTER XIV

THE MUSIC MUTE

A stillness falls, and there is heard only, far away in the Cherry Orchard, the thud of axes on the trees. . . .

How perfectly it symbolises the sad eve of change! And now the woodmen had come and felled the trees that surrounded Tchaikovsky's home at Frolovskoye, destroying all its appeal for him. He moved back to Maidanovo, to the house where he had lived before, though it was looking run down and had lost its charm.

There he settled down to work and there Modest and Bobyk joined him. In the intervals of composing music for the *Nutcracker* and *Iolanthe*, a one-act opera, he went with his brother and nephew and young Count Litke, a relation by marriage, first to Moscow to see the Franco-Russian exhibition, and then to St. Petersburg for a few days. He returned alone to Maidanovo.

Another occurrence, ill-omened, too, it must have seemed, distressed Tchaikovsky that summer when he had yet to receive the final rebuff from Mme. von Meck. Returning from his afternoon walk one August day he discovered that a costly black-and-gold clock, figured with Joan of Arc, and Apollo and the Muses, had been stolen from his room. Tchaikovsky had always been indifferent to material possessions and this loss would not normally have troubled him; but it was a gift, three years before, from his patroness.

Greatly upset at the theft, he sent for the police. Months went by and then one evening the police arrived not with the clock, of which nothing was known, but with a man they said was the thief. He could well have been the village idiot from what then took place. The whereabouts of the clock, he said, he would disclose to nobody but Tchaikovsky and then only in private. Tchaikovsky accordingly took him into another room where he threw himself at the feet of the composer and begged forgiveness. It was granted, and Tchaikovsky then asked him what he had done with the clock. He would not answer and began to deny he had ever stolen it. The police took him away and Tchaikovsky never saw the clock again.

Tchaikovsky told Bobyk, with humorous exaggeration, around this time that he was 'wearing out', losing his hair, teeth, and eyesight, beginning to drag his feet, and losing the capacity to accomplish anything. If the other particulars are no truer than the last, then the future composer of the *Pathetic* was not yet ready for the scrap-heap; but the common expectation of life was not as great then as now, and Tchaikovsky was conscious that he had not spared a never-robust physique. He decided that the time had come to make his will.

Looking into his affairs for this purpose, he found, as so often before, that he had no money. For his appearances at the Carnegie Hall he had received 2,500 dollars; but money earned on his tours always melted away before his return. 'One has to choose between never travelling, or coming home with empty pockets,' he said. The American fees must have seemed to him enormous, since for his first visit to London he was paid £20, to which the Philharmonic directors added a bonus of £5 in gratitude for his success.

When he consulted his lawyer about making his will, he was delighted to learn for the first time that a law formerly in force had been repealed and that the proceeds from his operas would benefit his heirs in consequence. Under the bad old law, all rights in the operas would have passed at his death to the Theatre Directorate. His ignorance on the point shows that he can scarcely have read his contracts for *Onegin* and subsequent works, as his rights were clearly stated in them.

He made allowances to various people during his lifetime, including 2,000 roubles a year to Modest, and was anxious that they should not all be left stranded when he died. He knew that his musical works had a substantial future earning capacity. He bequeathed the bulk of these royalties to Bobyk.

Moving once again, he now took a little house on the outskirts of Klin: his final home. It was surrounded by woods and fields, but the Moscow highway passed close by. What pleased Tchaikovsky particularly about it was its first-floor suite, unusually spacious for a small-scale country house in Russia, where he could offer any guest a pleasant bedroom and study.

But instead of settling there, he was still a traveller: touring in Estonia, Poland, Germany, Austria, France, spending as prodigally as ever. Some of the money went to Bobyk, who, like his sister Tatiana, had taken to drugs. Occasionally, Tchaikovsky was able to take Bobyk about with him. In 1892 they went to Vichy together for the waters. Both needed the cure: Tchaikovsky was suffering from what was diagnosed as catarrh of the stomach. But he curtailed the holiday to get back to some proof-reading. Apart from Modest and Anatol, Bobyk was the one remaining person in the world whom Tchaikovsky loved. Nevertheless, they did not meet frequently although many letters passed between them.

Tchaikovsky was being honoured everywhere and knew what he could command, these days. When Morris Reno sent him an offer of 4,000 dollars for a tour of twenty concerts in America, he cabled back curtly 'Non. Tchaikovsky.' He refused to conduct at a concert in Vienna when he found the orchestra incompetent at rehearsal and the hall like a restaurant, smelling of beer and tobacco. In Hamburg where he was to conduct *Eugene Onegin*, he found there had been changes in the recitatives and would not appear. This occasion provided a good example of his musical discernment, for he wrote to Bobyk that the local conductor who took his place was no mediocrity but a musician of genius. It was Gustav Mahler.

Onegin had notched its hundredth performance at the Marinsky Theatre in St. Petersburg and yet another wreath was presented to its composer. The French Academy elected him a corresponding member. He hastened from one capital city to another, deafened with applause, tired out with the nerve-racking work of conducting, riding on the tide of his fame, but aware all the time that it was neither satisfying nor necessary. Homesickness often reduced him to tears, and sometimes to such hysteria that he feared it would send him mad.

Modest attempted to divine the real reason for all this travel, admitting that the superficial ones were not enough. It was not simple deference to public demand: Tchaikovsky had learnt how to say no. Vanity, money, mere restlessness were not responsible. Something mysterious had taken possession of him and drove him on blindly. It was a deep anxiety, an inner despair demanding forgetfulness. 'It seemed that my brother had ceased to belong to himself,' Modest says.

He declares firmly that there is no ground for presuming a premonition of death, and contents himself with noting that Tchaikovsky went through similar periods of dejection and uncertainty before all his crossroads—his decision to make a career of music, his marriage, his emergence into public life. Presumably another big change was coming, something new and unknown would be brought forth.

When Tchaikovsky began to compose the *Sixth Symphony* it was as if a light broke through, and all the black devils that had possessed him for so long were exorcised. Serenity returned with the great act of creation.

Another interlude had helped to strengthen and calm him, although at its approach he trembled. A figure suddenly arose from the past: that of Fanny Durbach, his governess when he was very young, whom he had long supposed to be dead. Hearing that her 'porcelain child', now a celebrated man, was in St. Petersburg, she found someone to convey her greetings.

He was deeply disturbed. He longed to see this ghost of a love gone by, but was afraid she might be a pitiful, senile creature. However, he wrote her an affectionate note, with a photograph of himself, and asked if he could serve her in any way. He was reassured by her reply, cheerful, clearly phrased and written in a firm hand, and he decided to pay her a visit.

The powerful stirring of his emotions was not entirely due to the survival of Fanny Durbach herself, fond though he was of her. He knew the true cause: he felt as though his own mother had risen from her grave: as if the last forty-three years of his existence had been nothing but a dream, and he had awakened in the bedroom of his childhood.

The governess lived with her sister in the little Swiss town of Montbeillard, where she was born, and both of them were still teaching: they had indeed taught the whole educated population of the place, and were known and loved by everyone. Tchaikovsky wrote from Basle, en route: 'I have nothing to write about but fits of weeping. . . . I must confess to a morbid fear and horror, as though I were entering the kingdom of the dead. . . .'

Always delicately considerate of others' feelings, however shaken his own, he wrote in advance to tell Mlle. Fanny when he would be arriving, so that she should not be upset by his appearing unexpectedly. It was New Year's Day, 1893, when he entered the quiet street where she lived, found the inconspicuous six-roomed house and knocked.

Mlle. Fanny opened the door to him, and greeted him tenderly, simply, and as though it were no more than a year since they had met. He was overjoyed: she was so little changed, after all: her hair was not even as white as his. Nor was she haggard—her figure had grown stouter, her brown eyes twinkled, she still had the same rosy glow he remembered in her cheeks. He had been afraid she would shed tears, and that he would do the same; but their meeting was not at all like that. Perfectly at ease together, they sat and exchanged good-humoured recollections, and she told him forgotten details of his childhood. Out came his old copybooks, his letters, and—what he seized on with rapture—a few letters from his mother. As he looked at them he heard his mother's voice, clear and distinct, and smelt again the fragrant air of Votkinsk.

Talking peaceably with Mlle. Fanny, Tchaikovsky saw why he and his brothers, and his father and mother, had been so fond of her: she breathed, he found, 'an atmosphere of kindliness and integrity'.

She asked him which of his brothers he loved best, and he replied evasively that he was equally fond of them all. At this she was a little indignant, and told him he ought to care most for Nikolai, who had been his childhood playmate.

'And truly at that moment I loved you intensely,' wrote Tchaikovsky to Nikolai, 'because you had shared all my youthful joys.

'I stayed with her from three to eight o'clock without noticing how the time went. I spent the whole of the next day in her society. She gave me a beautiful letter from my mother. . . .

'In the evening I embraced Fanny when I took leave of her, and promised to return some day.'

This visit laid a calm hand on Tchaikovsky's forehead.

He began his new symphony at Klin in February, after a trip to Odessa, where among other honours he had his portrait painted by N. D. Kuznetsov. In this picture, which he himself thought very lifelike, he stands with lowered gaze and looks less serene than in the Napoleon Sarony photograph; in both he radiates a grave charm but with his white hair and beard, he appears far older than his age. Anton Door, who had known him in his Moscow days at the Conservatory, saw him in Vienna in 1892, and was shocked at his appearance. 'He had aged so much that I only recognised him by his wonderful blue eyes. A man old at fifty!'

Kuznetsov's picture of Tchaikovsky was a solid academic portrait, registering with candour the lines which suffering had delved in Tchaikovsky's face. The artist wanted to give him the painting, but Tchaikovsky declined because he could not bear the idea of having a picture of himself looking down at him from the wall!

Death forestalled the imminent change which Modest prognosticated, but it is obvious what it would have been: a genuine retreat from the world, an end of the exhausting travels and the public appearances, an autumnal dedication to composition and nothing else. Had he lived he might have turned the nickname 'Hemit of Klin' from a joke to a reality. He himself knew it was impossible for him to go on both composing and hurtling from land to land, without coming to a standstill and a choice; and his sane choice would always have been for the creative part of his life, unless, as his brother feared, he was at the mercy of a force too desperate to be withstood.

He had written to Glazounov in 1890 that he was in need of friendship and sympathy, as he was passing through a phase he did not understand. A strange life-weariness had come over him, he said. Sometimes he experienced a wild anguish, not of the kind that heralded a new flow of strength. (Only a year before he had spoken of a strongly renewed love of life.) The desire to write music was still strong. But places he had loved, Italy under its blue skies, the architecture of Florence, the teeming streets, no longer gave him pleasure, and he had to make a great effort to emerge from his shell.

This statement seems already to point to a coming withdrawal. Even more explicit is a letter written from England to Bobyk, during Tchaikovsky's last tour, when he asked if it were not strange that he had voluntarily undergone such torture. Unable to eat or sleep, he wondered what demon could have prompted him to take the journey. He would have fled back to his home, if it were not that he was ashamed to return empty-handed. His suffering was beyond words, but 'there is a place in my new symphony where I think I have expressed these feelings quite well,' he said. He went on to give details of his distresses: indefinable fear, dislike of meeting strangers, pains in the legs and belly, sensations of weakness. He was determined that never again would he go on tour, unless for very big rewards, and then for no more than three days at a time.

Unhappily, the test of this resolution never came. The decision was taken out of his hands.

The quoted reference to the *Sixth Symphony* is the first hint of its content. Previously, he had merely informed Bobyk that it was full of personal emotion, and that although it had a programme, he intended to let the public guess what it was, if they could; he would leave it enigmatic, and merely call it a Programmatic Symphony.

A week before beginning it, Tchaikovsky declared that he no longer believed in himself as a composer and considered he was played out. This remark, with which the reader must now be familiar, seems a fairly reliable signpost to a major work ahead.

During the early phase of composition he frequently cried—another good omen. The symphony was complete in his head within a week: he sketched out the first movement in four days, working eagerly and joyously, conscious that he had some original ideas as to form, and delighted to find that he had not yet dried up, after all.

To go straight ahead with the symphony was not possible, however: there were conducting engagements to be fulfilled in Moscow and Kharkov: he was also to go to Germany, and then to England, where Cambridge had invited him to receive an honorary doctorate of music, and London was waiting for him to conduct.

During the short visit to Moscow he was pleased to discover a new talent: an opera, *Aleko*, struck him as a work of great quality. Its composer, Rachmaninoff, then only nineteen, presented a set of five piano pieces to him.

Filling in time before the London visit, Tchaikovsky showed that his musical fertility was as great as ever. Jurgenson offered to take as many songs and piano pieces as he liked to send. To make a little money and to amuse himself, Tchaikovsky wrote eighteen piano pieces (Opus 72) in fifteen days, remarking, 'I am making musical pancakes—today I tossed the tenth.' He spent a single day of the same month on writing a military march for his cousin's regiment, and turned out a group of six songs to German lyrics in little more than a week.

His friends Grieg and Saint-Saëns were among the composers to be invited to Cambridge, but Grieg's health prevented him from making the journey.

London liked Tchaikovsky better than he liked London. He had not carried away very pleasant impressions of the city on his previous visits. Now, in 1893, arriving in green May instead of the season of fogs and smoky fires, and being surrounded by warm-hearted friends and fellow-musicians of several nationalities, he was happier, and he liked the look of London better, although its immensity and the tumult of its traffic overwhelmed him. Paris was a village by comparison, he remarked.

Sarasate, the great Spanish violinist, was giving a concert in London. Tchaikovsky attended and was also, of course, introduced to him; commenting modestly that Sarasate—who was three or four years his junior—was 'wonderfully kind' to him.

Tchaikovsky conducted his *Fourth Symphony* at the Philharmonic Society's concert with enormous success. Bernard Shaw was present, lending a cool ear to a programme that also brought Saint-Saëns on to the platform, but for the audience the occasion belonged to Tchaikovsky.

The conferring of doctorates in Cambridge took place on June 13. The Cambridge University Musical Society was celebrating its fiftieth anniversary, and the new doctors of music contributed to the programme of a jubilee concert. Stanford was the Society's president, and a work by him was also included. Tchaikovsky conducted his *Francesca da Rimini.*

The sun was hot, a maharajah in a gold turban and diamond necklace led the procession of doctors through the town. Five musicians of different countries were being honoured—Tchaikovsky of Russia, Saint-Saëns of France, Boito of Italy, Grieg of Norway, and Bruch of Germany. But as Field-Marshal Lord Roberts, in scarlet uniform under his doctor's robe, was also receiving an honorary degree, it was not the composers who captured the most applause.

There was a complimentary breakfast, with a loving-cup, and afterwards the vice-chancellor gave a garden party.

Tchaikovsky was able to sustain these public ceremonial events now with a poise he could never command in his earlier years.

His host and hostess were Professor and Mrs. Maitland, whom he found to be two of the most charming people he had ever met—'and Russophiles into the bargain, which is the greatest rarity in England'.

He liked Cambridge, its sense of the past and its monastic peace; but he did not linger. He returned to London the same evening and left for Paris the next day.

During this visit to England he met again his American host, Walter Damrosch, who also attended the Cambridge ceremonies.

Sitting next to him at dinner one evening, Tchaikovsky spoke of the *Sixth Symphony*, remarking that it was different in form from any he had previously written: the last movement was an adagio, and 'the whole work has a programme'. Damrosch pressed him for details of the programme but he replied, 'No, that I shall never tell. But I shall send you the first orchestral score and parts as soon as Jurgenson, my publisher, has them ready.'

On his return from his English visit, Tchaikovsky was consumed by a double eagerness: to get back to the symphony, and to be reunited with Bobyk Davidov, who was meeting him at Grankino, in the Poltava region. Tchaikovsky breathed the air of the steppes once more: his foreign travels were almost over.

All the news awaiting him was of death. His friend Albrecht and his once-beloved Vladimir Shilovsky had died, while another friend named Zvierev and the poet Apukhtin, who was very close to him in student days, were both dying. But Tchaikovsky's mood was remarkably and unshakably calm. One such grief, his brother remarks, would have affected him more, a few years earlier, than all of them together could now do. It was as if he had lost his own fear of death, or had come to think of it chiefly as a deliverance.

He did not begin orchestrating the symphony until his return to Klin, but did some small revisions on it and on his *Third Piano Concerto* during the three weeks he spent with Bobyk at Grankino: just enough work to keep boredom at bay. In mid-July, Bobyk departed. Tchaikovsky was taken ill the next day: 'they said it was from drinking too much cold water at dinner and supper,' he says: a grimly prophetic note. But he threw off the sickness, whatever it was, and recovering his good spirits went to Moscow for two pleasant days, spent a few days with his brother Nikolai at Oukolovo and then went home.

His little house pleased him. It looked 'very coquettish', with new gates and fence, the garden bright with flowers, the paths tidy, and everything trim and orderly, thanks to the labours of Alexei Sofronov.

Within a few days he was deep in the symphony and finding the orchestration more and more difficult. After sitting for a whole day over two pages that would not come right, he began to say he had lost his self-confidence, was turning coward, and no longer had the capacity of twenty years ago, when he would have rushed through it with unthinking ease and it would have turned out all right. His memory was tending to romanticise the past in this way.

Tchaikovsky had already decided to dedicate the work to Bobyk, though he playfully pretended that he had changed his mind about that to punish the languid young man for neglecting to answer his letters. The content of the symphony pleased him very well, he told Bobyk, but he was less satisfied with the orchestration. He considered this the best and the most sincere of all his works and affirmed to Bobyk, Jurgenson and others that nothing he had ever done before had filled him with such love and pride. He would, of course, not be surprised if it should be attacked or should fail to win much appreciation at first, for it was something new.

If he was working more slowly than usual, he decided on consideration that it was not because of a declining capability but because he now made stricter demands upon himself.

Once the symphony was finished, its composer was free to make his last trip abroad—to Hamburg, where *Iolanthe* was being played. When he returned, he went to St. Petersburg. Here a surprising fact emerges. Bobyk, whose education was completed and who now wore the uniform of the Tsar's crack regiment, the Preobashensky Guards, was going to live with another uncle—Modest himself!

What Tchaikovsky thought of this plan he never said in writing. Can he have approved? Was he unable to offer Bobyk his own roof, or unwilling to do so? Was he glad for his brother to take the dissolute young man into his charge? Modest merely records that he was very 'interested', which is not difficult to believe.

'At this time,' Modest remarks, in his careful, factual way, 'there was a change in the circumstances of my own life. Having finished the education of N. Konradi' (Kolya, the deaf-and-dumb youth), 'I decided to set up housekeeping with my nephew Vladimir Davidov, who had completed his course at the School of Jurisprudence and was now an independent man. My brother was naturally very much interested in all the arrangements of our new home.'

Tchaikovsky stayed only two days and then went into the country for what proved to be his last sight of Anatol. There, he wandered all day long in the forest, picking mushrooms. Back in Moscow, he found himself bored with city life, and soon hurried back to Klin. That was late in September. But he remained at home only three weeks or so. He still seemed unable to stay in one place for any length of time. In this case it was the funeral of Zvierev which drew him away.

When he arrived in St. Petersburg again, on October 22, to prepare for the launching of the *Sixth*, Modest and Bobyk were at the station together to meet him: they had now made their home together and were eager for him to see their flat. He complimented them on it and was glad to be their guest, for it enabled him to live quietly, his time his own, with only such visitors as he chose to notify of his presence, until the great musical occasion ended his privacy.

Tchaikovsky still maintained his secrecy about the programme of the *Sixth Symphony*, refusing to be drawn by Rimsky-Korsakov who questioned him after the first performance.

There had been a preliminary run through with students and staff of the Moscow Conservatory before Tchaikovsky took the symphony to St. Petersburg for rehearsals with the orchestra of the Musical Society.

The programme of the concert in St. Petersburg must have been very much to his liking. Adele Aus der Ohe was the soloist in his *First Piano Concerto*; there was an Overture, *Karomzina*, by his old friend Laroche, and dances from Mozart's *Idomeneo*. But his forecast that the public would fail to grasp or like his symphony at first hearing was correct; and what always disconcerted him, the musicians, too, seemed unimpressed—it was very important to him that the orchestra should show at rehearsal a warm understanding of his work, otherwise he found it impossible to conduct adequately.

He did not carry the *Sixth Symphony* into the hearts of his first audience: it was tepidly received. The old story! but for once, Tchaikovsky's own belief in his work never wavered, and he was quite unperturbed by the indifferent response, knowing it was only a question of time.

'I have put my whole soul into the work,' he had said; and he was past the phase of caring overmuch about applause, or regarding it as any kind of barometer: he had been deafened with cheers, smothered with laurels, flattered and fêted without measure, in a score of cities; and had lifted his head above it all, with a critical, self-appraising eye, and looked steadily at the new work he had created. He had expressed in it his deepest feelings, his love, his sense of the doom laid upon mankind; and he was satisfied that he had wrought it well.

The title was not settled until the day after the first performance. It was Modest's suggestion. He found his brother sitting at the breakfast table, brooding over the score, which he had promised to send that day to Jurgenson, for publication.

Tchaikovsky told him he had abandoned his original idea of calling it a 'programme' symphony, as he did not intend to expound its programme; but he did not want it to be known merely by a number. Modest proposed 'Tragic Symphony', but that did not please him. Several possible reasons for his rejecting it suggest themselves: one, that Schubert had given this title to one of his own symphonies (No. 4 in C minor); another that Brahms had written a *Tragic Overture*; more fundamentally, that 'tragic' did not seem to him the *mot juste*. Modest left him cogitating about the question, and then rushed back into the room to announce an inspiration: 'The Pathetic Symphony'.

'Bravo, Modest, splendid! "Pathetic"!' Tchaikovsky exclaimed at once, and wrote on the manuscript the title by which the symphony has ever since been known.

It is hardly necessary to add that the word 'pathetic', even in English, had not at that time acquired the damp, pitying tone that has since debased it. (Curiously enough the word 'pathos' retains the vigour which 'pathetic' has lost.)

After sending the score to Moscow, Tchaikovsky wavered about the title which he had accepted with such alacrity, and wrote to Jurgenson saying he hoped it was not too late to alter the title-page so that it would read simply 'No. 6', along with his name as composer, and the plain dedication, 'To Vladimir Lvovich Davidov.' Whether he changed his mind again, or whether after Tchaikovsky's death Jurgenson acted on his own discretion, the name 'Pathetic' was perpetuated.

There are differing opinions as to why the symphony did not conquer either the critics or the public at first hearing. One, the view of Modest, is that Tchaikovsky's conducting was at fault: having failed to inspire the orchestra, he could not carry conviction, through them, to his hearers. Rimsky-Korsakov and Tchaikovsky himself thought the trouble was simply the novelty of the composition. Certainly his public had never heard anything like the adagio movement. It made a far greater impact when Napravnik conducted it shortly afterwards, but by then it was transfigured by a tragic context in the mind of the audience: it had become nothing less than a majestic dirge for Tchaikovsky, twelve days dead.

Two stories of Tchaikovsky's last year belong to the realm of romantic sensationalism. One is that he had a premonition of death, and wrote it into the *Sixth Symphony*—that this is, indeed, the 'enigma', the 'meaning' of the symphony. The other, sometimes linked with it, is that Tchaikovsky really committed suicide, and that the cholera story was invented to conceal the truth. Modest's strong affirmation that his brother had no premonition of death, and was not even in one of his phases of depression, is seen as disingenuous and false.

Although Modest was certainly much concerned for his brother's moral credit, it is hard to believe that he would have tried to impose a deception of such magnitude on posterity. In any case, there are other important witnesses who had no reason for conspiring against the truth, including the doctor, who wrote to Modest on the very day of Tchaikovsky's death, speaking of 'the dread disease which carried off your brother'. Nevertheless, it is a fact, of which a biographer must take account, that a rumour of suicide did circulate immediately after he died. It is also true that a number of references to death are to be found, like warning shadows, in the days beforehand, although there are good reasons for them all and if anything they rebut the theory of a premonition. Also, it may well be that the *Sixth Symphony* is in some sense a meditation on death, or on the 'frailty of all things here'; but that has nothing to do with any personal foreboding.

The thought of death was never very far from Tchaikovsky's mind, throughout his whole life. Nor from the mind of any sensitive being of his time: thinking on one's latter end was a proper preoccupation. There was ample reason to do so, in an age when so many people died in infancy or youth, and when epidemics of killer diseases were a commonplace. Is it, indeed, ever far from the thoughts of men?

Travelling to the funeral of Zvierev, Tchaikovsky pointed from the train window at the graveyard of Frolovskoye and said, 'I shall be buried there, and people will point out my grave as they pass.' He repeated this remark to Tannaev at the memorial service; but he did not seem to be saying that his own end was imminent. The death of Apukhtin also prompted some gloomy reflections, but Tchaikovsky did not attend that funeral.

At the service to Zvierev, Tchaikovsky met his old colleague Kashkin and a couple of days later they supped together and talked over old times. Tchaikovsky told him about his visit to Cambridge, and then the conversation turned on the diminishing circle of their old friends and the gaps which death had recently made. They began to discuss the question, 'Who will be the next to go?'

Kashkin declared with conviction that Tchaikovsky would outlive all of them. He demurred, but admitted he had never felt better in health or spirits.

Tchaikovsky was leaving that night for St. Petersburg where he was to conduct the *Sixth Symphony*. He confided to Kashkin, who had not heard or seen the music, that he was still worried about the last movement, and thought that perhaps after the performance he would scrap the finale and write a new one. (He must quickly have discarded this notion as he sent the score to the publisher the day after the performance.) Before he left, the two friends arranged a meeting in Moscow a fortnight later. Kashkin did not see Tchaikovsky off at the station as they were to meet again so soon; and surely neither had any presentiment that they were parting forever.

Modest's impression was that during the last days before his mortal illness, Tchaikovsky was neither very cheerful nor yet despondent. With intimate friends he was jovial; among strangers he showed that nervous excitement which Modest so disliked in him, and ended tired out and dull. But 'nothing gave the smallest hint of his approaching end,' he says.

He was still in good health when on the last day of October he went to a private performance of Rubinstein's *Maccabees* and the following day when he dined with Vera, *née* Davidova, the girl who had been in love with him many years before and who was now married to an Admiral Boutakov. She of course was a living reminder of things past, Kamenka's delights and decay, Sasha's death and others'. Afterwards Tchaikovsky and Modest went to see *A Warm Heart*, a play by their old friend Ostrovsky. In the interval they talked to the actor Varlamov, a man with a richly humorous style, and the conversation in the dressing-room brought up the topic of spiritualism. The actor in a comic outburst denounced, 'all those abominations' which reminded people of death. Tchaikovsky laughed and rejoined, 'Yes, there is plenty of time before we need reckon with this snub-nosed horror: he will not come to snatch us off just yet. I feel that I shall live for a long time.'

A mediaeval painter of the scene would surely have put the snub-nosed horror looking over his shoulder as he spoke; for it was his last day of health.

A supper party at the Restaurant Leiner followed the theatre: Glazounov was there, so were Bobyk, Count Litke, and others. Modest did not join the party until they had already finished their meal, but later on he made inquiries to ascertain what his brother had eaten. Nothing that could have accounted for his illness: a macaroni dish and his usual drink, white wine and soda water (Byron's 'hock-and-seltzer'). They walked home at 2 a.m. Tchaikovsky perfectly well and uncomplaining. It does not seem to have been one of the high old Petersburg nights of over-eating and Homeric drinking, at any rate as far as Tchaikovsky was concerned.

But at breakfast next morning he was missing. Modest went to his room and found him haggard with dyspepsia—no new thing. He had had a bad night, he said. But he refused his usual medicine, castor oil. About 11 a.m. he rose and dressed and went out to see Napravnik. It was a short interview: he was back in half an hour, still feeling unwell, but firmly refusing to have a doctor. As the trouble seemed to be his old complaint, nobody insisted, and Modest did not think matters at all serious.

Lunchtime came: a family meal in the comfortable home which Modest and Bobyk now shared, and Tchaikovsky sat down at table with them, companionably; but he felt unable to eat. Refusing the food and wine, he talked while the others ate. Then came what Modest calls 'probably the fatal moment'. While talking he poured out a glass of cold water and took a long draught.

The others exclaimed in alarm: had he forgotten that cholera was raging? A man with a stomach disorder should not drink unboiled water! But he calmed their fears, and did not seem in the least frightened himself.

One cannot help protesting: what on earth was the unboiled water doing on the table at all? Presumably it was intended to be drunk with wine or spirits: but why unboiled, since everyone present seems to have known that it should be boiled for safety? Possibly they entertained the belief that to mix it with alcohol would sufficiently 'disinfect' it, and that the danger lay in drinking the water by itself. There still seems no reason why it should not have been boiled as a precaution and allowed to cool, before lunch. (One version of the story has Tchaikovsky take his glass into the next room and fill it from a tap; but Modest asserts that the water was poured and drunk while they were chatting round the table.)

The invasions of cholera known as the great pandemics rolled over the helpless populations at intervals through the nineteenth century. The first, beginning in India in 1817, spread to Russia six years later. The one scourging Russia at the time when Tchaikovsky drank the glass of water was brought to Europe by pilgrims returning from Mecca.

Modest says his brother 'dreaded cholera less than any other illness'. This is frankly incredible. His mother had died of it, with a cruel suddenness that left an everlasting wound on Tchaikovsky's mind, when he was fourteen, and soon afterwards it almost killed his father. All Russians dreaded cholera, with good cause. As has been said, Tchaikovsky avoided Italy because of the epidemic there when he was travelling from Trebizond to Paris in 1887.

The first of the three stages of cholera which brings vomiting and diarrhoea seems to have been developing in Tchaikovsky as the short November daylight faded, and he had to admit a worsening of his state. But he still refused to have a doctor, although his favourite physician, Dr. Bertenson, practised in the town. He blamed his pains on having gulped down too much Hunyadi, a Hungarian curative water, earlier in the day.

This raises the question of whether Tchaikovsky actually swallowed the cholera germs in the water at lunchtime, or was already by that time in the early stage of the disease—or both; for an unquenchable thirst is one of the first symptoms. Incubation is in any case short, and can be a matter of either days or hours.

Up to now, none of the household had taken the illness to be anything but one of the brief attacks of nervous indigestion to which Tchaikovsky was notoriously liable. He went to bed, however, helped and tended by Modest's manservant, Nazar Litrov, whom years ago he had taken with him to Italy.

Apart from the warning at the luncheon table, the first naming of the disease seems to have come from Tchaikovsky himself. Glazounov called to see him, and thought him in a bad way. Tchaikovsky murmured to him that he thought he might have cholera.

The visitor left, and by the time the candles were lit everyone had abandoned the notion that this was some passing ailment of no consequence.

Tchaikovsky was palpably weakening, and it was acknowledged that his sickness was serious and that his refusal to have a doctor must no longer be complied with. Modest took it upon himself to send for Bertenson, who arrived about eight o'clock.

Tchaikovsky was tossing feebly, and burning inside a cold skin, when Dr. Bertenson examined him. The doctor at once sent for his brother: the two Bertensons were the most renowned physicians in St. Petersburg. They took Modest aside and told him it was undoubtedly cholera.

Tchaikovsky was not told what they said but he had no illusions. He was struggling with a frightful sensation of oppression in the chest. Breathing fast and painfully, he said more than once, 'I believe this is death.'

The doctors were able to do singularly little for him.

The terrible second stage of the disease came on as evening passed into night: agonising cramps in the muscles, with all the time a weakening of the pulse, a wrinkling of the clammy skin. Modest and the others massaged his anguished limbs all night. Towards morning they seemed to be succeeding, the bouts of pain came at longer intervals. His courage, says Modest, was wonderful: he joked with them between paroxysms, constantly thanked them for their services and kept begging them to take some rest.

The next day, Friday, Tchaikovsky seemed markedly improved, though weak and hollow-eyed. Those around him were much cheered, and he himself declared:

'I believe I have been snatched from the jaws of death.'

Whether modern medicine, which knows how to go to the defence of the kidneys, the seat of peril in cholera, would have been able to take advantage of that rallying of his forces and save his life we cannot know. There is a phase of the disease when the cramps end, the breathing eases, the heart may strengthen and sleep brings refreshment—but it may be the prelude to either recovery or death. In Tchaikovsky's case, it merely raised delusive hopes in himself and those who loved him, whether or not it changed the private opinion of the doctors.

A message was sent to Klin, summoning Tchaikovsky's own servant, Alexei Sofronov. The illness and the nursing of it was being kept as far as possible a private, family affair. Nothing of it reached the newspapers. Glazounov was one of the only musicians to see Tchaikovsky on his sick-bed. Rimsky-Korsakov did not, and may well be exaggerating when he says in his reminiscences that the news of Tchaikovsky's illness 'was in everybody's mouth—the whole world filed to his apartment several times a day to inquire about his health'. The subsequent rumour that Tchaikovsky had killed himself could hardly have flourished if that had been the case.

Friday night came, and still the watchers at the bedside were hopeful: perhaps the night's rest would clear the road back to health.

But the twenty-four hour respite was all. On Saturday morning Tchaikovsky was worse: looked it and knew it. The doctors came to see him. 'Leave me,' he said to them. 'You can do no good. I shall never recover.'

Like many a timid, nervous man, he faced his last crisis with the greatest fortitude, in that spirit of acceptance which he had always rather dubiously hoped he might achieve in the end.

Nikolai, his eldest brother, had been sent for: of the Tchaikovsky brothers, only he and Modest were at the deathbed. Nikolai was head of the family: as for the others, they were probably not summoned: it was dangerous even to enter a house where there was cholera.

Most of Saturday Tchaikovsky slept, but fitfully and unrestfully. The gravest stage of the disease had come: his kidneys ceased to function, his distress increased, his fever heat rose. Now his mind began to wander during his periods of wakefulness and pain.

Modest heard him continually repeat the name of Mme. von Meck, with anger and reproach.

When he was lucid, his brothers asked him whether he would consent to the hot bath which the doctors wanted to administer that evening.

He agreed but told them he did not believe it would save him: his mother had had the cholera bath; like her, he would die after it.

The bath was postponed, as he was too sick that evening to be put into it.

Another night of watching over the fever-wasted body: all knew, now, that he must die. He himself, when he recovered consciousness for flickering instants, said the same thing to Dr. Bertenson, asking him to stop wasting his efforts.

The many bells of St. Petersburg called the people to church. The little group huddled silently round Tchaikovsky's sick-bed.

Sofronov had arrived but the dying man could no longer recognise him.

A third doctor was brought in by the Bertensons for consultation, and at two o'clock on Sunday afternoon the hot bath was prepared and the wasted frame of Tchaikovsky was lifted into it. This was the last faint hope but it was soon to be seen that it had failed. Back on his bed, Tchaikovsky was already half out of the world. His pulse was growing weaker and he became comatose.

Nikolai decided that a priest from the Isaac Cathedral should be asked to bring the sacraments. But when the priest arrived in the evening, he was unable to administer the rite, as Tchaikovsky was totally unconscious. Instead, he prayed aloud in clear, distinct tones. But there was no sign that any word reached Tchaikovsky's understanding.

Two brave young men ventured into the infected house and joined the vigil: Count Litke and Baron Buxhövden, another nephew. The doctors remained, for what they knew would not be a protracted watch.

The windy autumn night dragged on: the straining eyes of those around the bed saw nothing to indicate that Tchaikovsky was aware of this world, its discords or its harmonies, any more.

Thus it was until three o'clock in the morning of Monday, November 6.

About that time Tchaikovsky opened his eyes. His face was lit with a look of clear recognition: he saw about him in the candle-light the faces of those he had loved best—handsome Bobyk, faithful Alexei, and his dear brothers—and knew them again. For an instant, he was the man they had known, and they gave and received his love. Then the gleam faded, and with it his life.

So passed into silence one of the most prodigious talents of a great musical epoch.

Instead of seeking, in the current fashion, the secret of Tchaikovsky's art in his neuroses, we see his art as binding together the whirling particles of his personality, and his triumph as a music-maker giving unity and meaning to his life.

His countrymen when they learned of his death mourned and acclaimed him with characteristic public fervour and abandon. Thousands followed his funeral on November 9, and the streets of St. Petersburg were filled with weeping crowds. The body was blessed at Kazan Cathedral and buried in the Alexander Nevsky cemetery. Deputations from a hundred musical societies took part in the funeral procession.

'How strange,' wrote Rimsky-Korsakov, 'that although his death resulted from cholera, admission to the Mass was free to all!' He added that Alexander Vyerzhbilovich, a notable 'cellist, in his forties, 'totally drunk, kept kissing the dead man's head and face'.

The story goes that not one of the reckless people who flocked to see and even touch the body contracted the disease.

Slowly the rest of the world began to realise its loss. Press comments abroad were far from philistine, on the whole, although there were curious lacunae. Thus *The Times*, after reporting that 'the news of M. Tchaikovsky's death has been received with great regret throughout the country', spoke of him not as a symphonist but merely as the composer of 'several operas'. Apparently also *The Times* had nobody who could offer a knowledgable appreciation, as it contented itself with an excerpt by Edward Dannreuther from the *Dictionary of Musicians*.

The *Morning Post* said: 'The world is poorer for a great musician'; the *Manchester Guardian* called him—a trifle more cautiously —'one of the most remarkable of Russian composers'. *The New York Daily Tribune*, with his American tour fresh in mind, ranked him 'among the most brilliant and original of modern composers'.

Memorial performances were not slow to follow. England, where we have seen a considerable Tchaikovsky public had already been created, was the first country outside Russia to hear the *Pathetic*, and the performance was repeated a fortnight later. The first was given on February 28, 1894, and after it the Directors of the Philharmonic Society in London 'begged to announce that at the request of many subscribers, Tchaikovsky's latest symphony (No. 6 in B minor) will be repeated on March 14'.

The Times now saluted the symphony as 'among Tchaikovsky's finest works', and the *Morning Post* called it 'a perfect marvel of instrumentation'.

London was in this matter well ahead of New York, a fact which rather punctures a little balloon inflated by Walter Damrosch. In his autobiography, Damrosch, after speaking of his meeting with Tchaikovsky in England, says: 'We parted with the expectation of meeting again in America the following winter, but alas, in October came the cable announcing his death from cholera, and a few days later arrived a package from Moscow containing the score and parts of his Symphony No. 6, the *Pathétique*.

'It was like a voice from the dead.

'I immediately put the work into rehearsal and gave it its first performance in America on the following Sunday.'

The actual date of the first performance in America, however, was March 16—two days after the second London hearing, and five months after the composer's death.

Although in critical opinion Tchaikovsky has faded and brightened, receded and returned, over the years since his death, his public has remained great and constant through successive generations. Nor is there any sign of his music losing favour: the young crowd the concert halls to hear it, as did the young of half a century ago, touched by its emotional directness, enchanted by its melodies. As to the unknown Tchaikovsky, the composer of operas no longer played and scores of instrumental pieces and songs never performed outside Russia, it is to be feared that the extreme popularity of a few works tends to silence much else that would be eagerly enjoyed. But not all singers, conductors or impresarios prefer the safe and trodden path and one hopes that many unheard melodies will yet be heard and loved. If Tchaikovsky himself died prematurely old, his musical creation has eternal freshness. It offers more complexity of pleasure than is vulgarly supposed; but above all, the human heart is alive in it, pulsating still, communicating to new populations, reverberating in widening circles through the world.

Tchaikovsky's legend was assiduously cultivated in Russia from the very time of his death. Alexei Sofronov bought the house at Klin, having inherited his master's furniture, and began acquiring souvenirs of Tchaikovsky to turn it into a museum.

Four years later Modest and Bobyk bought the house from him. There Bobyk shot himself in 1906, and there ten years afterwards Modest died of cancer.

Hippolyte Tchaikovsky, when he retired as admiral, became curator of the Tchaikovsky museum, and retained a post there even under the Soviet regime; he died in 1927.

The Nazi invaders sacked the house, but it was meticulously restored after the war.

There is an imposing statue to Tchaikovsky at the Moscow State Conservatory. But his memorial is not a thing of stone, it is written on air, by plucked strings and sounding brass.

'Music,' he once wrote, 'is indeed the loveliest of all heaven's gifts to humanity, wandering in the dark. It alone can calm and illumine the soul. It is not the straw to which a drowning man clings, but the true refuge and comforter.'

BIBLIOGRAPHY

The Life and Letters of Peter Ilich Tchaikovsky, by Modest Tchaikovsky. Edited by Rosa Newmarch. (The Bodley Head.)

Days and Years of P. I. Tchaikovsky. Annals of His Life and Work. Edited by V. Yakolev. (Moscow-Leningrad.)

Reminiscences of Peter Ilich Tchaikovsky, by N. Kashkin. (Jurgenson, Moscow.)

The Diaries of Tchaikovsky. Translated Wladimir Lakond. (W. W. Norton, New York.)

Tchaikovsky, by Herbert Weinstock. (Cassell.)

Beloved Friend, by Catherine Drinker Bowen and Barbara von Meck. (Hutchinson.)

Tchaikovsky. A symposium edited by Gerald Abraham. (Lindsay Drummond.)

Tchaikovsky, by Gerald Abraham. (Duckworth.)

Recollections and Letters. Edited by Igor Glebov. (Leningrad.)

Recollections of P. I. Tchaikovsky, by H. A. Laroche. (St. Petersburg.)

Recollections of P. I. Tchaikovsky, by I. Klimenko. (Moscow.)

Recollections of Fifty Years of Russian Music, by Ippolitov-Ivanov. (Moscow.)

Tchaikovsky's Correspondence with P. I. Jurgenson. Edited by V. A. Zhdanov and N. T. Zhegin. (Moscow.)

Tchaikovsky's Correspondence with Mme. von Meck. (Three volumes, Moscow.)

Tchaikovsky's Correspondence with E. F. Napravnik.

Tchaikovsky, by E. Markham Lee. (John Lane.)

Tchaikovsky's Orchestral Works, by Eric Blom. ('Music Pilgrim' Series, Oxford University Press.)

Tchaikovsky, by I. Lipaiev. (Moscow.)

Tchaikovsky, by R. H. Stein. (Stuttgart.)

Tchaikovsky and Beethoven, by N. Miaskovsky. (Moscow.)

P. I. Tchaikovsky, by A. Y. Budyakovski. (Leningrad.)

P. I. Tchaikovsky, by Iwan Knorr. (Berlin.)

The Symphonies of P. I. Tchaikovsky, by K. Tchernov. (St. Petersburg.)

Russian Symphony: Thoughts about Tchaikovsky, by Dmitri Shostakovich and others. (Philosophical Library, Inc., New York.)

Music in London, by George Bernard Shaw. (Constable.)

Tchaikovsky's Correspondence with M. A. Balakirev. (St. Petersburg.)

Tchaikovsky's Correspondence with S. I. Tannaev. (Petrograd.)

Tchaikovsky, by Edwin Evans the Younger. (Dent.)

Tchaikovsky, His Life and Works, by Rosa Newmarch with a supplement by Edwin Evans. (William Reeves.)

My Musical Life, by Walter Damrosch. (Allen and Unwin.)

Tchaikovsky, by E. V. Schallenberg. (Sidgwick and Jackson.)

My Musical Life, by Rimsky-Korsakov. Edited by Carl von Vechten. (Alfred A. Knopf, New York.)

Impressions and Comments (1914–1918), by Havelock Ellis. (Constable.)

Gustav Mahler. Memories and Letters by Alma Mahler. (John Murray.)

Impressions that Remained, by Ethel Smyth. (Longmans, Green.)

Johannes Brahms, by Florence May. (William Reeves.)

Royal Philharmonic, by Robert Elkin. (Rider.)

INDEX

INDEX